CONTENTS

FOREWORD

With increased travel and an expanding interest in Europe as a whole, many books and field guides on its natural history have been published in the last two decades, but most either treat a wide field in general terms or cover a single class or group of animals or plants. At the same time, inspired by the need for conservation, the pendulum is swinging back from the specialization of the post-war years to a wish for a fuller appreciation of all aspects of natural history. As yet, the traveller-naturalist has to be armed with a variety of volumes and, even then, has no means of understanding the interrelations of plants and animals. We believe that this new series will help to fill that gap.

The five books cover the whole of the northern half of Europe west of Russia and the Baltic States, and include Iceland: the limits are shown by the map on pages 80–81, which marks the individual countries, and the various subregions with the abbreviations used for them. Four of the volumes deal with (a) towns and gardens; (b) broadleaved woods, hedgerows, farmland, lowland grassland and downs; (c) lakes, rivers and freshwater marshes; and (d) coasts, dunes, sea cliffs, saltmarshes, estuaries and the sea itself. This book is about coniferous forests, heaths, moors, mountains and tundra. Thus, in broad groupings of related habitats, the series covers the whole rural and urban scene.

Each book is divided into two. The first half is an ecological essay about the habitats, with examples of plant and animal communities as illustrations of interrelationships. The second is a field guide of selected species, each illustrated and described, with its habitat, the part it plays in food webs, and its distribution. Obviously there are limitations: about 600 species are illustrated in each book, or around 3000 in the series, but the north European total is probably at least 50,000. Whereas good proportions of the characteristic vertebrates (148 mammals, 364 birds, 18 reptiles, 22 amphibians and more than 300 fishes) are included, some single *families* of insects have more species than the total of these; there are over 4000 different beetles in Britain alone, and probably 8–9000 in the whole of our area, while some 3500 plants are also native or naturalized in north Europe. On the other hand, the identification of many insects and some groups of plants is a matter for the specialist and we believe that many readers will be satisfied if they can identify these at the family level. So our list of invertebrates and plants is selective, but we hope that it will form a useful groundwork from which interest in particular groups can be developed.

uas

ow...

...ivers

pa... ines

1999   90

9

31 10

conifers

Ranunculaceae

Cruciferae

Droseraceae

Rosaceae

Saxifrag...

...guminosae

Eri...aceae

Liliaceae

Orchidaceae

mosses

fungi

clubmosses

ferns

Umbelliferae

Compositae

0

rodents

bats

carnivores

1

newts

frogs

ungulates

THE NATURAL HISTORY OF BRITAIN
AND NORTHERN EUROPE

MOUNTAINS AND MOORLANDS
ARNOLD DARLINGTON
Editors JAMES FERGUSON-LEES & BRUCE CAMPBELL

Contributors Franklyn and Margaret Perring (Plants);
Paul Whalley, Frederick Wanless, Edward Easton, Roger Lincoln,
Peter Mordan (Invertebrates);
Tim Halliday (Amphibians and Reptiles);
James Ferguson-Lees (Birds); Gordon Corbet (Mammals)

Hodder & Stoughton
LONDON·SYDNEY·AUCKLAND·TORONTO

This book was designed and produced by
George Rainbird Limited,
36 Park Street, London W1Y 4DE
for Hodder & Stoughton Limited,
Mill Road, Dunton Green,
Sevenoaks, Kent

House Editor: Karen Goldie-Morrison
Designer: Patrick Yapp
Indexer: Stephen Walton
Picture Researchers: Barbara Fraser and
                    Karen Gunnell
Cartographer: Tom Stalker Miller
Cover Illustrator: Hilary Burn
Endpapers Designer: Marianne Appleton
Production: Sheila McKenzie

Printed and bound by
W. S. Cowell Limited
28 Percy Street, London W1P 9FF

ISBN 0 340 22615 3

Derbyshire College of Agriculture.
May 78
574,5264

All plants and animals are grouped into classes (*eg* Angiospermae, Insecta, Aves), orders (*eg* Campanulatae, Lepidoptera, Passeriformes), families (*eg* Compositae, Nymphalidae, Turdidae) and genera (*eg Aster, Inachis, Turdus*), groups of increasingly close affinity. Each plant or animal has two scientific names, the first of which is the genus and the second the species. These are often considered to be outside the scope of a work of this kind, but many invertebrates and some plants have no vernaculars and, at the same time, such names are invaluable in showing relationships. Consequently, each species is given its scientific name at the first mention in each essay chapter and again in the field guide, where the family name is also inserted in capitals.

The specially commissioned colour paintings which illustrate the field guide are a delight in themselves. It has become customary to illustrate plants and animals in field guides as individual specimens, but here they are arranged in attractive compositions. Scale has had to suffer, but the sizes are always given in the facing descriptions, as are the correct food plants of the invertebrates.

In contrast to the first book in the series, on towns and gardens, this one is concerned with the wildest, least cultivated habitats. Even coniferous forests, though now partly composed of introduced and planted trees, are still a natural resource of native species over great regions of our area. They march with both moorlands and mountains, just as moorlands may shade into heathlands and hill tops be covered with tundra vegetation. In terms of altitude, it is possible to walk from a coastal heath through a pinewood out on to moorland and up to a mountain top in a single day's transect, and we think that the same sort of naturalist is likely to enjoy and want to study all the habitats described in this book.

Arnold Darlington is just such a naturalist. He has had a distinguished career as a teacher of biology, with an important secondment as a group leader in the biology section of the Nuffield Science Teaching Project; he has a circumpolar knowledge of coniferous forests, moorlands and tundra and has done original research not only on heaths and moors in Britain but in the alpine mountain zone of continental Europe. Thus, he has had first-hand experience of the diverse wildlife systems dealt with here. More than that, he has an abiding affection for them, which informs his whole attitude. We believe that he has effectively communicated his feelings by what he has written in the pages that follow.

JAMES FERGUSON-LEES
BRUCE CAMPBELL

INTRODUCTION

This book is about four essentially northern wildlife settings and a fifth which is almost confined to northwest Europe.

Most widespread in the countries with which we are dealing and most productive from both the natural and the human aspects is the coniferous forest, in modern terms the source, as timber, of much of Fenno–Scandia's wealth. In Britain, where the native pine forest is reduced to a remnant in the Scottish Highlands, its place has been taken by great plantations of introduced softwood species, grown for commercial purposes; this process is taking place in continental Europe as well, so that the visitor needs to be as knowledgeable about Sitka spruce *Picea sitchensis* and Douglas fir *Pseudotsuga menziesii* as about Scots pine *Pinus sylvestris*, Norway spruce *Picea abies* and European larch *Larix decidua*.

Where the ancient forests have disappeared, they have been replaced, over a largely coastal strip running roughly northeast to southwest across our area, by heathland. This is the habitat which is virtually confined to northwest Europe and, therefore, one of its most precious ecological possessions. It has some of the characteristics of moorland, but in general it is drier and inhabited by many plants and animals which are also associated with fixed dunes and even with the dry aromatic heaths of Iberia and the Mediterranean. The Lüneburger Heide in west Germany is a classic example of heathland, now partly a nature reserve, with acid bogs and rolling expanses covered in heather *Calluna vulgaris*, shading into coniferous woodland. On a smaller scale is Die Hooge Veluwe in the Netherlands, and Denmark also still has some fine heaths. So have the New Forest and Dorset in England, though their future is precarious, while in southwest England, the Channel Islands and Brittany there are other examples, some quite small and some extensive. But, wherever there are reasonably large expanses, as in Jutland and East Anglia, they tend to attract the forester and so are returned to an artificial version of their pristine condition.

Heathland's wetter and peatier relation, moorland, covers enormous stretches of north Europe and has also been increasingly planted up in recent years, especially in north and west Britain and Ireland, where the great bogs, which to the dwellers on their fringes held much the same aura of mystery as the conifer forests, are now being exploited for their peat on a large scale. The

Moorland with Scots pine in foreground, rising through coniferous forests to mountain upland, north Norway.

extremely acid conditions, whether on sea-level 'mosses' or climbing to the 1000 metre contour, inhibit a varied wildlife, but some specialized plants and animals are adapted to the inhospitable conditions. Moorland is, of course, much favoured by the more active human visitor and, on grouse moors and deer forests, by the man with the gun or rifle, a feature especially of the Scottish scene over the past two centuries.

As altitude increases, both coniferous forest and moorland give way to the mountain top, the life zone until recently least affected by man, but now increasingly opened up to the mountaineer and winter sports enthusiast. Plants of the 'high tops', to use the Scottish term, show extreme specialization for survival, and shelter a surprising number of small and a few large animals. Mountains in our area range from the Polish Tatra, with its alpine affinities typified by wallcreepers *Tichodroma muraria* and alpine snowbells *Soldanella alpina* flowering as the snow melts, to the permanent snow cover of Norway's Jotunheim and central Iceland, with such minor but much studied outliers as the Scottish Cairngorms and the Welsh Eryri (Snowdonia).

Conditions on the tops may be classified as alpine tundra, closely related to arctic tundra, the vast circumpolar frontier of nature. In the arctic, life is adapted to a long, dark winter and a short, almost frenzied summer period of perpetual daylight, when the cushioned vegetation flowers brilliantly and a host of birds arrives for a short, intensive breeding season, sustained largely by myriad mosquitoes and blackflies *Simulium*, which also plague the human investigator.

No matter in which of these five major settings they live, plants and animals do work and therefore require energy. Its origin is the solar energy trapped by chlorophyll in the plants and utilized during photosynthesis to build up complex foodstuffs from simple raw materials: carbon dioxide and water. Plants are the primary producers, the factories of the world; animals are linked to plants and to each other by food-chains, the pathways along which energy progresses from one component to another in the system. The amount of energy available within each system depends first on the efficiency of the dominant plants. Herbivores, feeding on these primary producers, are the basis of animal food-chains. But we shall see that in the coniferous forest many herbivores feed not on the dominant trees, but on subordinate plants tolerating the shade and partial dryness of the tree cover.

Up the mountain slopes the highly productive forest gives way to moorland, rocks and near-barren tundra. The tundra, like the forest, is ecologically a climax situation, but it faces much harsher conditions in which little vegetation can survive above the surface. So anyone visiting the natural settings covered in this book has passed through many of the main terrestrial groupings, in terms of energy, that north Europe provides, as well as much of its wildest and most magnificent scenery.

CONIFEROUS FOREST

Northern forest and its setting

A forest is the most complex of the terrestrial ecological systems. It is also the most efficient in terms of productivity through the synthesis and storage of organic matter. Three features combine to ensure this productivity: (1) a high proportion of the sunlight becomes absorbed; (2) the tree canopy elevates a large area of chlorophyll-bearing tissue into a large volume of air, thus making a large amount of carbon dioxide available for assimilation; and (3) the tree roots exploit a considerable volume of water and dissolved soil nutrients. Thus, the three prerequisites for photosynthesis are fulfilled. As for the nutrients, the forest system capitalizes on the abundance of organic debris which reaches its floor from falling leaves and other waste.

The trees form a buffer for the ground against the full impact of sun, wind and precipitation and, in so doing, tend to conserve the soil against erosion. Their roots also bind the soil particles together.

Forests of some kind are the climatic climax systems which can develop wherever the average temperature is greater than 10°C in the warmest month and the annual rainfall exceeds 200 mm. Above these minima, various tree species are grouped into a number of stable forest types determined by the particular conditions of the environment. The forest system operates efficiently through time: its stability, imposed in the final analysis by its dominant tree species, is comparable only with the stability of tundra, a system where the climate is so severe that any changes are very slow.

The high-latitude northern forests, predominantly of conifers, form a circumpolar belt interrupted only by the Pacific and the Atlantic. Indeed, the coniferous forests of North America and Eurasia are very similar, and consist mainly of pines *Pinus*, spruces *Picea* and firs *Abies* as well as, in places, hemlocks *Tsuga* and larches *Larix*. In each landmass, too, the forests tend to change in composition from west to east, a feature associated with differences in ground-water, precipitation and atmospheric humidity.

Timbered systems made up partly of coniferous trees begin at the southern limit of our region as discontinuous mountain forests, in which the pines, spruces and firs usually have a lower belt of broadleaved, deciduous trees. The continuous belt of true northern coniferous forest lies between latitudes 60° and 80°N, except in Iceland. On the European mainland, these latitudes enclose a broad zone where the winter is long, the average winter temperature is 0°C or less, the growing season lasts a mere 1–3 months, and the precipitation is in the order of only 250–500 mm evenly distributed throughout the year. On the high ground of western Europe, where the surface drainage is good, the forest is of the Fenno–Scandian type, with an overwhelming predominance of Scots pine *Pinus sylvestris* and Norway spruce *Picea abies* and, where the canopy admits sufficient light, also birches *Betula*. Farther east, the terrain is lower and more swampy, and the forest becomes 'taiga', with larches as well as pines and firs. Altitude plays a part in bringing about a difference in the forests: an increase of only 300 m in vertical height is equivalent to a horizontal movement of 480 km closer to the Pole at sea-level. But the saturated condition of the ground is more important still.

Terrain and soil

Taiga

Taiga is a Russian term, in its strict sense denoting the type of coniferous forest found in north Siberia, where the land is more or less waterlogged and such species as Siberian pine *Pinus sibirica*, Siberian fir *Abies sibirica*, Siberian larch *Larix russica* and Dahurian larch *L. gmelinii* are native. Regionally, however, the word has a wider application: thus, the coniferous forests north of the Gulf of Finland, which stand on ground liable to inundation from nonsaline water, can be regarded as taiga.

Much of the terrain on which the northern forests have become established carries numerous lakes and swamps. These have formed in hollows gouged out, some 10,000 years ago, by ice moving south from the Pole during the last of the three glaciations which made up the Ice Age. Where standing water persists today, the configuration of the land has not produced an efficient system of surface drainage through erosion. In consequence, melting ice and the precipitation, although relatively low, together provide water which cannot run away freely, but has to drain through the soil instead. The wetness is increased by the slow evaporation in the cold air. The saturated soil is deficient in oxygen, earthworms (Lumbricidae) and such decomposers as bacteria. The fallen leaves and other debris decay slowly because, for the most part, they come from conifers which contain resin and whose leaves are surrounded by a tough cuticle – two features inhibiting attack by microorganisms. Year by year, they accumulate on the forest floor and form a peaty layer on its surface; the resulting soil water is acid.

Podsol

As the water seeps downwards, it leaches away nutrients, notably iron, manganese and magnesium salts. What remains near the surface is a grey soil of poor quality termed 'podsol'. During the downward flow, reactions take place which result in the formation within the subsoil of a layer of 'pan', consisting largely of compounds of iron and hard enough to impede drainage; it adds to the swampiness and resists penetration by plant roots.

LEFT *Larches, the deciduous conifers, can withstand long adverse conditions.* RIGHT *Scots pine seedling germinating on bare ground.*

In the absence of rapid action in podsol by earthworms and bacteria, fungi are important in the decomposition of dead plant matter. Normally almost invisible, they ramify through the surface layer of forest litter, and the soil immediately underneath, as a mycelium (meshwork) of hyphae (fine tubes). Their abundance can be judged from one estimate that the fungal hyphae in a single cubic metre of forest podsol would, if laid out, be sufficient to stretch unbroken half-way round the world. During the autumn, fruiting bodies (toadstools) arise from the buried mycelia and become a conspicuous feature of the forest floor. Having no chlorophyll, the fungi are independent of direct solar energy for feeding and survive in the darkest situations: they are more plentiful here than in most other forests. Fungi and, in clearings, lichens and mosses are the only plants that commonly grow beneath dense, northern conifers.

Conifers and forest conditions

Dryness and cold

Although the soil is wet, the trees are actually short of water, since this is frozen for much of the long winter and both precipitation and atmospheric humidity are low. Conifers are well adapted for dry conditions: their needle-like leaves have a small surface-area, a thick cuticle, and stomata (pores) sunk into grooves – three features which inhibit water-loss and make for survival at times when uptake from the ground is prevented by frost. In the northern extremes of the great coniferous belt, the deep cold keeps the soil-water frozen for most of the year and the period when absorption can take place is very short. There, evergreen conifers would be unable to make good the water evaporated from their foliage by drying winds, even if the needles themselves were not killed by the severe cold. Instead, larches become dominant: exceptional among conifers in being deciduous, they shed their leaves in autumn, remain dormant during the long adverse conditions, and produce new foliage and rapidly assimilate raw material when the short summer arrives. For most conifers, their evergreen foliage allows them to photosynthesize all the year round, not just in the summer which is too short a time for them to obtain sufficient food for maintenance and growth.

The smooth cuticles and small surface-area of the needles of conifers, and the downward slant of their boughs, allow accumulating snow to slide off the canopy. To some extent, their resin protects them from frost damage: where the wood splits, gum oozes out and plugs the wound against the inroads of bacteria, fungi and insects. Resin has the disadvantage, however, of enhancing combustibility and the consequent spread of forest fires.

Forest interiors

Conditions within the forests tend to be more equable than those outside: cooler by day, warmer by night; cooler in summer, warmer in winter. Being close together, the trees also give mutual protection against winds; the air inside is tranquil. The dense leaf canopy, however, often makes the interior so dark that shrubs and herbs are scarce; any development of subordinate plants is then also inhibited by the undecayed litter of needles.

Particularly during the 19th century, native conifers were much exploited for commerce. Increased land erosion was one result. Another was admittance for the first time of sunlight to the forest floor: this led to a general drying-out and, in turn, to disastrous fires which gained a hold in the dry, resinous litter and then worked their way through it, unnoticed, to break out afresh after the initial conflagrations had been extinguished. Regeneration of cleared forest is held back by a number of factors, but fire is probably the most potent and, except through lightning, almost invariably follows disturbance by man.

No artist or photographer seems ever to capture the eerie peculiarity of the northern coniferous forests, sombre to the point of night at noon-day, huge trees stretching away in an apparently endless vista, so mysterious as to suggest sinister forces at work unseen and imagined. The composer Jean Sibelius, inspired by the forests of his native Finland, succeeded better than most in his tone-poem 'Tapiola' (1925).

Insects feeding on conifers

Great numbers of insects occur in coniferous forests, but comparatively few species have overcome the difficulties of devouring the tissues of these trees, which tend to be hard, resinous, sticky and unpalatable. The insects which are so adapted, however, attack most parts of a conifer between them.

An insect with sucking mouthparts is at a disadvantage because the resin may block the fine tube leading into the head. One small sap-sucker able to drink the juices of conifer needles is the spruce gall aphid *Adelges abietis*, which produces a malformation of the needles on, most commonly, Norway spruce.

Another aphid, *Gilletteela cooleyi*, raises similar galls on Sitka spruce *Picea sitchensis*, and some of its generations migrate to Douglas fir *Pseudotsuga menziesii*; both these trees have been introduced from America. Spruces are attacked also by aphids of the genus *Cnaphalodes*, alternating on larches.

In fact, insects are not the only organisms which induce conifers to form galls. A tiny gall-mite, *Eriophyes pini*, which is another sap-sucker, causes lumpy swellings to develop on pine twigs in the soft wood of the new growth; its progeny dwell in them long after the galls have hardened. On silver fir *Abies alba*, the fungus *Melampsorella caryophyllacearum* brings about a witch's-broom gall of unusual character, a sphere with clusters of vertical twigs arising from it; like the aphids, this fungus completes its life-history on other plants – mouse-ears *Cerastium* and chickweeds/stitchworts *Stellaria*.

Defoliators

Few insects chew conifer leaves, or the buds from which they develop, but the larvae of certain sawflies and moths are among the exceptions: both can become serious plagues.

One of the most widespread of these pests is the pine sawfly *Diprion pini*. The adult female makes a row of slits in a pine needle, with an ovipositor toothed like a saw, and lays a single egg in each, capping them with a liquid which hardens into a protective lid. On hatching, the larvae devour the entire needle: a pine can be stripped to the bark by successive generations. Similarly, the large larch sawfly *Nematus erichsoni* has a bad reputation among larch-growers on the European mainland. Sawfly larvae look something like the caterpillars of moths and butterflies, but have more 'false' legs. When they have completed their feeding, the larvae drop to the soil, pupate underground in silken cocoons, overwinter, and emerge in spring as adults.

Moth caterpillars tend to go for the leaf-buds. The pine-shoot moth *Rhyacionia buoliana* is one which can cause much damage: its caterpillars bite their way into developing pine-buds and, by lining with silk the holes they excavate, prevent the resin from flooding them.

Some weevils (Curculionidae) also injure conifers badly. For example, the large pine weevil *Hylobius abietis* and another of these specialized beetles, *Pissodes pini*, both eat the leaf-buds and soft tissues, their effects being particularly significant on seedling trees.

Tunnellers in bark and wood

Most of the insects which bore through the bark and into the wood of conifers are beetles, usually well adapted for tunnelling with a narrow, elongated shape and minimal body protuberances. The mouths of their burrows are visible as neat, circular holes.

Beetles of the genus *Hylurgus* are notably elongated and live under the bark of pines; their larvae feed in the shoots, which turn brown and fall off. Another, *Dendroctonus micans*, is shaped like a bullet with parallel flanks; it burrows under the bark of pines or spruces and, as it bites out its tunnel, deposits eggs one by one along the sides.

Often, if the bark is stripped from a dead spruce or fir, a complex of tunnels, resembling the skeleton of a flatfish, is exposed. This is the work of the spruce bark-beetle *Ips typographus*. The horizontal main axis (the 'backbone') is a burrow hollowed out by the adult female; she lays eggs along its length, and the vertical side channels (the 'ribs') are made by the larvae moving away from the mother's gallery as they eat the wood. As the larvae grow, their tunnels become wider and they finally pupate in swollen chambers at the ends.

Another beetle, *Trypodendron lineatum*, often common in the fallen and dying branches of conifers, does not eat the wood itself. Instead, it devours a fungus whose spores are introduced by the female at the time of egg-laying. Although individually minute, the spores show collectively as a black pattern in the infected timber.

Wood-boring sawflies are far less numerous than beetles, but a conspicuous example is the greater woodwasp *Urocerus gigas*: startling in appearance, waspish in pattern, the female is larger than a queen hornet *Vespa crabro*, with a wing-span of 5 cm and a stiff, rapier-like ovipositor nearly 2 cm long. The woodwasp selects a diseased tree, frequently a larch or a fir (whereas the lesser woodwasp *U. noctilis* often attacks Scots pine) and at a right-angle to its body forces the ovipositor, which is hinged, through the thick bark to the solid wood. It seems remarkable that it should be able to drive this awl through such resistant material; yet a number of investigatory punctures may be made in rapid succession before an egg is passed, and a woodwasp is said to lay up to a hundred eggs. The whitish larvae excavate long, twisting tunnels and commonly take three years to reach pupation.

Even more remarkable are the wood-boring activities of an insect which specifically parasitizes the woodwasp. One of the larger of the ichneumon flies, it is delightfully named the persuasive burglar *Rhyssa persuasoria*, because it is not kept out by thick walls. Although the woodwasp larva is tunnelling deep beneath the bark and is wholly concealed, the ichneumon has some method of locating it. By means of a slender, flexible ovipositor up to 4 cm long, which seems absurdly flimsy for the work, but which it can rotate back and forth like a drill, it pierces the wood and deposits an egg next to the woodwasp grub. The ichneumon larva then parasitizes and finally kills the other.

Seed-eaters

Not surprisingly, some insects have become adapted for eating conifer seeds, which are rich in protein but non-resinous. Among these are certain of the small chalcid wasps, such as *Megastigmus spermotrophus*, whose larva feeds solely on the seeds of Douglas fir. Its manner of egg-laying somewhat resembles that of a woodwasp: the female drives her slender ovipositor through the outer scales of a young cone and inserts a single egg in each seed. The grub eats the seed and grows until, after 6–7 weeks, it fills the husk; it pupates inside the cone and may stay there for one or more winters before it emerges as a flying adult.

Just as the woodwasp has a particular enemy in the ichneumon *Rhyssa*, so the chalcid is parasitized by another wasp, *Mesopolobus spermotrophus*. The female must first obtain protein from a chalcid grub to produce eggs: having no long ovipositor or proboscis, she waits until the cone has opened sufficiently for her to creep in between the scales, cut a hole in an infested seed, and suck some body-fluid from the grub inside. Several days later she returns and lays an egg near the grub, on which the hatched larva then feeds.

Birds feeding on conifers

Food derived directly from conifers is usually limited; even the more edible parts are tough and resinous. It has been estimated that not more than 50 bird species are physically adapted to such an environment and able to survive on its peculiar foods.

Shoot-eaters

Three grouse wholly or partly adapted to conditions in coniferous forests are the capercaillie *Tetrao urogallus*, the black grouse *T. tetrix* and the hazel grouse *Bonasa bonasia*. The black is more a bird of clearings and the border between forest and moorland, while the hazel grouse needs an undergrowth of deciduous scrub. The capercaillie, however, is confined to upland coniferous forest: though in summer it takes a variety of vegetable foods, in winter it feeds almost exclusively on the buds and shoots of pine, larch and, to a lesser extent, spruce. The black grouse browses more on birch buds in winter, but its wide range of other foods includes conifer shoots. Unlike those of the two moorland grouse *Lagopus*, the males of black grouse and capercaillie meet the females only to mate, and they play no part in raising the young. A male may couple with several females during the season, and this promiscuity has led to competition. Male black grouse and, less consistently, capercaillies display communally at gatherings called 'leks'. Dense forest provides little space for such assemblies, however, and male capercaillies often posture and utter their cork-popping 'songs' alone, sometimes in trees. In a black grouse lek, which is attended for much of the year, even in snow in midwinter, each of the regular males has his own territory, those in the centre covering about 200 square metres. They posture to show their brilliant white undertail-coverts, hiss and flash their white underwings, flutter-jump, utter their powerful 'rookooing' song and, when necessary, actually fight; in the breeding season, the females wander through the territories and each eventually solicits a male.

Seed-eaters

Finches have short, stout bills with strong muscles. Some have evolved specialized beaks for particular diets: crossbills *Loxia*, which are essentially conifer birds, are a notable example. There are only three species – the 'common' crossbill *L. curvirostra*, the parrot crossbill *L. pityopsittacus* and the two-barred crossbill *L. leucoptera* – and all occur in the forests of north Europe. The adults are unique in having the mandibles crossed at the tip, the lower being turned to the left or right, but the young are hatched with straight bills and they leave the nest before the mandibles cross. The beaks of all three species are well adapted for extracting seeds from the woody plates of cones. When a crossbill inserts its beak between two of the plates and then closes it with its powerful neck muscles, the leverage exerted by the protruding tips of the mandibles, combined with a twisting action, is sufficient to force the plates apart; the cutting edges of the mandibles, moving one across the other, are used to shear the plates and the bird is able to extract the seed with its long tongue. Characteristically damaged cones can often be found on the ground. The parrot crossbill, breeding mainly in Fenno–Scandia and feeding largely on pine cones with thick plates, has the heaviest bill. The 'common' crossbill, widely distributed in Europe and living chiefly on spruce cones with thinner plates has a less stout beak. The two-barred crossbill, the western limit of whose range is Finland and which attacks the softer cones of larches and firs, has the slenderest beak of the three.

Crossbills are specialized in other ways. They are parrot-like acrobats which clamber about the branches and feed at any angle. They commonly breed in February and March, or even earlier, when the snow is on the ground. If the female leaves the nest for any length of time, the young are capable of surviving low temperatures by passing into a state of torpidity when their bodies become cold; they quickly recover when she returns and broods them. So closely linked are crossbills with the fluctuating cone crops that years of plenty often result in high populations and many of the birds then move restlessly away to other areas, thus avoiding starvation when the food supply fails: these are the years of the crossbill irruptions into Britain and adjacent parts of the Continent; some remain to breed for a year or two, but these immigrants seldom stay for long. Crossbills seem to be thirsty birds: they often nest within easy reach of water and drink frequently and copiously. Perhaps their diet of conifer seeds is a particularly dry one.

The pine grosbeak *Pinicola enucleator*, another finch of coniferous forests, is a muscular bird which looks something like a large crossbill, but it does not feed much on cones. A high proportion of its diet is berries of the forest undergrowth, especially juniper *Juniperus*, crowberry *Empetrum*, bearberry *Arctostaphylos* and bilberry *Vaccinium*, but in winter it turns to the berries of rowan *Sorbus aucuparia* and the buds and seeds of larch and spruce. Its powerful bill is used mainly to roll and crush the hard seeds of berries, and it attacks cones by hammering at them. The nutcracker *Nucifraga caryocatactes*, is a crow and not a finch. It, too, is characteristic of forests which are predominantly coniferous and its bill is powerful enough to hack open cones (and the nuts of hazels *Corylus avellana*), which it holds in its foot on a branch or the ground. In the Alps and in north Russia and Siberia, its main food is the seeds of the arolla pine *Pinus cembra* and, as in the case of the crossbills, large cone crops and high populations are often followed by eruptive movements which occasionally reach western Europe. Nutcrackers often perch on the tops of conifers and can thus damage the terminal buds.

Mammals feeding on conifers

Again, because of their toughness and resin content, the buds, shoots and bark of conifers seem to be unacceptable to most herbivorous mammals. Rodents are best equipped for such foods because of their chisel-like incisors, which grow throughout life, do not become worn away, are suited for gnawing and seemingly enable them to thrive in environments which would be fatal to many mammals. They are also adaptable to changing conditions and extremely prolific. Where trees are concerned, small ground rodents are largely limited to fallen seeds, but the arboreal squirrels come into their own.

Although the red squirrel *Sciurus vulgaris* is distributed virtually throughout our region, except for Iceland and parts of Britain and Ireland, it is found above all in coniferous forests. The staple food is conifer seeds, which the squirrels obtain by gnawing through the hard plates of the cones, a time-consuming process which has been estimated to yield a mere 15 g of consumable seed matter from 200 cones. If the cone harvest is poor, red squirrels turn to coniferous buds and cause serious damage by cutting off the leading shoots and stripping the bark; they are wasteful feeders, destroying much more than they actually eat. They have no true hibernation, but sleep for long periods during the winter. In autumn, they collect provisions in hollow trees or push seeds haphazardly into the soil; some of these sites are forgotten and entire stands of trees are said to have resulted.

Two other tree squirrels are found in north Europe. The flying squirrel *Pteromys volans*, which extends no farther west than Finland, is strictly a conifer species, while the American grey squirrel *S. carolinensis*, introduced into Britain and Ireland, is as much or more at home in broadleaved woodland.

A large herbivore which does browse on conifers in winter is included in the next section.

Mammals of forest margins and clearings

A forest provides cover for a variety of mammals, ranging in size from large herbivores to small bats and shrews. The cover screens them from predators and allows many to remain active during winter by sheltering them from the worst of the weather. But conifers supply few of them with food and the herbivores especially are constrained to feed where there is sufficient light for an undergrowth of softer, non-resinous plants to develop. Such places include the margins of lakes and swamps, often with lush aquatic shrubs; forest edges; and gaps left by felling, where there may be lichens, mosses, grasses and herbs.

The moose of North America, and the slightly smaller elk of the north Eurasian coniferous forests, are the same species, *Alces alces*. This is the biggest of all deer and is well adapted by sheer size, as well as by its thick hide, to withstand the cold of high latitudes. As an animal grows, its volume increases as the cube of its linear dimension, but its surface enlarges as the square: thus, larger mammals lose proportionally less heat by surface radiation. Structurally too, the elk's long, stilt-like legs are an asset for striding through deep snow in winter, when plant food is scarce and so scattered that much ground has to be covered. An adult bull elk may weigh 450 kg or more, be 2 m tall at the shoulder and have an antler-spread equal to its height. Such an animal is said to require 700 kg of vegetable food to survive the winter; the emaciated appearance of many elks in spring is a pointer to the difficulty they have. For most of the year, these are solitary animals: they are so large that each requires an extensive browsing territory and, while the bulls roam the forests alone, the cows are accompanied only by their calves. In spring and summer, they feed in lakes and swamps, submerging their bodies when necessary to obtain water-lilies and other aquatic vegetation. Once the water has frozen, however, the territories break down and the animals assemble where they are likely to find winter food. They either trample away the snow to expose berries and the lower shoots of willows, birches and conifers, or heap it into mounds on which they can stand to reach the higher growths. In Sweden and Russia, many are now accustomed to living near cultivated lands.

Two small rodents which live in the more open parts of forests and feed on roots and plants in the undergrowth are the root vole *Microtus ratticeps* and, on mossy ground, the wood lemming *Myopus schisticolor*. The vole is the more widely distributed and extends into the open arctic tundra. Both are prolific and subject to marked fluctuations in numbers. They remain active through most of the winter by sheltering between the soil surface and the lid of snow resting on top of the undergrowth: the snow serves as an insulator and the temperature of the air beneath it seldom falls much below freezing-point. In particularly severe weather, even mountain hares *Lepus timidus* sometimes enter the forest edges to find lichens. They also chew fallen cones to reach the seeds.

Feeders on invertebrates
Northern forest animals which feed on insects and similar prey have four

Great spotted woodpecker, vegetarian and predator.

ways of surviving the long winter, when most small invertebrates are inactive
and concealed: they can hibernate, migrate, change their diet, or have specialized methods of locating and extracting the hidden food. In general, the
majority of mammals of this kind either hibernate or alter their diets, while
all but the more specialized or adaptable birds tend to migrate from the far
north in winter.

Birds
Huge numbers of insectivorous birds, such as warblers and flycatchers, fly
from the tropics to the northern forests, clearings, scrub and marshes each
summer. There, they find an abundant food supply and long hours of day-

light for rearing their young, but in winter they would quickly starve. They are joined by others such as ducks and waders. Each has its own niche, of course, but the general pattern is the same and so this section concentrates mainly on some of the species which remain throughout the year.

The woodpeckers (Picidae), which as a family are mostly non-migratory, are good examples. Of the ten European species, all of which breed in at least part of our area, three are particularly associated with coniferous forests, these being the great spotted *Dendrocopos major*, the black *Dryocopus martius* and the three-toed *Picoides tridactylus*; a fourth, the lesser spotted *Dendrocopos minor*, occurs widely in conifers in Fenno–Scandia. All four extend north to the tree-limit. True woodpeckers, strongly built, are able to climb vertical trunks, aided by a short, stiff tail which acts as a prop; most have strongly clawed, zygodactyl feet (two toes directed forwards and two backwards), but the three-toed has only a single hind toe. They get their name from their habit of hammering holes in trees to obtain insect grubs; they also excavate their nest-holes in the trunks and 'drum' on wood as a form of spring advertisement. Their adaptations for these activities include a hard, chisel-like beak, bristly feathers round the nostrils which filter out the wood dust, powerful neck muscles and a peculiar head structure which absorbs the shock of the beak's blows by flexible joints between the skull bones. The tongue is also well adapted for extracting insect prey deep in holes and crevices: enormously long, worm-like and equipped with small barbs and a sticky tip, it is capable of protrusion up to three times the length of the bill, owing to the great length of the cartilaginous and bony supporting framework which extends right round the back of the skull and forward over the crown to the base of the bill. The entire apparatus moves forward when the tongue emerges and it is theoretically possible for a black woodpecker to protrude its tongue for 15 cm, though in practice it is usually only 5–9 cm. The characteristic foods of most woodpeckers are the larvae of wood-boring insects, such as beetles, moths and sawflies, but they also take a wide variety of prey from ants, beetles and other insects to spiders, earthworms, gall-causers and the numerous invertebrates living in mammal droppings. Great spotted woodpeckers, in particular, break into the hole-nests of tits *Parus*, pied flycatchers *Ficedula hypoleuca* and redstarts *Phoenicurus phoenicurus* to remove the young and, in winter especially, do the same to beehives to obtain the workers. In autumn, winter and early spring, this species eats berries, particularly rowan, and in the far north habitually breaks open pine and spruce cones.

Several species of tits are common on conifers. Most typical of pine and spruce forests north to the southern half of Fenno–Scandia are the crested tit *Parus cristatus* and, less exclusively, the coal *P. ater*. Largely to the north of these two and extending as far as the tree-limit, the Siberian tit *P. cinctus* is also confined to coniferous woodland, often with an admixture of birch or alder *Alnus*. Lastly, the willow tit *P. montanus*, reaching well north in Scandinavia, is frequently found in coniferous and mixed trees, often in damp places. Apart from the coal tit, which breeds in holes in walls, trees or the ground, the other three are unusual among perching birds in often partly or wholly excavating their own nest-sites in the soft, rotten wood of dead tree stumps. All tits feed primarily on a range of insects and larvae from aphids to beetles, also spiders, but are adaptable and in winter turn to weed seeds, beechmast and the berries of rowan and juniper; crested, coal and Siberian tits also extract pine and spruce seeds from ripe cones.

Treecreepers *Certhia familiaris* often move about with tit flocks in winter and, except in Britain and Ireland, are confined largely to coniferous and mixed woodland. They nest behind loose bark. Their long, decurved bills enable them to pick spider cocoons and other invertebrates from cracks in the bark and they are insectivorous throughout the year, though they do occasionally take seeds of weeds and even conifers.

The brambling *Fringilla montifringilla* is a finch, adapted for eating seeds, which breeds north to the tree-limit in Fenno–Scandia and which nests in open coniferous forests, or along their edges, notably where there are birches: here in the summer it feeds mainly on the larvae of looper moths (Geometridae). There is an advantage to the growing nestlings in receiving such a rich source of protein, and many finches feed their young on insects; in this case the adults live almost exclusively on these caterpillars. In autumn, bramblings quit the forests and migrate south and west in Europe, where they feed on a variety of seeds including wheat, grass seeds, berries and, above all, beechmast.

Mammals

Shrews (Soricidae) are among the smallest and most voracious of the insectivorous mammals. Two which are widespread in more open parts of the northern forests are the common shrew *Sorex araneus* and the pygmy shrew *S. minutus*. Even the former is only 62–85 mm long plus 30–55 mm of tail, and weighs 5–14 g, while the pygmy justifies its name with a body length of 45–60 mm and a weight of 2·5–7·0 g; the rarer least shrew *S. minutissimus*, a much more local species in Fenno–Scandia, may be as little as 35 mm long and weigh a mere 1·5 g. Being small, shrews have a relatively large surface, rapidly dissipate energy, and have to feed continually to stay alive. They consume at least their body weight of food daily, even up to three times this amount when it is plentiful, and sleep in short 'cat-naps' between bursts of frenzied searching for things to eat. In winter they subsist largely on invertebrate eggs, larvae and pupae which they dig out of the ground: like lemmings and voles, they remain active in the narrow space beneath the capping of snow held up by the undergrowth. But, despite their feverish activity, they are short-lived: even in temperate latitudes a common shrew has a life expectancy of only 18 months.

Bats are another major group of insectivores, but the northern coniferous forests are generally unfavourable to them: the flying insects on which they depend are seldom abundant and, at best, tend to be localized in clearings or swamps. A particularly widespread bat that occurs north to the limit of tree growth is the whiskered *Myotis mystacinus*. It flies moderately high when feeding and, like the long-eared bat *Plecotus auritus* (which also extends north to south Fenno–Scandia), picks insects and spiders off trees. It hibernates in caves, in holes in trees, quarries or river banks, or in spaces under the roofs of houses. The bat confined mainly to arctic Europe is the northern bat *Eptesicus nilssoni*. Best known in Scandinavia, although there are a few scattered records in central and western Europe, it flutters through the forests at tree-top level where it feeds on flying insects. Throughout the year, it rests by day in buildings, where it is more often seen than high up within forests. On the approach of unfavourable weather, some individuals have been known to migrate long distances.

Larger predators
A number of birds of prey, both diurnal and nocturnal, and carnivorous mammals are characteristic of the northern forests.

Hawks
Whereas the high-flying falcons *Falco*, with their long, pointed wings and ability to dive on their victims at high speed, belong to open country, the round-winged hawks *Accipiter* are birds of the forest, either coniferous or broadleaved. They are somewhat slower, but are better equipped for sudden twists and turns when chasing small birds between trees. The sparrowhawk *A. nisus* and the larger goshawk *A. gentilis* are both widespread in Europe, north to the very limit of the trees and the forest tundra, although the northern populations, particularly of the sparrowhawk, tend to move south in winter. Both feed mainly on birds, but many goshawks take a fair proportion of mammals, while sparrowhawks eat some mammals and a good many insects. As is the case with some of the falcons, the males of both species are noticeably smaller than the females and so tend to take smaller prey.

Another widespread raptor of the northern forests, often nesting in the very crown of a pine or a spruce, is the osprey *Pandion haliaetus*, but it feeds almost exclusively on fish up to nearly 2 kg in weight and is always found within a few kilometres of a lake. The northern waters are frozen in winter, so it is a summer visitor.

Owls
Because of their specializations for night vision, owls are well suited to the deep shade of the northern forests. Some are able to distinguish objects in light 100 times less intense than that needed by man, though they cannot see in complete darkness. Their eyes, set in front of the head in a flat face, give good binocular vision and the head can be turned through more than 180°. Hearing is also acute. Owls depend more on their silent flight than on speed

for seizing prey, an obvious advantage between the obstacles of trees: their feathers are bordered with loose fringes which reduce the disturbance of the air.

Seven owls, five large or medium-sized and two small, are widely distributed in the north European conifer forests. Most are generally resident throughout the year, some periodically become locally abundant in seasons of plentiful food, and all tend to reduce interspecific competition by being spaced out and adopting different nesting and feeding habits. The largest species, the eagle owl *Bubo bubo*, lays in a scrape on rocky ground, in a hollow tree or in the old nest of a bird of prey, and is powerful enough to kill a small deer or a bird as big as a capercaillie; it has even been recorded preying on all the other northern owls, except the great grey *Strix nebulosa* which is of comparable size. The great grey and the hawk owl *Surnia ulula* also take over the old nests of large birds, but often prefer the hollow tops of broken conifers; despite their very different sizes (the great grey is nearly twice as big), both feed largely on small mammals. The hawk owl, however, does take a certain number of small birds and the same applies to another rodent predator, the Ural owl *S. uralensis*, but the latter also kills larger prey and nests in a range of sites from hollow trees to rocky crevices and even flat ground. The long-eared owl *Asio otus* breeds almost exclusively in old nests, more rarely on the ground, and preys on a wide variety of small mammals, birds and insects; in turn, it is much the most frequent of the owl

The eagle owl, capable of killing a small deer.

victims of the eagle owl. The two small owls, the Tengmalm's *Aegolius funereus* and the pygmy *Glaucidium passerinum*, the latter smaller than a starling *Sturnus vulgaris*, both nest in old woodpecker holes or other enclosed tree cavities and feed on small birds, voles and mice, but the Tengmalm's is largely nocturnal except where it has to hunt in the arctic twilight, while the pygmy is partly diurnal.

Weasels and wolverines

Apart from brown bears *Ursus arctos*, which are omnivorous, and wolves *Canis lupus*, which wander only sporadically into northern forests, the mammalian carnivores most typical of the coniferous belt belong to the weasel family (Mustelidae). They range in size from the weasel *Mustela nivalis*, with a body length of 13–23 cm and weighing only 100 g, to the wolverine *Gulo gulo*, which can be as large and heavy as a big dog.

That they are adaptable animals is shown by the range of environmental conditions they exploit. For example, the stoat *M. erminea* and the weasel are common from temperate latitudes through the coniferous forests to the tundra, and the farther north they live the whiter they become in winter. In fact, they are found wherever there are sufficient small animals for them to eat. As in the case of the owls, competition is to some extent lessened by different feeding habits. The weasel, the smallest carnivore, can work its way under the snow cover to hunt voles and shrews in their runways; it even climbs trees, but never wanders far. The stoat, which is half as big again, also takes larger prey up to the size of hares and, since such animals are more dispersed, has a feeding range at least ten times as great. The pine marten *Martes martes* is an arboreal hunter, particularly in coniferous forests, but also takes rodents and birds on the ground; when pursuing a squirrel in the branches, it approaches stealthily and finally takes a leap of 2 m or more to fall on its victim. The European mink *Mustela lutreola*, an animal of conifer settings mainly to the east of the Baltic, avoids the forest interior, but lives near water in rock crevices and river banks, swims well and captures fish and aquatic mammals such as water voles *Arvicola terrestris*.

The most formidable of all is the wolverine, which, like the stoat and the weasel, ranges north into the tundra. The prey it kills itself includes small mammals and birds up to the size of grouse, some of which it stores in snow against winter shortage, but it is capable of destroying animals as big as young elks and other deer. It is, however, chiefly a carrion-feeder and a pirate: it will challenge another large mammal for its kill, and its ferocity is such that even a wolf will abandon its prey in the face of its intimidation.

HEATHLAND

Distribution and origin

True heaths are confined to a limited part of northern Europe, mainly between the latitudes 50° and 60°N. They are unique to this quite small area, but have been much fragmented by developments of all kinds. Today, they vary in extent from the 4000 square km of Lüneburg in west Germany to the narrow strips of *côtil* along the tops of the cliffs in the Channel Islands.

Heaths are usually below 200 m and maritime, as in Ireland, in Brittany and along the European coast to Poland (as well as on the north side of the Baltic, though there they are more infrequent). In southern Britain, on the other hand, inland heaths extend northwest to meet the moorlands. But numerous ancient heaths – for example, Hampstead in north London and Mousehold at Norwich in Norfolk – have been urbanized, while many small rural areas have grown up into woodland, with perhaps only bracken *Pteridium aquilinum* to indicate their former nature.

Many of the sandy heathlands scientifically investigated occur in regions formerly covered by primeval forests. These were obliterated, more often than not in Neolithic times by man using fire to burn down trees and clear the soil for agriculture, and have not recovered; their failure may be due to several causes, often their exposed situation or man's continued activities. Like heaths, lower moorlands are the 'degenerate' replacers of forests but, though both coastal dunes and heaths are sandy and notably exposed, their origins are quite different: a heath results from a process of decline, whereas a sand dune is built up from raw materials.

Soil

Heathland soils undergo few changes. They remain acid throughout, and relatively infertile. They lie in regions with a drier climate than that giving rise to moorland, but certain characteristics of their soil must be considered in relation to the peat layer, which is one of their diagnostic features and which forms a shallow, firm but rather dry accumulation near the surface, made up of vegetable debris not completely decomposed. Peat does produce some mineral salts, but these are insufficient in both quantity and range to maintain a high level of fertility and tend to be leached away so that the surface remains impoverished.

Acids diffuse from the peat layer; if, say, before the establishment of peat, the soil contained traces of alkaline material in the form of limestone, this has long ago been lost by leaching. Peat is the main factor in acidifying heathland

LEFT *Southern shrub heath of gorse and heather invaded by pines, Dorset.* RIGHT *Soil profile on heathland shows residual podsol (grey) and pan (orange).*

soil, but its sandy components may also derive from acid rocks. The peat readily absorbs the sun's rays and so promotes one of the most striking features of heathland soil – the great temperature variation through which it often passes during the 24 hours of a summer day; at times this can be as much as 50°C between day and night. The quivering of the air just above the ground on sunny days shows that the surface has become very warm. Owing to the large amount of water which peat absorbs, it tends to stop rain water reaching the lower levels. Most of the precipitation evaporates in warm weather and the shallow peat soon dries out again. Being close to the surface, the peat acts as a lid in another way: it hinders the flow of gases from the atmosphere into the gaps between the soil particles, so that these remain poorly aerated.

Pan is a normal feature of the soil on well-established heaths. This is derived from ferrous compounds leached from the upper levels and carried below in solution; the yellow-orange colour of many sands and gravels is due to the presence of iron, which, mainly in the form of hydrated oxides, gradually accumulates at a depth as a well-defined hard layer, the pan. Eventually this becomes so impenetrable that only plants with shallow root systems can become established above it, and it is therefore one of the factors holding back the return to a forest climax. In short, heathlands provide arid, desert-like environments, lacking easily accessible water and subject to the drying effects of wind and sun. Altogether, heathland top soil is not conducive to a lush vegetation.

Heathland environment

This aridity applies strictly to flat, plain-like areas with negligible undulations. Hollows in the ground cause the water content of the soil to vary, which is reflected in varying vegetation and animal life. Where depressions permit water to stand, the resulting pools comprise three categories: they are either permanent or temporary; if temporary, they are either intermittent, re-forming at the same sites after periods of drying, or ephemeral, in which case they do not reappear because of changes in the configuration of the terrain. All three call for different adaptations by colonizing plants and animals.

Hollows infer elevations. Where these are windswept, they may give the impression of being without vegetation, but, in fact, hillocks with no plant colonizers seldom persist as they are generally eroded and levelled. Those exposed to all but the strongest wind are often capped with wavy hair-grass *Deschampsia flexuosa* and are defined as 'hair-grass hills'; the grass fixes the soil against erosion. Animals occupying such localities are largely dependent on the vegetation, obtaining their food from flowers or from prey in the cover.

The activity of many heat-loving animals is due to the high surface temperatures in summer. Others, less tolerant of heat, dig themselves into the soil; a well-developed propensity for this is often characteristic of heathland animals, especially bees, wasps, beetles, flies and spiders. Adaptations to wind resistance are shown by species which have lost their wings altogether, have reduced wings, or show special abilities for clinging to plants or to objects on the ground. In general, the animal life of heaths is rich, but many of the invertebrates are tiny and more or less concealed 'cryptozooites'.

Of the larger species, butterflies, which require both warmth and direct sunlight for successful mating, are often comparatively plentiful but some other invertebrate groups are poorly represented. Although snails occur on heathland, they are neither as numerous or as varied as on lime-rich soils: snails require calcium carbonate for building their shells. Earthworms and millipedes are few: most worms require accumulated humus or a rich supply of dead vegetable matter, such as fallen leaves, while millipedes need damp surroundings to survive, because, unlike insects, they lose water through their integument. Similarly, woodlice, being crustaceans and therefore representatives of a mainly aquatic class, are even rarer on heaths.

Plants of heathland include many adapted to a particularly dry environment, which are known as 'xerophytes' or, more accurately, 'xeromorphs'. This condition is apparently correlated with a number of structural peculiarities, including a reduction of the transpiring (evaporating) surfaces into spines or very narrow leaves, reminiscent of conifer needles; stomata (pores) sunk in pits or grooves which curtail evaporation; the presence of hairs which trap a layer of moist air close to the surface; and the development of water-storage tissue in the stems or leaves of succulent plants. Heathland plants show all these modifications, the reasons for which seem to be the aridity of the habitat, the acidity of the soil water, which makes its uptake by vascular plants difficult, and the drying effect of the wind in exposed situations.

A casual glance shows that a heath is not homogeneous: in addition to permanent or temporary pools, quite tall-growing shrubs and trees occur in groups, entirely replacing low-growing plants. Such differences are due probably to the soil rather than to climate or biotic factors, although man, the most important of these, may organize heathland to suit his convenience and plant trees to act as windbreaks screening arable areas. Large plants can be expected to induce microclimatic changes which affect the dependent animal and plant species, and are conveniently considered under the two major subdivisions of herbaceous and shrub heaths.

Herbaceous heath

Strictly this is a misnomer since the dominant heather *Calluna vulgaris* is an evergreen undershrub, but the term may conveniently be used for areas of low vegetation, though some of the components have woody structures. On old heaths, heather occurs in almost pure stands; in wetter parts it commonly associates with cross-leaved heath *Erica tetralix* and in drier with bell heather *E. cinerea*, which may also 'go it alone' on large stretches – for example, on Tresco in the Isles of Scilly. Particularly acid conditions favour bilberry *Vaccinium myrtillus*, which is often transitional between heath and moorland.

Owing to the deep shade under richly branched heather, typical heath has a rather scanty flora made up almost entirely of lichens and mosses. Where the heather is not so pure, common associates are the two gorses *Ulex minor* and *U. gallii*, tormentil *Potentilla erecta*, heath bedstraw *Galium saxatile*, heath speedwell *Veronica officinalis* and wood sage *Teucrium scorodonia*, as well as bracken and various grasses, the most typical of which is wavy hair-grass. Many of these are intolerant of lime-rich soils, while heath speedwell, hair-grass and common thyme *Thymus drucei* are adapted to the dryness of heathland. Where bracken moves in, it can take over from the heathers as the dominant plant, spreading long distances vegetatively. It is promoted by grazing rabbits *Oryctolagus cuniculus* and sheep, because neither eat it, and by fires, because it colonizes burnt ground rapidly. A noteworthy subsidiary plant is the parasitic dodder *Cuscuta epithymum*, found entwined round various hosts, especially heather, and rampant on some Breton heaths.

Heather is of special interest because of its lack of root-hairs: their job of absorbing nutrients is taken over by fungal hyphae (tubes) in the symbiotic association called 'mycorrhiza'. Quite apart from water intake, the fungus probably fixes nitrogen from the soil atmosphere and so adds to the supply of combined nitrogen normally available in richer soils. Heather also illustrates xeromorphy: besides being narrow and rather tough, its leaves have their margins rolled downwards to form a groove and enclose the under-surface from which most water is transpired. Water loss may be further slowed down by hairs which partly fill the cavity within the groove.

Shrub heath

This contains a range of species so varied that many of them may properly be regarded as casual. Those which are sufficiently widespread include gorse *Ulex europaeus* and broom *Sarothamnus scoparius*. Both occupy the lighter, more silicious soils, but gorse is the more liable to be cut by frost in exposed situations. Gorse leaves are rigid, furrowed spines with a small surface area tending to reduce transpiration. Only immediately following germination of the seeds are flat, non-specialized leaves produced. Morphologically, broom is equally remarkable. Its small true leaves are shed early in the year. Thereafter its green, strongly angled stems become its assimilating structures.

Shrub heath is invaded on the Channel Islands *côtils* by brambles *Rubus* and honeysuckle *Lonicera periclymenum* which, associated with gorse, makes it an almost impenetrable cover for small breeding and migrant birds. Inland English heaths may be colonized by hawthorns *Crataegus*, brambles and briars *Rosa*, formerly the breeding habitat of the red-backed shrike *Lanius collurio*. Where parts of an old heath are reverting to forest, silver birch *Betula pendula* may proliferate: it tends to colonize dry, silicious soils and forms an intermediate stage between the herbs and shrubs and the forest climax. It is often attacked by a fungus, *Taphrina turgida*, causing the bunched, twiggy growths known as witches'-brooms. Scots pine *Pinus sylvestris*, although not part of the heath's main road to forest succession, has a widespread distribution, native or planted (as in England) and then regenerating; in some places, it forms woods so dense as to kill off the usual heathland flora.

For any heathland colonizer, the greatest single problem is that of shelter. Many plants respond to exposure by developing a compact, cushion-like form of growth. Normally, heather grows as a diffuse undershrub, spreading widely with branched, twisted stems which root at the base and bear numerous short axillary shoots. When, however, the plants are more or less isolated from one another, each tends to become a dome-shaped mass, rarely more than 35 cm high and with few shoots projecting laterally, presumably because they have either been 'burnt' by wind or shortened by grazing animals, but with others arising thickly within the domed enclosure. This provides shelter for many small animals, which is enhanced by a dense growth of lichens. Even gorse, a much larger shrub, assumes a more compact form than usual when it grows scattered on the drier parts of exposed heaths: should grazing animals be active, a bush may be bitten short and maintained as a dense mass only a few centimetres high and wide, also giving cover to a varied and populous fauna. If these clumps were shaken out above a sheet of paper, some of the animals they shelter would appear.

That the microclimate inside a plant cushion varies less than in the open

Bracken is able to recolonize burnt heathland rapidly by means of its underground stems, Surrey.

can be tested over several consecutive days. Temperature and humidity are notably more stable within the clump than outside. This relative stability generally favours the small animals which take shelter there.

Invertebrate colonizers

Arthropod colonizers, which include the insects, are legion, since many species are well adapted for dryness. Commonly, their horny exoskeleton of chitin has an additional covering of wax; the exposure of heathland to solar radiation suits their metabolism and they become very active in sunshine. The most obvious connection between the vegetation of a habitat and its colonizers is shown by those herbivorous animals which feed directly on the typical plants.

Notable among herbivorous insects are butterflies, moths and certain crickets and grasshoppers. The larvae of the small heath butterfly *Coenonympha pamphilus* feed on various grasses, especially those growing in the open on dry soils, and the adults fly in numbers on heaths. But few insects, which are particularly liable to attack by predators, remain conspicuous for long in such open surroundings: they either hide or are protectively coloured. Thus, this butterfly, when it comes to rest with its wings closed and held vertically, reveals a blotchy underside of tawny and greenish tints which merges with the colours of sandy heaths. Another grass feeder, the grayling butterfly *Hipparchia semele*, suns itself on exposed sandy soil and other warm surfaces; when the caterpillar pupates, the chrysalis is normally in a hollow space about 1 cm beneath the surface of the soil, the particles of sand cohering slightly to form a protective enclosure near the roots of a grass tussock. The heath rustic moth *Amathes agathena* is typical of larger heaths and moors: the larva feeds on heathers, but conceals itself in daytime. A heathland moth caterpillar normally never seen is that of the map-winged swift *Hepialus fusconebulosa*: it feeds underground on the roots and rhizomes of bracken and the adult generally flies about over heaths where this plant is plentiful. Some of the heathland bees and wasps are closely associated with specific plants. Thus, the heath bumblebee *Bombus jonellus* takes nectar from the flowers of heather and bilberry; the girdled colletes *Colletes succincta* is a small solitary bee which shows a preference for heather flowers and so is often to be seen on heaths in August; and larvae of the gall wasp *Xestophanes brevitarsis* can develop only inside galls induced on the aerial parts of tormentil, a common plant of dry, acid soils.

Aphids are bugs which normally take food from two species of plants in the course of their life-cycle; if one of these is typical of heathland, the aphid can be regarded as a heath-dweller. But some of the related capsid bugs (Miridae) show a merging of feeding habits. For example, *Orthotylus ericetorum* occurs on plants typical of dry heaths such as heather and bell heather; *Systellonotus triguttatus* feeds on tormentil and heather, but is also partly predatory and kills and sucks the body-juices of aphids and other small animals; and *Globiceps cruciatus*, although closely associated with creeping willow *Salix repens* in the damper parts of heaths, is largely predatory.

Several grasshoppers, normally herbivores, are notable among the insect fauna of heaths. They are closely related to the migratory and desert locusts of Africa and, like them, can feed successfully on a range of fresh plant material although they seem to prefer the foliage of grasses, wild and cultivated alike. Probably several factors combine to make sandy heaths attractive to them: these places become hot in summer and the loose, sandy soil facilitates the insertion of the abdomen when the female deposits her egg-pods underground. *Psophus stridulus* is a grasshopper with powerful lift; at rest, its predominantly khaki upperparts make it unnoticeable on heaths, but, as soon as it takes off, the hindwings display a flash of red, brilliant and unexpected. Bright colouring is also revealed in flight by both the blue-winged grasshopper *Oedipoda caerulescens* and the blue-winged steppe grasshopper *Sphingonotus caerulans*. The red or blue shows its survival value as soon as an attempt is made to net the insect: more often than not, the grasshopper drops to the ground, closes the forewings over the hind pair, and seems to vanish. A bird or other animal predator is likely to be confused.

Regrettably, no grasshoppers with colour flashes on their hindwings are found in Britain. Those mentioned have a wide distribution on the European mainland, certainly up to south Sweden and, in the case of *P. stridulus*, as far north as Finland. All require heat and colonize sun-baked, sandy places. A less brilliant species which does occur in Britain and is also widely distributed on the Continent, closely associated with sand, is the mottled grasshopper *Myrmeleotettix maculatus*: tawny in colour with a patch of green, it is well camouflaged on heaths.

Subterranean builders

Insects which utilize the looseness of the sand particles in heathland soil to make a variety of shelters form a high proportion of the fauna. Of 361 species recorded from a heath in the English West Midlands during a three-year period, 84 or nearly a quarter were of this kind.

It is probably because of the warmth of the soil and the ease with which it can be worked that such general feeders as ants are widespread and often numerous on heaths. *Formica rufibarbis* frequents the more open, warm and sunny parts, where it excavates subterranean nests, the entrances to which are usually difficult to locate; in contrast to the situation in the colonies of most European ants, only a single egg-laying queen is present. The negro ant *F. fusca* tends on heaths to be commonest in places with access to damp patches, since its nests are constructed from a mixture of sand particles and mud.

Bumblebees are social, their society consisting of a single egg-laying queen, a few males and a more or less numerous retinue of sterile females (workers) whose function is that of taking over from the queen the enlargement of the nest, the collection of food and the rearing of the larvae. Several species establish their nests on the surface of the ground, sheltered within a tuft of grass or similar cover, but the heath bumble, probably the most characteristic social bee where heather and bilberry are plentiful, makes its nest in a hole in the soil, often taking over a mouse hole.

Indeed, solitary bees are generally more in evidence than social bees on heaths. Nearly always smaller, they obtrude by numbers, not size. In this environment, most are mining bees, which excavate shafts in light soil. One of the most primitive genera of solitary bees is *Hylaeus*, with about 17 species in north and west Europe. The one most likely to be found on heathland is *H. confusa*, but it does not mine into sand; instead, it occupies holes in the stems of bushes or makes use of hollows in old timber and, consequently, occurs on shrub rather than herbaceous heath. It is primitive because it has no specialized apparatus on the exterior of the body for packing pollen; it collects both pollen and nectar in the stomach and ejects this as a viscous, yellow paste for its larvae.

Two genera, *Lasioglossum* and *Andrena*, predominate among the true mining bees. Their shafts may be on their own, but are usually in groups. On a south-facing bank of sand – for instance, alongside a track worn into a depressed pathway – hundreds of holes may be arranged close together within a few metres. Members of the large genus *Lasioglossum* often develop extensive colonies, with a range of aspects for the entrances. I have noted a group of more than 200 shafts of the white-zoned mining bee *L. leucozonium* in the sandy soil of a path trodden firm by walkers, where people passed hourly on foot and sometimes even cycled.

Several *Lasioglossum* species are on the wing from early spring to late autumn. Typically, the males die after mating in August–September, whereas the females bury themselves in sand to hibernate. In spring, these females then excavate shafts, laying their eggs singly in each of a row of cells; after they have provisioned all the cells with a paste of pollen and nectar, they die. On hatching, the larvae devour the paste, grow, pupate and, as adults, leave the shaft in reverse order to that in which the eggs were deposited. These are the bees which appear in autumn, the females surviving the winter. Unlike *Hylaeus*, *Lasioglossum* species carry pollen on their legs: thyme, willows *Salix*, cinquefoils *Potentilla* and hawkweeds *Hieracium* seem to be the flowers most often visited in heathy places.

Andrena bees are numerous, with more than 60 species recorded from Britain alone. These are the miners that are most liable to be confused with hive bees *Apis mellifera*. Like *Lasioglossum*, they tolerate a range of aspects in the sandy soils where they excavate in dry, grassy banks or small paths, nearly always in colonies with a few to several hundred burrows close together. Members of this genus are often about early in the year. The hairy-legged mining bee *Dasypoda hirtipes* also normally nests in colonies, but seems to be restricted to sandy heaths, sand hills and disused gravel pits near the coast. The entrance hole to its unlined burrow is often framed by a small bank of sand; the main shaft can be as long as 50 cm and from it side burrows branch out, each ending in a cell. Long hairs on the thighs and tibiae are used for gathering pollen, but this species can be said to obtain pollen with the whole of the body as it performs virtual somersaults in the flowers; by the disturbances it must cause to the essential parts, it can be regarded as an exceptionally effective pollinator. It is a fairly common and familiar bee in late summer, often found on the flower-heads of the daisy family (Compositae).

Wasps which burrow in heathland are active, rather restless insects and differ from bees in their feeding habits: they are predatory, obtaining their protein from small invertebrates, while bees are herbivorous and get theirs from pollen. Both visit flowers for nectar. Two groups which excavate the soil are digger wasps and spider-hunting wasps.

Each of the several species of digger wasps tends to restrict its feeding to herbivorous prey of a particular kind. A mode of life typical of digger wasps

Hairy-legged mining bee excavating its burrow in sandy soil, August.

is that of the red-banded sand wasp *Ammophila sabulosa*, which is widespread throughout the summer in sandy areas, notably coastal heaths and dunes. The female first excavates the nest, a small cell at the bottom of a vertical burrow; the entrance is camouflaged with particles of sand and gravel. The prey, a caterpillar bigger than the wasp, is paralyzed by several stings in the thorax and dragged often some distance to the nest; on the way, the wasp occasionally releases its prey to reorientate itself and the injured caterpillar may then be seized by another predator. When the burrow has been reopened, the prey is dragged into it and a single egg deposited on its underside; the nest is closed again and camouflaged, the egg is left to hatch, and the larva to feed on what amounts to a supply of fresh meat, while the adult moves away to dig another shaft.

Although not, in fact, a digger, the heath potter wasp *Eumenes coarctata*, restricted to the southern part of our area, also paralyzes small caterpillars to provision its nest. This is an exceptionally beautiful structure in the form of a broad, low flask with a diameter of 1–1·5 cm, fashioned from clay pellets cemented together with the insect's saliva and attached to a heather stalk. The single larva is provisioned with up to ten caterpillars.

Spider-hunting wasps have a specialized diet and are an example of one predator devouring another, instead of the commoner relationship of predator attacking herbivore. The dark anoplius *Anoplius fuscus* is widely distributed and can be seen throughout the summer in sandy places. The fertilized females overwinter and start to excavate their burrows and hunt for prey in spring. Large wolf spiders, such as *Trochosa terricola*, are stung twice in the nerve centres of the cephalothorax and paralyzed; when, after a few seconds, the spider ceases to struggle, it is dragged to the nesting site. Here it is wedged temporarily between plant stalks while the nest is being completed. After the spider has been pulled into the burrow, the egg is laid and the mouth of the shaft is closed and camouflaged.

Relationships are sometimes complicated by parasitism. Thus, the spotted ceropales *Ceropales maculata* is a wasp specialized, not as a hunter, but as a parasite on other spider-hunting wasps. The female flies over the ground, searching for a spider-hunting wasp in the act of dragging its own prey to its nest. Should there be some hesitation by the hunter, so that momentarily it relinquishes possession of the spider, the female ceropales drops on to the spider and quickly inserts a single egg in one of its lung-books (respiratory organs). Occasionally, the ceropales makes a direct attack on the hunter and succeeds in placing an egg during the ensuing struggle. The ceropales's egg is laid before the hunter's egg and so hatches sooner; the larval parasite kills the hunter's larva when this emerges and thereafter eats the spider.

A possible derivation from the habit of catching food to provision larvae protected in an underground burrow is adaptation of the burrow for catching the food as well. The tiger beetles (Cicindelidae) are a widespread family of heathland insects which excavate such burrows. The antlions (Myrmeleontidae) are another; they are not found in Britain, but have several representatives on the Continent.

The adult green tiger beetle *Cicindela campestris*, an active wanderer during spring and early summer on heathland, is fiercely predatory. The larva lives in a vertical burrow excavated in somewhat firm, sandy soil, its head and large prothorax close to the entrance and held horizontally somewhat in the manner of a manhole-cover. Should a small insect pass near the hole, the larva darts from its lair, seizes the prey with its stout mandibles and drags it to the bottom of the burrow. By the time the larva has attained full size, the shaft may be 30 cm long. Antlions frequent sunny parts of sandy heathland where there is protection from wind. The adults are seldom seen: they reach maturity in June–July, hide in vegetation during the day and fly at dusk. The larvae occupy funnel-shaped snares dug in the sandy soil: that of *Myrmeleon formicarius* has a diameter·of 3–4 cm and a depth of 2 cm. Only the sharply pointed mandibles of the larva protrude above the sand surface. Small animals, such as ants, falling into the funnel are gripped by the mandibles and held until their body fluids have been sucked out. Pupation takes place in the burrow.

One advantage of the burrowing habit is that both the larvae and their food supplies are out of reach of possible competitors. For example, burying or sexton beetles (Silphidae) locate the fresh carcases of vertebrates by smell and, if these are small, bury them underground in graves of fairly specialized form. They avoid fly-blown meat and attack and drive away bluebottles *Calliphora*. After a cleaned corpse has been interred, the female beetle lays her eggs at a short distance from it. While the eggs of bluebottles are to be counted in hundreds and may hatch within 12 hours, those of a single sexton beetle seldom exceed 20 and may take as long as five days to hatch: clearly the relationship between the two insects is strongly competitive.

Dung beetles have similar habits. The minotaur beetle *Typhaeus typhoeus* rolls the manure pellets of rabbits or sheep into its burrows, which are sometimes as long as 1·5 cm; it lays its eggs on the surface of the buried dung. Dor beetles *Geotrupes* are nocturnal: they excavate a number of shafts below deposits of manure, and two working together can put an entire cowpat underground during a single night. Both these genera of dung beetles occur in a variety of places, including heathy commons where there are grazing farm animals; the minotaur seems to be decreasing, but is especially characteristic of sandy heaths where rabbits feed.

Predators and parasites

Although far less numerous in population and less in total biomass than the plant-eating forms, those invertebrates which devour other animals tend to be conspicuous because of their prowling habits. Beetles, the largest of the insect orders, form one of the major sections of the invertebrate carnivores, among which the rove beetles (Staphylinidae) are especially noteworthy. One widely distributed and locally common in heathlands is *Stenus geniculatus*, which lives mainly on hillocks, under the cover of heather, moss and lichen. This beetle preys on springtails (Collembola), which it captures by extruding a sticky tongue.

But the predators which exceed all others numerically in almost any land habitat, and certainly on heaths and moors, are spiders: most are so small they are easily overlooked, but their numbers compensate for lack of size. Their role in controlling flies, many of which are in some way injurious, is a most important environmental factor. Among the larger species which frequent heaths are the various wolf spiders (Lycosidae), so named from their habit of running rapidly over the soil and leaping on their prey instead of spinning a snare. A member of another family, the labyrinth spider *Agelena labyrinthica* does spin a snare: it looks much like a house spider *Tegenaria*, but is found only out-of-doors, typically in heather or dry grass. Its large web consists of a vertical retreat-tube opening at the top into a closely woven carpet often 30 cm across. Over the carpet, threads are stretched criss-cross up to a height of 20–30 cm. Flying or jumping insects which strike these threads fall on to the carpet, whereupon the spider darts out and kills them. *Araneus quadratus* is closely related to the garden orb-web spider *A. diadematus* and makes a similar web with sticky threads: its circular nets are commonly attached to the branches of broom or gorse on shrub heaths.

Related to spiders, and still more readily missed than even the smallest, are the false scorpions (Pseudoscorpiones), bizarre-looking animals seldom longer than 3 mm, which lurk in the dense cover of small plants or ground litter. *Neobisium muscorum* is one of the commonest in Europe; on heaths, it occurs in sand underneath mosses and lichens, although it may turn up wherever any very small invertebrate prey is hiding. Springtails make up much of its food: these are seized with its pincers and broken up, digestive fluids are poured over the remains, and the product is sucked up.

Parasitism is really a specialized form of predation, in which the predator budgets so well and achieves so stable a relationship with its prey that the host is kept alive, providing the parasite with a continuous supply of food until it has itself finished feeding and is ready to disperse. Then the host is killed. This is the mode of life of the parasitic wasps of the families Ichneumonidae and Braconidae, which typically lay eggs in the living bodies of caterpillars of butterflies and moths early in their metamorphosis. Structural modifications are seen in *Stylops muelleri*, a beetle-like insect of the order Strepsiptera, which parasitizes the heathland mining bee *Andrena vaga*. Only the male ever leaves the host: his flying wings are fan-like and his elytra modified as club-shaped organs. In contrast, the female has lost all resemblance to a beetle: her abdomen has become a soft sac lying inside the bee's abdomen and her head and thorax a flat brown plate protruding between the host's abdominal segments. *A. vaga* appears early in the year and, on warm spring days, *Stylops* males swarm around the burrows searching for the females inside the bees. A single female *Stylops* produces numerous eggs, from which develop thousands of active larvae each about 0·3 mm long. These leave the host bee when it is visiting flowers and transfer to other bees which come to the same flowers; they are thus carried back to the bees' nests where they work their way into the bee larvae and further development takes place. Stylopized bees are widespread among *Andrena* colonies in many regions.

Parasitism tends to be so concealed a phenomenon that it is often not noticed, but some organisms attack living plants and cause them to respond by developing the monstrous growths called galls. The vascular plants of heathlands have their share of gall causers. In wetter places with willows, two locally common species are a gall midge, *Rhabdophaga rosaria*, which induces the so-called 'rosette gall' at the apex of a twig, and a gall mite, *Eriophyes tetanothrix*, which colonizes pustulate galls on the upper surface of a leaf. In drier places, broom may carry galls of another midge, *Jaapiella sarothamni*, which develop in the flower buds. Herbaceous plants are also galled: flowers of thyme are sometimes converted into cylinders covered by thick, whitish hair, in response to the activities of a gall mite, *Aceria thomasi*; and lady's bedstraw *Galium verum* may be attacked by yet another gall midge, *Dasyneura gallicola*, which causes the host to develop a gall like a diminutive globe artichoke at the growing point of a shoot. Galls are so widespread and seem to reduce the reproductive potential of plants so little that they well illustrate the equilibrium between host and parasite.

Vertebrate colonizers

Heathland vertebrates include reptiles since these, like insects, are active in warm places and have a scaly and keratinized exterior, which conserves body water. Adders *Vipera berus*, the most widespread of the European snakes, are commoner on heaths, where mice provide much of their food, than in cooler and wetter situations. In Britain, the smooth snake *Coronella austriaca* is a rare reptile with a distribution largely restricted to certain southern heaths; the common lizard *Lacerta vivipara*, although widespread, tends to be as plentiful on heaths as anywhere; and the sand lizard *L. agilis* is particularly a denizen of such sandy places as dry heaths.

The sort of cover available largely determines the bird life. Some require little in the way of vegetation. The wheatear *Oenanthe oenanthe* is found on open ground in heathland; the whinchat *Saxicola rubetra* needs rough grass, low heather and exposed perches; and the stonechat *S. torquata*, equally characteristic of dry heaths and slopes, prefers longer heather and gorse. The stone curlew *Burhinus oedicnemus* is largely restricted in Britain (but less obviously so on the Continent) to such places as sandy heaths and barren, flint-strewn chalkland, where the openness is evidently more significant than any state of acidity or alkalinity. Kestrels *Falco tinnunculus*, hovering over exposed heathland soil, can detect beetles and rodents running over the surface more easily than where the ground cover is thicker, although the disturbance of plant shoots by rodents working their way across grassland helps to position the prey for these raptors. The linnet *Carduelis cannabina*, which is common on heathland, requires bushy cover, while the nightjar *Caprimulgus europaeus* is often found where there is bracken: its extraordinary camouflage is effective, both when it is perched horizontally along the bough of a silver birch and when it is on the ground, perhaps close to fallen wood. Two other species characteristic of heathland, particularly in southern England and on the adjacent Continent, are the woodlark *Lullula arborea* and the Dartford warbler *Sylvia undata*; both are scarce and local in much of our area, and absent from the north.

Mice *Apodemus*, voles (Cricetidae) and the badger *Meles meles*, which burrow in the ground, probably find the sandy material easy to work. Badgers take such a remarkable variety of food that only the barest of heaths are likely to provide too little. But they need water and normally eat earthworms in great numbers, so wetter heaths tend to suit them more than drier ones, though they need well-drained soils for their setts.

Exploitation of temporary pools

Although many pools on heaths are only temporary, they provide habitats where animals adapted for short-term living in aquatic conditions can survive. The natterjack toad *Bufo calamita* is one of the most interesting of these: its numbers are declining and its range contracting, but it persists in such areas as heaths and dunes where loose sand allows it to find shelter by burrow-

The natterjack toad exploits temporary pools in heathland for breeding.

ing into the ground and where there is water for spawning. Its breeding season is so lengthy and its metamorphosis so rapid that its exploitation of temporary pools is facilitated: its egg-laying period encompasses 18 weeks (compared with only six and nine respectively for common toad *B. bufo* and common frog *Rana temporaria*) and yet its tadpoles are in the water for a mere 6–8 weeks (compared with 10–15 and 12). In addition, it is something of a wanderer, able to run fairly quickly, and thus tends to come across disconnected waters when these form. Like the common toad, it is apt to return year after year to the same breeding pools and so commonly uses intermittent rather than ephemeral ponds. So tolerant is the natterjack tadpole of certain kinds of pollution, including sea-salt and the derivatives from metallic waste, that its increasing scarcity invokes surprise.

Many kinds of invertebrates colonize temporary waters. The mosquito genus *Aedes* includes species which lay eggs in successive groups at intervals, thus reducing the risk of all the larvae being killed off by the premature drying-out of temporary pools. The fairy shrimp *Cheirocephalus diaphanus* is a heathland aquatic whose life-history is closely geared to periodic drying-out. Its thick-walled eggs can survive for long periods in dry mud and may become dispersed by such agencies as wind or the feet of animals. So long as the depth of water remains greater than 20 cm, development is arrested; when dry conditions supervene and the depth is reduced by evaporation, slow development begins and the extent to which it proceeds depends on the time the water remains shallow, at least 11 days of suitable conditions being needed for the hatching stage to be reached. Partly incubated eggs lying in dry mud resume development on becoming wetted.

MOORLAND

Climate and soil

Heaths and moors are similar in origin in that they frequently develop on the sites of cleared forests; both commonly represent degenerate ecosystems. The difference between the two settings is rather one of degree than of a shift in soil conditions. There is no clear demarcation, and transitional situations are frequent; both are acid and peaty places. In general, however, it can be said that a moor is wet and a heath is dry.

The immediate origins of the water are rainfall and the holding capacity of the ground. In Britain, typical moorland develops on level hill-tops or on gentle slopes with an altitude of 250 to 700 m in England and up to 1000 m in Scotland; these are upland moors which form where the precipitation is heavy and hill fogs are frequent. Lowland moors arise where the precipitation is not necessarily high, but where the peat holds sufficient water for the flora and fauna to differ from those characteristic of heaths. Some of these lowland moors appear to have developed, not from the destruction of forests, but from the silting-up of river valleys or estuaries where marshland vegetation has become dense enough to impede the flow of water, thus bringing about a gradual rise in the floor through the accumulation of solids falling out of suspension. The lowland moors of the English New Forest are evidently of this type; many of the moors on the Continent are also lowland and some, at least, could differ from upland moors in being the product of a building-up process.

The thickness of the peat is the chief feature distinguishing a moor from a heath. Heathland peat is shallow and relatively dry. Moorland peat is deeper and wetter; its depth may vary from 1·5 to 10 m or more, and the shallower it is the closer the moor will be to the heathland condition. Where the peat is thick and well-bedded, moorland is practically independent of the character of the rocks over which it lies. The amount of sand mixed with the peat is less than in heathland soil. Added to the depth, this gives it a greater capacity for holding water, and so it is commonly saturated and poorly aerated; as well as being acid, it is usually cold. Because the conditions favour the formation of peat, the processes of decomposition are so retarded that the soil water tends to be deficient in those mineral salts normally replenished from fully decayed organic remains. Thus, direct evidence that some upland moors have replaced forests appears in the form of well-preserved tree-stumps, particularly of birch *Betula* and Scots pine *Pinus sylvestris*, embedded in the peat in the growing position. Confirmation comes from analysis of the pollen-grain components of successive layers of moorland peat. Similar preservation is shown by the long-dead human corpses and perishable artefacts excavated from Continental peat-bogs.

Although water is usually plentiful, many moorland plants give the impression of being adapted for life in dry surroundings. Two possible reasons for this are that the entire ecosystem is so exposed and wind-swept that non-xeromorphic plants might be expected to lose water rapidly by transpiration; and that the rate at which plants take up acid water through their root systems tends to be reduced when the supply is cold and low in oxygen.

Three types of moorland
Few moorlands are homogeneous. The subdivisions fall into three major groups, determined partly by the water-content of the soil and partly by the degree of acidity and the amount of nutrient salts, features related to the formation rate, depth and mineral content of the peat.

Heather moor
This is the driest and most widespread type of moorland and the one most like a heath. The dominant plants are heather *Calluna vulgaris*, bell heather *Erica cinerea* and bilberry *Vaccinium myrtillus*, all of which possess xeromorphic foliage and are without root-hairs, their function being taken over by mycorrhizal fungi; the commonest shrubby associates are cross-leaved heath *E. tetralix* and crowberry *Empetrum nigrum*. Together these form a somewhat low vegetation, all more or less equal in height, so that the plants afford one another protection. Bilberry has leaves with a thick cuticle and in winter becomes a 'switch-plant' (its assimilatory processes carried out by its green stems), while the rest have the stomata lying in grooves: these are xeromorphic features. Other frequent plants of heather moor include purple moor-grass *Molinia caerulea* (notably where the soil is slightly calcareous and tends towards alkalinity), mat-grass *Nardus stricta*, heath rush *Juncus squarrosus*, bracken *Pteridium aquilinum* and hard fern *Blechnum spicant*, in addition to numerous mosses, of which the chief is hair-moss *Polytrichum commune*.

Bilberry moor
On the deeper peat, bilberry sometimes grows so thickly as to become dominant. It tolerates both exposure and shade better than heather, so this dominance tends to occur in the higher zones (up to 1300 m in Britain) and in the field layer of more shaded woods. Another species, bog bilberry *V. uliginosum*, is sometimes abundant on high moors in the far north of Europe, but it seldom reaches the upper limit of *V. myrtillus*, petering out at around 1000 m.

Cottongrass moor
In some areas, where the peat is deeper still and contains a much smaller pro-

Scottish moorland, Perthshire : the heather is burnt rotationally to provide both food and cover for red grouse.

portion of sand, the soil is saturated with water and cottongrasses *Eriophorum* become dominant. These plants rapidly form peat. Their narrow leaves with a thick cuticle show xeromorphy and they creep through the peat by rhizomes traversed by numerous air-canals, a structural adaptation for survival in soil poor in oxygen.

The wettest parts of moorlands are blanket-bogs with thick mats of *Sphagnum* moss, in which some insectivorous plants are locally common. The digested insects apparently supply the nutrients vital to the plant, which are deficient in these wet, acid soils. Sundews *Drosera*, the commonest, have leaves bearing numerous filaments whose sticky tips secure small flies; butterworts *Pinguicula* trap flies under the rolled margins of their horizontal leaf-blades.

Invertebrates

Understandably, the invertebrate fauna has affinities with that of heaths in the occurrence of burrowing forms, which reflects the need for shelter, and in the small number of snail species, which reflects the deficiency of lime. Three snails, however, which can tolerate even acid bilberry moors are a crystal snail, *Nesovitrea hammonis*, the tawny glass snail *Euconulus fulvus*, which occurs well inside bogs, and a chrysalis snail, *Columella aspersa*, which is

ABOVE *Cottongrass moor, Pennines : the 'cotton' indicates the seeding stage, not the flowers.*
BELOW *Wet moorland, characterized by red Sphagnum moss, lichen, heather and bilberry.*

thought to feed on algae and lichens on the stems of bilberry and its associates.

The differences in the invertebrate fauna are related to differences in the species of colonizing plants and to moorland's higher atmospheric humidity and greater prevalence of standing water. The humidity of moorland is probably responsible for the increase in the populations of such cryptozoic forms as myriapods and woodlice, which tend to desiccate in dry air. The wetness of the soil permits the survival of an adaptable earthworm, the octagonal worm *Dendrobaena octaedra*, which lives under moss tufts between the lichens growing around the bases of heathers and the unresolved plant litter underneath; although little known on heaths, it is so resistant to periodic drying and to cold that it is one of the few worms able to colonize moorland. As a breeding species, one of the smallest of the blue-tailed darter dragonflies, the keeled orthetrum *Orthetrum caerulescens*, is practically confined to peat bogs where *Sphagnum* moss has left open water in the pools.

Most moorland moths are small species whose larvae defoliate the various heathers: the smoky wave *Scopula ternata*, the narrow-winged pug *Eupithecia nanata*, the grass wave *Perconia strigillaria* and the clouded buff *Diacrisia sannio* are four examples. A larger and altogether heavier-looking moth is the emperor *Saturnia pavonia* which, though widely distributed, is sometimes abundant on moorland, where the handsome caterpillar is commonly found feeding on heathers. Possibly wet conditions are more significant than the species of food plant in determining its whereabouts, for in low-lying areas it tends to occur in damp places where meadowsweet *Filipendula ulmaria* and creeping willow *Salix repens* often become the caterpillar's sources of food.

A moth which periodically attains high populations is the antler *Cerapteryx graminis*. Though the adults are often observed flying over heather moors and grassland alike, the feeding larvae seem to be restricted wholly to grasses. When the caterpillars are abundant, rooks *Corvus frugilegus* and gulls *Larus* fly on to the moors and devour them, even where these areas are outside their usual feeding ranges. (This behaviour is similar to that of short-eared owls *Asio flammeus* in coming to the moors in larger numbers in years when there are 'plagues' of voles *Microtus*.) At times, the caterpillars occur in such abundance as to choke drainage ditches with their bodies when dislodged by heavy rain. Notwithstanding these natural forces operating to control their numbers, antler moths are often plentiful in the summer following a population explosion.

Another insect sometimes reaching plague proportions is the heather leaf-beetle *Lochmaea saturalis*; it can cause extensive damage to heather shoots, leaves and bark. A number of beetles are plentiful on moors and the majority are herbivores.

Wet peat does not favour the excavation of breeding-shafts, but conditions are sometimes dry enough, notably on tracks crossing heather moors. Certain mining bees *Andrena/Lasioglossum* burrow in such places, as do the larvae of tiger beetles (Cicindelidae); the latter seem particularly liable to attacks from one of the velvet ants, the ant wasp *Methocha ichneumonides*. This parasitic or, better, predatory insect shows marked sexual dimorphism: the female is wingless, looking much like a red ant *Formica*, and the male fully winged. When the female has located the burrow of a tiger beetle larva, probably by smell, she lures its occupant into the open, partly by running around the opening and partly by waving her antennae in the mouth of the shaft. If the tiger beetle larva comes out, the ant wasp stings it, inducing semi-paralysis; if it does not emerge, the predator crawls into the shaft and stings it there. The method of attack calls for a specialized pattern of movement if the ant wasp is to evade the powerful mandibles of so active a host. She then lays a single egg on the ventral surface of its abdomen, fills in the top of the burrow with soil, thus completely disguising its position, and then repeats the process with other larvae. When the egg hatches, the grub absorbs the fluid contents of the host's living body.

On high moors, the social bee more likely to be found than foraging bees from a hive is the attractive little bilberry bumblebee *Bombus lapponicus*, one of the red-tailed species and restricted in range to where bilberry is thickly established. Of the many spiders, one of the smallest, commonest and most widespread is *Dictyna arundinacea*, which seems to require open situations with low vegetation, such as moors. The web is spun in the tops of heather or grass clumps and is made up of long, spreading strands with sticky, crisscross threads. In summer, up to half a dozen cocoons, each containing about 18 eggs, are fixed to the central part of the snare.

Vertebrates

Vertebrates, being generally larger than invertebrates, are at a disadvantage on moors in winter, in that it is harder for them to find shelter in the low-growing plant cover. Size itself, however, gives a certain amount of protection to warm-blooded species, since a large animal has a lower ratio of surface area to mass than a small animal and, therefore, tends to lose heat more slowly.

Birds

Clearly one method of gaining protection from severe winter weather is to leave an area altogether. Birds, having the capacity of flight, are able to move long distances. Some species which breed on moors migrate, or at least shift their ground seasonally, irrespective of the weather.

Among the birds which frequently nest on high moors are some of the waders, a diverse group of often long-billed and long-legged species which are probably more familiar in lowland waterside habitats, on migration or in winter. The seasonal movements of the dunlin *Calidris alpina* are typical of moorland waders in general. It breeds on various kinds of open terrain, especially where there are peaty pools; the soft ground provides it with a harvest of insect larvae and other small invertebrates, which it takes by picking from the surface or probing with its beak. As soon as the young can fly, the dunlins move off the uplands to such places as muddy estuaries and the seashore where, joined by others from Greenland and the USSR (this is a circumpolar species), they become usually the commonest waders of the Atlantic and the North Sea coasts of Europe. Others travel on to winter in, for example, the Mediterranean area and equatorial Africa.

One of the most conspicuous waders, on account of its size and loud, liquid song, is the curlew *Numenius arquata*, which nests mainly on moors, marshes and damp pastures and which, like the dunlin, moves down to coastal mud-flats throughout west Europe in autumn and winter; Iceland is outside its breeding range, but it nests widely in many other parts of north Europe. The closely related whimbrel *N. phaeopus* is a more northerly breeding species altogether, nesting plentifully in Iceland and north Fenno–Scandia; after spending the summer on boggy, heath-clad moors, it also moves to the coasts in August, but almost the entire population then migrates to winter in Africa. The greenshank *Tringa nebularia* also winters largely in Africa north to the Mediterranean region; it breeds on moors in north and central Scotland, but in much of north Fenno–Scandia it is commoner in coniferous forest where there are open patches of bog or heather-covered ground. Another wader widespread in north Europe, but restricted as a breeding species to both upland and lowland moors, is the golden plover *Pluvialis apricaria*; in winter, on the other hand, it is a familiar bird of arable farmland, often flocking with lapwings *Vanellus vanellus* and sometimes associating with woodpigeons *Columba palumbus* and rooks.

Many of the seed-eating birds which do not depend upon soft ground for feeding also leave the moors in autumn. That upland finch, the twite *Carduelis flavirostris*, is one example. It nests, often in groups, in open country in west and north Ireland, north Britain and Norway, mainly in upland areas from bleak moorland to rough pastures; it feeds almost entirely on seeds. At the onset of winter, it leaves its exposed surroundings for such places as open fields, low-lying marshes and the sea coast; sometimes wintering twites even enter stackyards and join up with other finches feeding there. In these circumstances, it is not surprising that the merlin *Falco columbarius*, the least of the European falcons in size and an habitual nester beneath moorland heather, should also move in autumn from the exposed ground where little of its bird prey remains. During the breeding season, it feeds mainly on the small birds which share its moorland environment, notably meadow pipits *Anthus pratensis*, twites, linnets *Carduelis cannabina*, yellowhammers *Emberiza citrinella*, skylarks *Alauda arvensis* and ring ouzels *Turdus torquatus*, the last being summer visitors to the moors of north Europe which migrate south in autumn to the Mediterranean region. In winter, merlins hunt over open country, marshes and coasts.

A number of aquatic birds are commonly associated with moorland pools, lakes and bogs. These include red-throated divers *Gavia stellata*, greylag geese *Anser anser* and various ducks. Three ducks – mallard *Anas platyrhynchos*, teal *A. crecca* and wigeon *A. penelope* – often make their nests in moorland heather or bracken 150 m or more from the nearest water. Like most of the species already mentioned, these water birds also move to such places as coasts and lowland lakes in winter.

Grouse, on the other hand, are well adapted for exposure in elevated situations. The willow grouse *Lagopus lagopus* is resident over much of Fenno–Scandia on moor with scrub willow, birch or juniper *Juniperus*. Evidently the cover the scrub provides is important, since the ground nest is normally within its shelter. In summer, both sexes are rufous with white wings; in winter, they are entirely white and thus blend very well with snow-covered ground. In Ireland and north and west Britain, the characteristic game-bird of moors is the red grouse *L. l. scoticus*, formerly regarded as a distinct species, but now treated as a race of the willow grouse; it has dark brown wings and does not turn white in winter. The moors it colonizes are typically those where heather and crowberry are plentiful. So well adapted are red grouse to moorland conditions that they mostly remain throughout the year, though some from very exposed areas descend to lower ground in winter to feed in such places as stubble fields. Because of their importance in sport, red grouse have been studied more thoroughly than most birds. The adults are almost entirely vegetarian, feeding on the shoots, flowers and fruits of heather, often the most abundant plant in their immediate surroundings. The chicks take a high proportion of insect food, which presumably supplies the protein their rapidly growing bodies require; by the time winter sets in, the need for such a diet has passed and, with it, the need to locate small, weather-sensitive, invertebrate prey. In snowstorms, grouse survive on open moors by crouching with their heads into the wind, avoiding burial by constantly treading the falling snow so that each is surrounded by a melted patch, and obtaining their heather shoots by burrowing into the lying snow.

Mammals

Few mammals are wholly restricted to heaths or moors. The field vole *Microtus agrestis* is distributed over a range of altitudes and terrains, but it is especially the vole of rough ground and, probably because it drinks much, tends to be commoner on wet moors than on dry heaths; otherwise, it chiefly inhabits damp grasslands and plantations. Much of its food is grass, but it will take almost any vegetable material. Light soil facilitates the excavation of its burrow, a vertical hole about 60 cm deep ending in a small nest cavity which contains a tight ball of grass serving as a winter food store. Numerous runs bitten in the surrounding vegetation radiate from the entrance and dip under obstacles and bare spots; sufficient overhanging cover is left to conceal the burrow from above. The vole appears particularly alert to overhead dangers, rarely leaves the shelter of these runs, never climbs above the ground, and 'freezes' if surprised in the open too far from the entrance to dive underground. This is the vole whose populations in some years increase so much that large tracts of vegetation become devastated. Such 'vole plagues' appear to follow a series of mild winters, and at these times nests may even be constructed on the surface of the ground. Field voles move short distances in winter from land on which the grass has perished to places where coarser grass persists.

Two mammals whose association with moors is altogether more exclusive are the mountain hare *Lepus timidus* and the wild cat *Felis silvestris*. The mountain hare breeds in Iceland and Fenno–Scandia, and on moors above the level of cultivation in Scotland, north England, parts of Wales, and Ireland; it eats a variety of upland plants from heathers to lichens and mosses. In some areas it turns white in autumn, except for black ear-tips; the change is not due to a moult, but to the action of cells which absorb the colour of the fur at low temperatures. Thus, the hare is protected to some extent from predators by matching the winter snow; a new dark coat grows in spring. Its zigzag style of running and its speed, notably up slopes, are further defences against attack. During severe winters, it sometimes descends to arable fields at lower levels. The wild cat is found in the more rugged parts of Europe, including the northern Scottish Highlands where it frequents the rockiest and most mountainous areas of the upland moors. In central Europe, it lives mainly in woods; in Britain, on the treeless moors called 'deer-forests'. Its prey spans a variety of moorland vertebrates, from young deer, full-grown hares and grouse to voles.

Like the wild cat, the red deer *Cervus elaphus* inhabits forested regions on the Continent. Originally it occupied dense woodland in Britain, too, but today it lives chiefly on the bare moorland tracts of the Scottish Highlands and of parts of northwest and southwest England. So adaptable are these deer that they survive if they can reach shelter at certain periods of the year – notably in January, when the stags lie up in the thickest cover available, and again in May, when the hinds drop their calves in tall heather or bracken.

MOUNTAIN UPLAND

Structure and scenery

Both scenically and climatically, the most spectacular of the environments in our region are the mountain areas. Many of their plants and animals are also largely peculiar to them.

North European mountains tend to run northeast/southwest. Those in the southernmost part of the region are offshoots of the great chain of fold mountains which winds its way across Europe from the Pyrenees to the Black Sea, separating the Mediterranean basin from the broad north European plain which extends from Ireland to Russia. Elevations in the northern part of this plain, where it adjoins the Baltic, are particularly low: thus, few places in Denmark rise as high as 150 m above sea-level, and much the same can be said of south Finland.

But north of the Baltic the great mountain backbone shared by Norway and Sweden runs for 1800 km; numerous rivers flow from it, those on the Swedish side being relatively long and supplying lakes, and those on the Norwegian relatively short and soon passing into coastal fjords.

Some of the oldest mountains in Europe appear to be the Caledonian foldings of west and north Britain and the large Scandinavian peninsula, generally put at some 300 million years; these overlie masses which are even older and which form the substructure of the European continent. At the opposite extreme, Iceland is still undergoing disturbance and re-formation as a result of recent volcanic activity. Volcanoes elsewhere in north Europe have long been inactive although their sites are recognizable and sometimes spectacular: two Scottish examples are the volcanic plugs of Ailsa Craig, in the Clyde, and Arthur's Seat, in Edinburgh.

The work of ice

At various times during the three major glaciations which made up the Ice Age, sheets of ice stretched south from polar regions. They wore away the jagged profiles of high mountains and, in the form of glaciers (rivers of ice), they carried off rocky debris and piled it elsewhere in masses termed moraines. They gouged deep valleys with vertical sides and U-shaped floors; some of these became lakes through damming by moraines, others formed fjords where they entered the sea. But the notion of an Ice Age as belonging wholly to the past is mistaken. The tops of the mountain formations each bore their own ice-caps from which glaciers descended to carry out their work of cutting, grinding and moulding. Today, the main polar ice-sheet may

Active glacier in Jostedal, Norway.

have retreated, but it has left behind numerous pockets on the higher ranges from which glaciers still arise. Here the Ice Age has not ended, although European glaciers generally are shrinking.

That mountains now free of snow and ice must have had a past history along these lines is clear from their appearance today. The English Lake District, for instance, is a dome and its lakes are arranged like the spokes of a wheel: the hub is the mountain Helvellyn (1000 m) and the lakes lie in valleys cut by glaciers descending from this high point. Similar patterns can be recognized in many other upland districts, although they do not necessarily hold lakes. So worn down and smoothed off are all the British mountains that permanent snow-caps can survive no longer, although residual patches of snow sometimes persist in sheltered hollows on the highest parts of the Scottish Grampians. In contrast with the barren wildness of the European snow-mountains, those in Britain and Ireland give the impression of being clothed in a mantle of lush vegetation; indeed, one of the American astronauts described these islands as the greenest-looking lands in the world.

Two additional points should be made. First, the direction of the trend-lines along most of the mountains of northwest Europe evidently made it easy for the ice flowing southwards to reach them. Farther east, the Carpathians

Romsdal, Norway, U-shaped by glacial action.

have different trend-lines and form a great arc about the Hungarian plain; curiously, the inside of this arc was protected from the glaciation of the Ice Age, when most of the precipitation was on the north side of the mountains. Second, in view of Iceland's volcanic past and present, it is strange that fjords are also found there, with the biggest of the glaciers remaining in Europe.

Plants and animals of glaciers

The main groups of living organisms that survive the cold of glaciers are certain algae, lichens and mosses and a few small invertebrates. Some of these, particularly the animals, are able to survive because of, rather than in spite of, the snow: it serves as a protective blanket against extremes of temperature, and prevents damage by ultra-violet radiation and desiccation.

Particularly remarkable is the occurrence of algae in the snow of the accumulation zone at the tops of glaciers. This is where the so-called 'red snow' is recorded from time to time, the causes of which are unicellular algae of the aquatic genus *Haematococcus*. Each cell is only 0·05 mm or less in diameter, but on occasions they develop in quantities sufficient to colour patches of snow large enough for the effect to be visible through binoculars from a distance of several kilometres; caught by the rays of the rising or setting sun, the effect is arresting. The colour of the algae varies considerably: the red pigment, haematochrome, becomes predominant in conditions of intense illumination, as when the plant develops in strong snow-glare or very shallow water. *Haematococcus* can endure somewhat extreme conditions, including immersion in hard-packed snow and desiccation: it is common as a reddish incrustation on the stones of intermittently dry hollows in the rock debris of moraines deposited by glaciers.

Lichens are the most conspicuous forms of vegetation at the higher levels of a glacier. They become a coating, not unlike paint, on many of the rock surfaces, including the walls of the valley and the stones of the moraines. Upland species fall into two main groups: crustose lichens, which form a powdery coating; and foliose lichens, which take the form of flat sheets pressed against the surface and often raised slightly at the margins. Lichens are commonly held to be effective agents in the formation of soil from bedrock. A foliose lichen tends to retain water from rain or snow between its body and the rock face: should the water hold carbon dioxide in solution, it is slightly acid and may erode the rock; subsequent evaporation deposits the eroded matter as minute particles which eventually make up the framework of new-formed soil. But the process is less significant at high altitudes: much of the carbon dioxide is lost through its own weight from the rarified atmosphere, and exposure to strong winds carries away the deposits of eroded rock.

Animals colonizing the upper slopes of mountains depend for much of their food on a continuous airlift from lower down where conditions are less severe. Warm winds rise by convection, for much of the year carrying pollen-grains, seeds, spiders, insects, and a vast array of organic debris; the invertebrates are either frozen to death or drift as aerial plankton in a state of suspended activity. Part of this material falls on snowfields and glaciers, where the accumulation becomes a kind of larder for large numbers of mountain animals: the snow preserves the food and shelters the feeders. Apart from the resident fauna, wandering birds and insects also visit the icy slopes.

Of decisive importance in maintaining communities resident at high altitudes are the profusion of springtails (Collembola). Some of these tiny, wingless insects are pollen feeders, but between them the various species take so wide a range of foods as to resolve much of the organic matter blown on to the snowfields. As long as they are protected from desiccation by the snow, their power of survival in the physical severity of mountain climates is phenomenal. Few animal communities support a higher proportion of predators than do the springtails. This, their huge numbers and their ability to withstand cold account for their value in a diversity of food-chains. Among the most remarkable of their predators are certain arachnid mites which are so hardy that they can survive being frozen solid throughout the winter. On the snow and ice of glaciers and high mountains, swarms of such mites, as well as beetles and flies, may assemble to devour the springtails and organic waste.

Moraines provide a framework for soil where some of the vascular plants of high altitudes may become established. Coarse grasses and members of the pea (Leguminosae) and daisy (Compositae) families are typical of the non-woody kinds. Where woody species appear, these often include birch *Betula*, willow *Salix* and alder *Alnus*, the last especially characteristic of wet situations in the terminal moraines of the outwash at the bottoms of glaciers.

Alder is commonly infested by three species of mites of the genus *Eriophyes* that bring about conspicuous malformations in its leaves: one causes pouch-galls, which invariably form in the angles between the midrib and the primary veins; a second causes diffuse blisters over much of the leaf-blade; and the third induces compact pimple-galls clustered on the upper surface. Although plant galls are widespread, owing their formation to five major groups of parasitic organisms, those of these three mites are the only ones which develop in glacier valleys close to the near-freezing waters of the outwash. Galls caused by the other four groups – bacteria, fungi, roundworms and insects – appear lower down.

Vertical zonation

That mountain vegetation changes with increasing altitude is common observation. Above the grasslands and broadleaved woodlands of low valleys, the coniferous forests reach the timber line; highest of all come the rock faces and snowfields of the arctic-alpine zone, misleading in its superficial impression of barrenness.

Of the several reasons for vertical zonation, the most important are imposed by the atmosphere. Both arctic tundra and high mountain ranges are cold; the atmosphere is largely responsible, although it operates differently in the two settings. Near the Pole, the air is dense, and usually humid, and the sun is at a low elevation so that its rays have a long, oblique journey through the air, during which much of their heat is removed. On the upper parts of high mountains, the atmosphere is made thin by gravity (at 2700 m, its density is only threequarters of that at sea-level); thin air holds less moisture and thin, dry air retains less heat. Though the mountain surface is warmed during the day by the sun's rays, which are nearer the vertical and have only a shorter passage through the air before they strike the ground, the blanketing effect of the atmosphere is insufficient to prevent much of the heat being radiated back into space after sundown. The daytime temperatures of ground and air show greater differences than those of lowlands; at night, these differences are reduced. An additional factor is the strong wind at high altitudes.

A mountain arising at sea-level and reaching a height of 3000 m or more passes through zones which correspond to the vegetational types of their particular latitude, for zonation is equally associated with latitude. Thus, at 80°N (*eg* Spitsbergen), there are only tundra and alpine grassland; between

'Red snow', caused by minute algae.

70°N and 60°N, boreal (north coniferous) forest also develops; between 60°N and 50°N, mixed coniferous and temperate broadleaved forest comes in; and below 50°N, mixed temperate deciduous and evergreen forest. In short, the nearer the equator the greater the number of zones, and the more southerly ones are those lower on mountain slopes.

Above the tree-line, which may be as low as 700 m in Scandinavia and little higher in Scotland, several other zones supersede one another. The first is a shrub zone, which typically comprises dwarf, hairy forms of local forest trees, gnarled and windswept, their hairs and squat, mat-like shape helping to protect them from frost or wilting. Above this comes alpine tundra, similar to arctic tundra in its exposure to harsh conditions but differing from it in the absence of permafrost and, because the ground is sloping and becomes frozen only intermittently, in having better drainage; its lower levels may be clothed by a continuous carpet of alpine pasture, in which the viviparous sheep's-fescue *Festuca ovina*, mat-grass *Nardus stricta* and alpine lady's-mantle *Alchemilla alpina* are often conspicuous. Beyond this continuous carpet, there follows the vegetation of the higher and more rocky parts, the arctic-alpine community, so-called because its distinctive plants are found mostly within the Arctic Circle; some, indeed, probably moved into our region during the

Ice Age and have survived only on mountain summits, among them the dwarf willows *Salix herbacea* and *S. reticulata*, mountain avens *Dryas octopetala*, moss campion *Silene acaulis* and purple saxifrage *Saxifraga oppositifolia*, all characterized by their low, mat-like growth. Heaths are often found in drier parts and mosses in wetter ground below snow banks, but the cover is discontinuous, partly because little soil persists except in crevices. The zone of sub-snow, where thawing is sufficient to uncover the ground during the growing season and which stands immediately below the permanent snow, may be colonized by a few hardy flowering plants, but otherwise it is inhospitable and chiefly supports only lichens on the rock faces. Nunataks (pinnacles and bare crags protruding into the air through the capping of permanent snow) must surely rank among the places least favourable to life.

Adaptations to mountain environments
Although its actual height varies with latitude, the upper edge of the tree-growth follows a line where the average monthly temperature never exceeds 10°C. The mountain-life zones are commonly taken as beginning at this well-defined level, but their upper limit is more arbitrary. Resident communities tend to die out at somewhere around 2700 m, where the air is not only three-quarters as dense as at sea-level, but also, assuming a temperature drop of 1°C for every 170 m increase in altitude, 16–17°C colder.

Plants and animals living above the tree-line must be especially adapted to cold, high winds, strong solar radiation, low humidity, low oxygen, low carbon dioxide and steep terrain. Each of these conditions has its own implications. For example, steep slopes allow precipitation to drain away quickly; consequently, they tend to become unexpectedly dry, as is most apparent on a sunny day when the ground warms up temporarily. Low atmospheric humidity also contributes to the surface dryness. But the configuration of the rocks may so channel the water as to bring about the formation, here and there, of wet patches and even large mountain lakes.

Slow metabolism in plants
Some of the above conditions are unfavourable for the rapid synthesis by plants of organic foodstuffs. Ninety per cent or more of mountain plants are small perennials which grow slowly over a number of years until they have accumulated sufficient reserve food to start reproduction.

Many alpine plants are succulents, equipped for dry conditions by their capacity to store water in fleshy leaves and stems. Other common xeromorphic developments, such as the growth of a thick cuticle, a reduction in leaf-size and the formation of a barrier of hairs over the stomata (pores), reduce the rate at which water is lost from a plant by evaporation. A change in growth-form may also be functional: particularly where they are exposed to strong light, a good many plants develop as rosettes with the undersides of their leaves, where the stomata are situated, pressed close against the ground.

There are several striking adaptations for withstanding exposure to cold. First, many plants acquire a cushion form and, in consequence, tend to look alike when not in flower: a typical example is the moss campion, which grows as a dense clump of short stalks holding a layer of still air, whose temperature is sometimes as much as 10°C higher than that of the surrounding atmosphere. Another feature of the cushion form is that the surface area is small in relation to the mass, so that losses of both water and heat are reduced. A second method of resisting cold is to generate warmth: the alpine snowbell *Soldanella alpina*, limited in our area to the extreme south, actually melts the adjacent snow by fermenting its sugars and releasing heat-energy from the disintegrated molecules. A third way, this time of reducing frost damage, has been developed by the glacier buttercup *Ranunculus glacialis*, which grows at high altitudes in Scandinavia and Iceland: it builds up an exceptionally concentrated sap in its cells and, because this depresses the freezing-point of the cell fluid, it functions in the same way as antifreeze in a car radiator.

Conditions on high mountains tend to reduce the success of the typical forms of sexual plant reproduction, and alternative methods have evolved in some cases. The mountain buttercup *R. montanus*, found in the south of our region, is one of a number of species which can set seed without any fusion of sex cells. The purple saxifrage, although often visited by small moths, seems usually to be self-pollinated. The drooping saxifrage *Saxifraga cernua* certainly produces flowers (which are white, fairly conspicuous and visited by flies), but they seem to be on the decline and its fruits are unknown; many of its flowers have become replaced by small, red bulbils (and there are larger bulbils in the angles between the leaves and stems) which become detached in late summer, fall to the ground, overwinter beneath the snow, and give rise to new plants in the spring. Alpine meadow-grass *Poa alpina* is one of the 'viviparous grasses' occurring at high levels: wind pollination is followed in the ordinary way by fertilization, but the seeds are retained on the parent until, well advanced in germination, they fall off as young plants which have a better chance of establishment in the harsh conditions.

Apparently correlated with reproductive difficulties is the fact that so many mountain flowers are brilliantly coloured. Presumably, they are then more noticeable to wandering insects.

Animal metabolism and behaviour

Problems arising from cold are countered by animals in various ways. Some of the small invertebrates common in exposed places tolerate the cold itself to a remarkable degree. Springtails have been known to revive after being frozen in a glacier for three years. And some species of 'water bears' (Tardigrada) and roundworms colonizing the snowfield moss-cushions have been found in laboratory experiments to survive a temperature of −272°C: absolute zero is only 1°C lower.

Many birds simply migrate. Others, such as the alpine accentor *Prunella collaris* and the grey wagtail *Motacilla cinerea*, move to lower altitudes in winter; among mammals, the same applies to the chamois *Rupicapra rupicapra*, though this is limited in our area to the Vosges mountains and the Black Forest, where it is introduced, and the north Carpathian. Mice and, particularly, voles are the commonest small mammals on mountain slopes, as in many lowland environments, and their habits of burrowing and storing food favour survival at high altitudes; here, they include the snow vole *Microtus nivalis*, which just extends north to the Polish Carpathians. The alpine marmot *Marmota marmota*, one of the ground squirrels which, again, just reaches Poland, differs from its lowland relatives in not hoarding food. It lives in an underground burrow up to 3 m long, with a grass-lined nest chamber at the end, and hibernates there after building up reserves of fat during the summer. In view of the reproductive difficulties of plants in mountain areas, it is interesting that the marmot does not breed until the third year and then produces only a single litter in two years. Like mountain mammals generally, it has a shorter breeding season and longer fur than related species at lower altitudes.

Decreases in the oxygen available at progressively higher levels seem to be associated with modifications in the blood systems of some mammals. Individuals on high slopes have sometimes been found to have a larger heart and more haemoglobin (more red blood-cells per unit volume of blood) than those on lower ground.

Apart from the penetrating cold associated with the high winds in mountains, their velocity also brings difficulties and these are greatest for the smaller flying animals. Thus, more than half of the insects resident above the tree-limit never leave the ground; the mountain grasshopper *Miramella alpina*, for example, has greatly reduced wings and cannot fly.

Influence of solar radiation

One effect of exposure to radiation is to produce mutations in plants and animals. As a result, new forms arise. Whether these survive depends upon the extent to which they fit the conditions of the environment.

There are, for example, two form of crowberry *Empetrum*. The species on the moors of central and northwest Europe is *E. nigrum*, whose genetic composition is diploid, that is to say its chromosomes are in pairs, commonly represented as 2n = 26. (The chromosomes carry the genes which control much of the development and metabolism of the whole organism.) But the species found mostly on mountains and higher moors from Iceland eastwards is *E. hermaphroditum*, and this is tetraploid, the chromosomes having doubled to become 2n = 52. Multiplication of the chromosomes is a feature of many alpine species: evidently the extra genes result in greater vigour.

Animals exposed to strong radiation at high altitudes have developed dark pigmentation in the same way as the black human races living in the tropics, where radiation is also strong: this absorbs short-wave ultra-violet light and thereby protects underlying tissues from injury. Mountain races of a number of butterflies and moths are distinctly darker than those of the same species in lowland areas. The alpine Scandinavian form of the pearl-bordered fritillary *Clossiana euphrosyne obscurior*, for example, is more heavily pigmented than the typical *C. e. euphrosyne* of Britain and elsewhere in lowland Europe. Dark pigmentation also serves as a heat absorbent and thus warms the body. The alpine salamander *Salamandra atra* is glossy black all over, in contrast to the paler European salamander *S. salamandra* of the valleys; it is also better adapted for reproduction on high ground, where pools may be infrequent, since it bears live young without a free egg stage, thus avoiding the need to return to water to spawn.

The thick coats often grown by mountain mammals, which are warm-blooded, could serve to insulate them from radiation as well as from variations in environmental temperature. The relative hairiness of mountain flies and other insects, which are cold-blooded, may also have developed more as a screen against radiation.

Movement over rocky surfaces

No bird is better equipped for life on precipitous rocks than the wallcreeper *Tichodroma muraria*, a beautiful species which is mainly grey and black, but with conspicuous white spots and large areas of crimson on its wings. Related to the nuthatches *Sitta*, it extends into our area in south Germany, Czechoslovakia and south Poland; in Europe, it breeds mostly between 1000 m and 2700 m, with a few pairs in Switzerland as low as 350–550 m, and the higher populations provide another example of altitudinal migration, descending even to lowland ruins and quarries, but still maintaining the association with rocky faces. Its long, spreading toes end in long, strongly curved, sharp claws, with which it can climb up vertical rock-walls by taking advantage of tiny irregularities in the surface. Unlike treecreepers (Certhiidae) and the woodpeckers (Picidae), it does not use its tail as a support in climbing, but rather its wings; indeed, it makes only small hops with the feet alone. At times, too, it actually walks up, moving the feet alternately. The nest is built deep in a hole or crevice, often above a rushing stream. The wallcreeper's food consists entirely of invertebrates, including the adults, eggs and young of a wide variety of insects, and also spiders; with its sharp eyes it searches every rocky nook and cranny, using its long bill like a pair of curved forceps to extract its prey. Often it feeds on the sunlit faces of rocks, where the warmth has caused small insects to gather. For its growing young, it collects larger prey, notably owlet moths (Noctuidae) and small grasshoppers (Acrididae).

Among mammals, goats are wonderful climbers, whether they be truly wild chamois or, in Britain and Ireland, feral domestic goats *Capra* which, no less wary and difficult to approach, maintain themselves in the mountains. Both species are equally agile on the shifting stones of screes, firm

The wallcreeper, a specialist climber of rock walls.

talus, ledges or precipices, and are capable of scaling almost vertical rock-faces. Their small, two-toed hooves are better suited for rock-climbing than at first they might appear to be: each hoof has dew-claws at the heel which are normally raised from the ground, but which, when the foot is pressed against a rock, come down to form a hollow cup on the underside that clings to the surface like a rubber suction-pad. Even the small size of the hoof is an advantage: the goat's full weight is so distributed as to force each of the four small suction-pads hard against the underlying rock and thus secure firm adhesion. When the animal needs to move, it frees itself by working its toes to change the shape of the hollow and admit air into it.

Worlds of small animals

Potentially, high mountains hold many habitats for small animals. Snow itself provides the water essential in surroundings from which it otherwise tends easily to be lost, and snow and ice alike can serve as protective blankets; invertebrates occur even on glaciers. Other habitats range from within screes of loose stones, heaped-up moraines and cracks and fissures to open rock faces. No animal life can, however, survive on bare rock until such pioneers as lichens and mosses have gained a hold, entrapped drifting particles, and set up a measure of shelter. The same applies to holes in rocks, which become enriched when wind and other agents deposit finely divided matter in them.

Where mountain soil becomes sufficiently deep and set, it supports a complex community, almost invariably dominated by springtails, but including mites and the larvae of weevils (Curculionidae) and other beetles. With time, the community undergoes succession: older soils tend to have fewer mites and more beetles. In exposed places, the topsoil rapidly absorbs heat, but then radiates it again, and so tends to dry out quickly: in consequence, most of the animals live deep down where conditions are more stable. This contrasts with what happens in the soil of sheltered places, such as lowland forests, where the animal populations are at their maxima just below the unresolved leaf-litter in the upper layers of the topsoil. On mountains, the food of soil animals is derived principally from organic debris and the underground structures of alpine plants, sources which become increasingly meagre as the altitude increases.

The most favourable conditions for many small mountain invertebrates prevail under rocks where the temperature variations between day and night, and the fluctuations in humidity, are comparatively small. Where sufficient soil accumulates in crevices, mats of alpine plants become established and these provide shelter, as well as food, initially for springtails and thrips, then for mites and flies, and eventually even for some butterflies. But the feeding period is limited to a few months in a short summer. The higher the level, the more restricted to a scattering of sites are those conditions of temperature and humidity favourable for activity. The decline in food is accompanied by a decrease in the number of animal species. But this, in turn, brings about a decline in competition: sometimes, the result is high populations of individual species in relatively small spaces.

Insects at high altitudes present a number of surprises. For example, it might be expected that snowfields would be particularly unattractive at the onset of winter, but several species of ladybirds (Coccinellidae) have been known to assemble in late summer in sheltered localities well above the snowline. Here they hibernate, congregated together under the snow throughout the winter, though many are killed by cold or eaten by animals. This behaviour seems especially to follow hot summers when the populations of ladybirds in lowland regions become unusually large.

Despite their fragile appearance and dependence on a narrow range of food-plants, butterflies and moths are often hardy insects which either live on high mountains or periodically pass that way. The apollo *Parnassius apollo* is a butterfly largely restricted to mountainous regions, mainly between 800 and 2000 m, but at lower levels in Fenno–Scandia. The idas blue *Lycaeides idas* and the marbled white *Melanargia galathea* are two of many wide-ranging butterflies which are common alike both in lowlands and in mountains to about 1500 m. Like the burnets generally, the mountain burnet *Zygaena exulans* is a day-flying moth; in most European mountains it lives at between 2000 and 3000 m, but in Scandinavia and the Braemar district of Aberdeenshire – its British station – it occurs 1000 m lower down.

Two small amphibians with a wide distribution in north Europe, from sea-level to at least the lower pools on mountains, are the alpine newt *Triturus alpestris* and the palmate newt *T. helveticus*. On plains, as in north France, the alpine newt appears to breed normally, but in some mountainous areas it shows neoteny, in which the metamorphosis of the tadpole is so retarded that it remains a gill-breathing larva for an abnormally long period, often for life. It may even reproduce while still a larva, as does the North American axolotl *Ambystoma tigrinum*, probably the best-known example of neoteny. The alpine newt's retarded development seems to be brought about by cold. Despite the wide distribution of the palmate newt, population densities show that it is primarily a montane species; in Britain, it has been recorded from upland pools at altitudes of around 1000 m.

Worlds of large animals

As food diminishes with altitude, so does the biomass of the larger animals which an area can support. Mountain species are fewer in number, and there is less competition for the same food supply than in the lowlands. Populations tend to be controlled by aggressive territorial behaviour and a low rate of reproduction: many mountain vertebrates breed only once a year.

Mountain herbivores, such as the two goats, subsist by feeding on meagre plant growths widely scattered in places so inaccessible as to put the browsers beyond the reach of predators. Otherwise, apart from rodents, which tunnel under the ground, birds are probably the vertebrates best equipped for living where the terrain is swept by cold and violent winds. Perching birds, such as wheatears *Oenanthe oenanthe*, ring ouzels *Turdus torquatus* and snow buntings *Plectrophenax nivalis*, roam about very little, grip surfaces with their claws, and allow the air to flow by them. But large predators, which need to wander from place to place in search of prey, have become powerful fliers able to withstand the buffeting by their own strength and, indeed, to make use of the air currents.

The golden eagle *Aquila chrysaetos* is a characteristic predator in wild mountain tracts. Its distribution is virtually circumpolar, but nowhere in Europe is it very common. Its strongholds in the north are Scotland, with 250–300 pairs, and Norway. Each pair has a large hunting area, which in Scotland varies from 2000 to 7000 ha; though these 'home ranges' often overlap, they obviously set a limit on the size of any population. Much of the golden eagle's food is red/willow grouse *Lagopus lagopus*, ptarmigan *L. mutus*, mountain hares *Lepus timidus* and, not infrequently, sickly or dead young lambs and various forms of carrion. Its eating of dead sheep has given it a bad name among some hill farmers, who mistakenly regard it as a threat to their flocks, and it is also said to cause serious disturbance on grouse moors. As a result, too many golden eagles are illegally killed. Further, the use of pesticides in sheep-dips was followed by a serious decline in the breeding success of this species in Scotland in the early 1960s: pesticides tend to accumulate in the bodies of all such predators which are at the ends of food chains.

Another mountain bird of prey which has been still harder hit by the cumulative effects of pesticides is the peregrine *Falco peregrinus*. This magnificent falcon nests on rocky crags inland, and also on sea-cliffs. It preys very largely on other birds, especially wild rock doves and feral and homing pigeons (which are all one species, *Columba livia*); in some areas it often takes grouse or sea-birds and, indeed, it has been known to strike down a wide range of species from ducks to the smallest song-birds. In the mid-1950s pesticide residues began to be found in dead birds of many kinds, and the bird-eating raptors came off worst: by 1963, the peregrine population of Britain had dropped to 44 per cent (and only 16 per cent were capable of rearing young). Corresponding declines were reported throughout north Europe – a 'disastrous decrease' in Poland, for example – and over much of the species' almost cosmopolitan range. Fortunately, with restrictions on the use of pesticides, there has now been a partial recovery. The gyr *F. rusticolus* is a second large falcon of open, rocky country in the mountainous areas of Iceland and Fenno–Scandia; its chief foods are ptarmigan, willow grouse and a variety of waders and ducks.

Of the various grouse, the ptarmigan lives the highest on mountain slopes, where the rocky ground has an adequate growth of bilberry *Vaccinium*, crowberry, heather *Calluna vulgaris*, and its other food-plants. Many ptarmigan stay there all through the year, except when particularly harsh weather forces them down, for they are well adapted for life at high levels. In the course of a year they undergo three moults, two partial and one complete. As a result, they are almost entirely white in winter (when much of the habitat is covered in snow); brown or yellow-brown barred with black in summer, apart from white wings and underparts (thus blending with the broken patterns of the arctic-alpine zone); and much greyer, particularly the male, in autumn.

Ravens *Corvus corax*, the largest of the crow family, are widespread through a diversity of environments, but in north Europe they are characteristic of wild mountain country up to about 700 m, where they usually nest on rock ledges, but sometimes in trees. They feed particularly on carrion, including the placentae of ewes, but they will also attack and kill sickly lambs, small mammals, reptiles and frogs. A closely related and equally important predator of mountains and moorland, with similar habits, is the grey-and-black hooded crow *C. corone cornix*.

The more varied its food, the better are the chances of any animal's survival. This applies particularly to the large predatory mammals which appear periodically on mountain levels above the tree-limit. Like birds, they have the advantage of being able to withstand the cold by maintaining a constant body-temperature. Conservation of body-heat is assisted by the growth of thick, hairy coats and also by size.

All the same, few can survive for long without shelter: more often than not, this means vegetational shelter. The wild cat *Felis silvestris*, being a predator of only medium size, is able more easily than some to find shelter among rock formations: in Scotland, its lairs are often inside mountain screes or rock caves on treeless deer-forests, although it readily makes use of fallen trunks or old fox-earths. In continental Europe, on the other hand, the wild cat is typically found in timbered areas. The lynx *F. lynx*, although not in Britain and now a scarce animal over most of Europe, still prowls where it is unmolested. It remains by day in the cover of forests and emerges at dusk or dawn to catch food, sometimes venturing above the tree-line into more open ground to a branch 3 m above. Generally, it creeps close to its prey and then sense of smell; large feet, like snow shoes, enable it to move silently over snow without sinking. It is exceptionally agile and can leap vertically from the ground to a branch 3 m above. Generally it creeps close to its prey and then takes it in a single pounce. The lynx eats any birds or mammals it can kill.

Although lynxes have become scarce, they seem never to have been as plentiful as brown bears *Ursus arctos*. In north Europe, both have disappeared from western parts but remain in a few localities in Scandinavia and are still relatively common in the east.

Like other bears, the brown tends to be regarded as a somewhat alarming carnivore, a view warranted by the structure of its teeth. In fact, however, bears are catholic when it comes to food and eat practically anything they can find. Brown bears give the impression of being clumsy, slow-moving animals. They are certainly too slow to prey upon active, large-hoofed herbivores, but are capable of killing those handicapped by injury or disease, as well as smaller, weaker mammals, birds and insects.

Actually, they are neither as clumsy nor as slow as they seem: they are great wanderers and, if need be, can run at speeds of up to 50 km an hour. They also take large quantities of roots, leaves and fruits and, if all else fails, resort to garbage cans and rubbish dumps. What they eat is, to some extent, seasonal: in spring, they forage for the young of susliks *Citellus* and lemmings *Lemmus/Myopus*, which they dig out from the burrows, and also search for birds' eggs; and in autumn, they fatten themselves for the approaching winter on fruits, berries and nuts. From October onwards, they sometimes stay in their dens (holes and caves) for several weeks during hard weather, but this is scarcely true hibernation since their body-temperature falls very little.

Brown bears emerge at times in search of food on to the exposed snowfields of mountains, where they have been known to find and eat buried ladybirds. Here they may encounter cold as severe as that of the tundra frequented by polar bears *Thalarctos maritimus*. Their shaggy coats are an effective protection and make them look bigger and more formidable than they really are. They are not particularly aggressive and it is mainly when they are cornered or defending cubs that they turn vicious.

TUNDRA

Appearance and distribution

Tundra is one of two kinds: alpine, which clothes the upper parts of mountain slopes in temperate regions; and arctic, which encircles the North Pole and with which this section is mainly concerned.

In concept, arctic tundra is a vast, frozen, treeless plain dotted with lakes and bogs and crossed by meandering streams. It supports a patchy mantle of low-growing vegetation, such as grasses (Gramineae), sedges *Carex* and dwarf shrubs, which gives the appearance of a greenish-brown, low grassland; blossoms are generally large and showy, but of short duration. It is inhabited by a meagre variety of animals, although their actual numbers are often surprisingly large. In distribution, it can be compared with the ham in a sandwich, where the two slices of bread represent two very different situations: on one side, it is bounded by the polar seas, covered by ice and snow, rich in plankton but poor in mammals, except for such types as polar bears *Thalarctos maritimus*, seals (Phocidae) and whales (Cetacea); on the other side, its southern limit follows the northern edge of rich coniferous forest. Over the world as a whole, arctic tundra accounts for one-tenth of the entire land surface. In Europe, it is restricted largely to latitudes above 70°N.

Arctic tundra is held back in lands influenced by the Gulf Stream. Much of the northern two-thirds of Iceland, for example, is under arctic tundra; but the southern third, the shores of which are bathed by warmer water, is subarctic – notwithstanding the presence in this part of Vatnajökull, the largest ice-cap in the country – and the lower levels, with their shrubby plants, accord more with heath and moorland. Again, well to the south of Iceland, the warm current reaches the entrance to the Baltic and then flows northeast along the Norwegian coastline: there is little tundra here, and it is only after the Gulf Stream has merged with the cold waters beyond the North Cape that eastern Lapland carries wide expanses of this terrain.

As in deserts and other severe environments, changes in the composition of species with time – commonly defined as succession – are very slow in tundra. Any which do take place tend to be cyclic rather than directional; such climatic factors as wind and needle-ice serve to erode the soil and plants and, in so doing, to retard succession. In other words, changes are mainly

ABOVE *Tundra, a greenish-brown landscape illuminated in sunshine by numerous pools.* BELOW *Looking towards the great ice-cap of Vatnajökull, Iceland.*

shifts in the relative numbers of the species and not total replacement. Of the five environments examined in this book, only the climax of coniferous forest alters as little as tundra.

Climate and light

Arctic tundra is characterized more by low temperatures in summer than by deep cold in winter, and in coastal areas the tundra is cooler and foggier than it is inland. By early autumn, so much flooding has resulted from the summer thaw of ice-bound rivers that the ground has become saturated and an abundance of standing water is available for evaporation. Consequently, this is the cloudiest season; clearer skies return when the first freeze of the winter sets in.

Tundra climates are variable. They range from those of severe polar deserts, with temperatures averaging $5°C$ in midsummer and falling to $-30°C$ in midwinter, to those of alpine conditions where the summers are cool and the winters moderate, with temperatures seldom dropping below $-18°C$. Precipitation falling as rain is usually less than 38 cm; with snow, the total commonly reaches 64 cm, but rarely exceeds 191 cm.

In arctic latitudes, the sun's elevation is low. Its rays have a long journey through an atmosphere with high humidity, and much of their heat becomes absorbed before they reach the ground: this is the primary cause of the coldness. The exposed nature of the terrain is secondary. Winds are not as strong in arctic as in alpine tundras, but their influence on snowdrift patterns and whiteouts (blowing snow) is an important climatic factor; blizzards may reduce visibility to 9–10 m.

Arctic light prevails for three months continuously, and metabolic and behavioural rhythms among the colonizers are induced more by other variables than by a daily period of darkness. Many of the plants flower abundantly only when they are exposed to light which is continuous or nearly so. Insect rhythms of feeding, flying and swarming, normally controlled by light/dark cycles, respond rather to the prevailing temperatures or to the intensity of the sunlight. Many birds and mammals tend to undergo a quiet period in the early mornings, although this seems to be less pronounced than it is with corresponding animals on the alpine tundra in temperate regions. Although the light is not as strong as on mountains, conditions for photosynthesis are in two respects more favourable: gravity bring the heavy gas, carbon dioxide, down to the low levels of arctic tundra; and more water is available because there is less run-off.

Soil and permafrost

Patterned ground is a conspicuous feature of most tundra and is a somewhat bizarre result of differential movements of soil, stone and rock, on slopes and level land alike, plus a downward creep of the soil mantle. The cause is the expansion and contraction of water when it freezes and thaws. Terraces and

Water-logged tundra under the midnight sun.

lobes arising in this way are common in alpine tundra where there is adequate moisture for soil lubrication. In arctic tundra, where the ground tends to be more level, rock slabs may be found standing on end.

Permafrost is commonly given as the unique feature of arctic tundra, which serves to place it apart from any other environment. It denotes ice in the subsoil, which never melts, and the term is applied to soil whose surface has remained colder than 0°C continuously for two years or more. In patches, at least, permafrost is ever-present in arctic tundra, but it is seldom encountered in alpine tundra. Even in arctic tundra, it may be continuous or discontinuous. Where the permafrost is continuous, the ice extends throughout, except beneath lakes which do not freeze to the bottoms; probably 20 per cent or more of the land areas under tundra have continuous permafrost. In lower latitudes, permafrost occurs as patches which become progressively smaller and more scattered as one proceeds southwards, until they peter out altogether; practically all the permafrost in north Europe is discontinuous.

The most obvious effect of permafrost appears after the annual thaw, when the subterranean ice is so great an obstacle to drainage that extensive flooding occurs. Clearly, the underlying geology is one important factor governing the extent of waterlogging. In Iceland, the slope of the ground effectively reduces it by facilitating run-off from what otherwise would be normal tundra. On mountains, despite the generally heavier precipitation, the water runs away so quickly that alpine tundra seldom remains saturated for long. In the lower levels, at least, the soil of arctic tundra is usually peaty and thus it has some affinity with those of heaths and acid moorlands. The capacity of any particular area of tundra to support life, especially vascular plants and burrowing animals, must depend to a large extent upon its ability to thaw.

Vegetation

Succession in space

The vertical transition in mountains from evergreen forest on the middle slopes to alpine tundra on the upper levels is roughly similar to the horizontal transition in the far north from coniferous forest-belt to arctic tundra. One obvious difference is that the transition in the mountains takes place over a rise of only a few hundred metres, whereas the corresponding changes in the arctic can occupy many kilometres.

In mountains, the timberline trees are mostly pines *Pinus*, firs *Abies* and spruces *Picea*, and there are few broadleaved species. Above the timberline, trees become increasingly stunted and scattered; they include clumps of willows *Salix* less than 60 cm tall. Meadows are common on gentle slopes with soil, and there are cushion plants on windswept ridges. As rocky slopes and peaks emerge, the vegetation survives in smaller and increasingly scattered patches; vascular plants vanish at, or just below, the line of permanent snow.

Much the same pattern can be seen on a journey from the northern forest across the plains of the arctic tundra to higher ground, but here it is affected by a number of factors, of which the wetness of the land is one.

Across the southern parts of the arctic tundra lie vast areas of low relief. Their soil is boggy and peaty, and there are numerous lakes, ponds and meandering streams. They are dominated by various sedges, cottongrass *Eriophorum* and mosses, of which bog-moss *Sphagnum* is one of the commonest. Where the ground is slightly elevated – only some 15–60 cm above the wet, peaty areas – low willows, grasses and rushes *Juncus* are plentiful. Taller willows are common on the sands and gravels of river banks, in the lee of rocks, and in basins on the leeward sides of ridges where the winter snows tend to be deep. The sands and gravels seem also to be the particular setting for representatives of the Compositae (daisy family) and Leguminosae (pea family), which are often numerous. On higher ground, where the tundra passes into the foothills of the arctic mountains, the vegetation becomes sparse.

Succession in time, resulting in the replacement of one group of species by another, although very slow in the high tundra, does occur along the shores of lakes and ponds, on river flood-plains and near mammal burrows.

Adaptations for climatic severity

Adaptations to alpine tundra are often found among the plants characteristic of arctic tundra. A great many of these colonizers die back at the beginning of winter and persist underground from one season to the next; or else they have shoots which stay viable even after being buried for long periods under snow and ice. Nearly all of those which lose their aerial shoots in winter are vascular plants. Lichens and mosses contrast with them in having green parts above ground tolerant of exposure to conditions unfavourable for metabolism, including cold, dark, inundation and drought. The reindeer moss *Cladonia rangiferina*, which is a bushy, greyish-green lichen and not a true moss, is among the most widespread of the non-vascular plants succeeding alike in arctic tundra and in more temperate regions with no coastal tundra, such as Britain. This is the plant commonly represented as the great mainstay of reindeer *Rangifer tarandus* during their winter feeding. These animals certainly use their splayed hooves to uncover the lichen after snowfalls, but, in fact, they eat practically any sort of emergent vegetation they find in this way.

An adaptation noted already for some mountain plants, and also characteristic of several arctic tundra species, is the reduction of frost damage through the density of the cell fluid operating to lower its freezing point. This is the so-called 'glycerol effect'.

A somewhat unexpected feature, and one which could be a functional adaptation in cold situations, involves flowering: during cloudy periods, in shade and at night, the temperature of flowers is close to that of the surrounding

Patterned tundra, with reindeer moss.

air, but in sunlight it may be as much as 10°C warmer. Several tundra plants, among them cottongrass, are able to maintain a similar temperature difference around their flower stalks all the time; where the air temperature falls to near-freezing during the period of flowering, this could be metabolically significant. Much the same has been noted for louseworts *Pedicularis* and willows. Save for willows, none of the plants mentioned can be regarded as having particularly hairy flowers – the dense white threads of cottongrass are on the fruits, not the flowers – but hairiness has been suggested as part of the explanation for the temperature differential. Perhaps numerous small flowers in close-packed inflorescences achieve the same result as hairs.

Beginnings of food-chains

The outstanding feature of arctic tundra is the rapidity of the plant growth following the spring thaw and the increase in light and warmth: there is a profusion of colourful flowers and ample grazing for herbivores. In fact, however, the actual growing period lasts for only about six weeks, and the successful plant species are those which can speedily exploit favourable conditions of short duration as soon as they arise. In both alpine and arctic tundras, the plant communities are influenced by soil drainage, by snow cover and time of melting, and by localized microclimates with differences in temperature, soil moisture, nutrients and exposure to wind. The increase in plant matter is accompanied by the breeding of herbivores, and later by that of the animals which prey upon them; the increase in standing water results in an enormous upsurge in the population of mosquitoes (Culicidae).

But over the span of a full year, the vegetation remains sparse. It is no accident that man harvests herbivorous animals from the tundra, including reindeer and geese and ducks (Anatidae), rather than native or cultivated plants as is his usual practice in other environments.

Although comparatively few species of spiders and insects live on tundra, their actual numbers are often high. Certain adaptations to cold have been described already: the ability of some to withstand being frozen in ice and the dark coloration of others, which absorbs the sun's rays, are two. Further peculiarities separate tundra arthropods from those inhabiting temperate regions. One is the 'glycerol effect', which functions in some of the invertebrates as in some of the plants. Another is the fact that the mosquitoes and black-flies *Simulium* of the tundra include species able to deposit eggs without first encountering a vertebrate host and drinking its blood – evidently an advantage where large animals are scattered. Many of the insects are herbivorous, at least in their larval stages, and might therefore be expected to act as a link between vegetation and predators. But the most important herbivores are the small mammals.

Of the three species in northernmost Europe of the hamster-like rodents known as lemmings, the commonest in the mountain uplands and coastal tundra is the Norway lemming *Lemmus lemmus*, an animal of marshy places where it can find its basic foods of grasses and sedges. Lemmings are burrowing rodents which, by their tunnelling activities, destroy their own plant food, so modify the soil as to bring about erosion, and cause successional changes to develop in the vegetation. They are the main prey of many flesh-eating mammals and birds, and the fluctuations in their populations affect, directly or indirectly, the food supplies of practically every species of animal in their surroundings.

A second species, the arctic lemming *Dicrostonyx torquatus*, also occurs in arctic tundra along the northeast fringes of our region. On the whole, it is found in better-drained areas; its staple foods are cottongrass and the sedges of drier ground. Where these two lemmings coincide, the arctic occupies ridges running into the low-lying, wet plains favoured by the Norway. The third species is the wood lemming *Myopus schisticolor* which, as we have seen, is confined largely to coniferous forests.

In winter, lemmings are protected from the cold and predators by their subterranean tunnels. These lie a metre or more underneath the surface and contain rough nests of grass. The warmth of the animals' bodies is sufficient to maintain an air temperature of $10°C$ in their nests when that of the exposed tundra is below zero. Each burrow forms an extensive network, with short side branches leading from the main one, which may be 7–10 m long. The side tunnels result from the lemmings' feeding activities: in winter, they spend most of their time digging for underground stems and roots and they appear on the surface only for short periods. The arctic comes above ground more frequently than does the Norway.

Lemmings breed throughout the year, but at a slower rate in winter. When the snow melts in June, there is an upsurge. Because both the gestation and lactation periods are short (21 and 14 days respectively), the young themselves have reached mating condition by autumn.

Norway lemmings' populations are cyclic, with peaks every four years. High numbers supply abundant food for middle-sized predators, such as snowy owls *Nyctea scandiaca*, stoats *Mustela erminea* and arctic foxes *Alopex lagopus*; a decrease is followed by a decrease in the predators. The effect of a lemming climax on the vegetation of the tundra is devastating: plant life is destroyed both by overgrazing and by tunnelling, aggravated in winter when the plants cease to grow but the animals continue to feed. The summer following a peak year sees both food shortage and a deficiency of cover against predators, so that the numbers of lemmings fall away and remain low throughout the winter. During the next two years, while the vegetation is slowly building up again, the populations increase in winter, but decrease in summer when predators take their toll. By the fourth summer, the plants have recovered sufficiently for a new peak in the lemming population and the cycle begins again.

When their numbers are low, Norway lemmings are confined to the tundra, though some migrate each year, either singly or in small groups, moving away from winter terrain when the vegetation has been eaten or flooded, and returning in autumn after conditions have improved. These are not the legendary 'suicide rushes to the sea', but in peak years normal movements build up into mass migrations in all directions. The animals have damaged the food supply to such an extent that their swollen populations are forced by hunger to travel long distances in search of fresh grazing and cover. Many often move in a body to reach pastures new, swimming streams and small lakes on the way. But their inability to distinguish between waters which they can cross and larger expanses which they cannot causes many to drown.

Voles *Microtus* and *Clethrionomys* fill a broadly similar niche in the food supply of carnivorous animals on the tundra. Although far less accentuated, their numerical fluctuations follow a similar pattern.

Birds

During the time of plant-growth and flowering, there is a profusion of bird life on arctic tundra. Many of the species are aquatic, including some which are partly or wholly flesh-eaters. Most of the carnivorous birds depend in the long run on a rich supply of vegetable plankton. This is devoured by small crustaceans and these, in turn, are eaten by the fishes and other animals which constitute the bulk of the birds' food. But when the plants on the tundra turn brown, and ice starts to form on the inshore waters, the vast majority of the birds leave the exposed ground and either winter along coasts farther south or on the open sea. Only a few land-birds remain to face out the cold and darkness of the arctic winter.

In this last category, grouse seem to be particularly successful on open tundra in winter. Both the willow grouse *Lagopus lagopus* and the ptarmigan *L. mutus* remain, protected to some extent from the cold by their thick plumage and feathered legs and feet, and from enemies by their white winter coloration, although gyr falcons *Falco rusticolus* locate and kill many ptarmigan on the tundra. Another resident species faced with extreme seasonal variations of light is the snowy owl; it nests on mossy hills in the arctic tundra and, though normally diurnal, also hunts by night in winter. Its numbers are closely linked with those of the Norway lemming, one of its principal foods: in years when the lemming population is minimal, many snowy owls starve or at least fail to breed.

Skuas (Stercorariidae) and gulls and terns (Laridae) breed colonially in numbers on tundra or nearby shores. Arctic skuas *Stercorarius parasiticus* are basically predators which have developed the habit of harassing smaller sea-birds, especially terns, until they disgorge food they are carrying: this lightens the bird under attack, facilitates its escape, and the skua takes the food instead of the bird. Such a habit is more piratical than predatory, but arctic skuas are general predators also: they take the eggs, the nestlings and even the adults of a variety of birds, as well as lemmings and other small to medium-sized mammals. Indeed, the long-tailed skua *S. longicaudus*, which is more typical than the arctic of the tundra and high moorland of Fenno–Scandia, feeds very largely on lemmings in the breeding season.

Waterfowl leave the tundra in September and return in May. At these times the sky is filled with swans, ducks and, especially, geese flying in loose, straggling lines or V-formation. Tundra-breeding has to be completed during the short time available for feeding and growth. Many of these larger birds pair for life, or overwinter together, and return to the same site year after year, thus reducing time needed for preparatory courtship. As a rule, their nests are uncomplicated structures and quickly built. The pink-footed goose *Anser brachyrhynchus* breeds colonially on the Iceland tundra, where talus slopes and other rocks provide sheltei from such predators as the arctic fox. Like many other ducks, the long-tailed duck *Clangula hyemalis* merely lines a clump of grass or heather with down plucked from its own breast. The nest of the whooper swan *Cygnus cygnus* is a large but roughly built crater of coarse vegetation. The downy young of waterfowl become active shortly after hatching and grow rapidly. Most of the food of ducks comes from plants growing close to or within the marshy pools of the tundra, either from the vegetable matter itself or from molluscs, crustaceans and other small invertebrates living on it. Waterfowl have various adaptations for dealing with food: for example, swans use their long necks and broad beaks for underwater grazing; some ducks have serrated margins to their beaks, which enable them to filter small particles of organic material suspended in the water; and all have buoyant bodies and webbed feet, and swim well.

Waders are plentiful on the open ground of the arctic tundra or the adjacent coasts. Many have long legs which give them access to flooded land and they use their elongated beaks like forceps to extract from wet mud such small invertebrates as worms, crustaceans and insect larvae. Many of the waders familiar in autumn or winter to observers in west and central Europe nest on the arctic tundra. Typical are the jack snipe *Lymnocryptes minimus*, with its exciting flight-song like the sound of a horse galloping across the sky; the colourful, jousting ruff *Philomachus pugnax*; the purple sandpiper *Calidris maritima* and, much more restricted in their Fenno–Scandian breeding ranges, the bar-tailed godwit *Limosa lapponica* and little stint *Calidris minuta*. A less familiar, but perhaps more famous, wader of tundra and the high tops of northern mountains is the dotterel *Eudromias morinellus*, one of the few species of birds with a reversed sexual role. The males alone incubate the eggs and rear the young, while each female may lay several clutches; this is an interesting adaptation to preserve the females, since a predator may kill a male on the inevitably exposed nest and yet other clutches and the egg-layer then survive.

Among small birds on the tundra, the arctic redpoll *Carduelis hornemanni*, restricted in our area to Finland and a small part of Sweden, breeds in low scrub or on the ground in open areas. More widespread in Fenno–Scandia are the Lapland bunting *Calcarius lapponicus* and the snow bunting *Plectro-*

phenax nivalis, the latter also extending to Iceland and in very small numbers to Scotland; both nest on the ground in treeless tundra, the snow bunting among rocks. Another typical small bird of the tundra is the red-throated pipit *Anthus cervinus*. All these species move south to a greater or lesser extent for the winter, with the exception of some of the arctic redpolls and most of the Icelandic snow buntings. Incidentally, the snow bunting, which commonly winters along coasts, is hardy enough to have been recorded from ice-floes within 300 km of the North Pole.

Mammals

Winter camouflage

Both herbivorous and carnivorous mammals appear on open tundra throughout the year. A similar form of camouflage to that of the mountain hare *Lepus timidus* – dark in summer, but white in winter – is acquired by some of the carnivores which attack it. One of these, the arctic fox, lives throughout the tundra, usually in burrows in hillocks or low cliffs, and takes meat of almost any sort, but its chief prey is the Norway lemming, especially in summer; it accumulates dead lemmings and stores them in nature's deep-freeze, the snow. The arctic fox does not hibernate, but forages throughout the winter, burrowing to escape blizzards; it has been known to hunt in temperatures of −50°C. Often it becomes a scavenger and carrion-feeder; when polar bears are around, it may follow them to the sea, living off the remains of seals and whales that they have killed and even eating the bears' droppings. It breeds in March, at which time the supply of lemming litters ensures that the vixen is likely to remain in good condition during pregnancy.

Like the mountain hare and arctic fox, the stoat is a tundra mammal which is brownish in summer and white in winter; in the white phase, it is commonly known as the 'ermine'. It is strictly carnivorous and, at all latitudes, is less nocturnal than most predatory mammals. At any time of the day or night it hunts its prey relentlessly, both by sight and by smell, finally rushing in to seize the throat or the artery behind the ear. More or less cylindrical in shape and phenomenally agile, it is able to penetrate a burrow in pursuit of lemmings, without, like the arctic fox, tearing it apart. It, too, stores some of its prey in refrigerated caches underneath the snow: evidently, this is an adjustment to the hazards of acquiring sufficient food in a climatically severe environment, since no such behaviour seems to have been detected among stoats in temperate latitudes.

Reindeer

Four subspecies of the caribou *Rangifer tarandus* are among the herbivores most characteristic of the circumpolar tundras. Three are restricted to North America, and the fourth is the reindeer of Europe and Asia, *R. t. fennicus*. They are the only deer in which the cows as well as the bulls grow antlers.

Reindeer in Finland.

Herds of both wild and domesticated reindeer are common in northern Fenno–Scandia. They are the largest herbivores in the tundra, and commercially the most important, although their niche is not a central one in the economy of the system as a whole, like that of the Norway lemming. They are practically essential to man in the thinly populated wastes between the northern forests and the sea, providing meat, milk and its derivatives, and hides, and serving as haulage beasts for pulling vehicles. Big animals with a small surface relative to their mass, so that heat loss is reduced, they are well adapted for survival in the arctic: they have an effective insulating coat, the hairs of which are hollow; long and muscular legs, facilitating lengthy migrations when the local supply of food runs low; and splayed hooves which they use to uncover vegetation from the snow. (The American Indian word 'caribou' means 'shoveller' and refers to this habit.)

Wild reindeer undertake their own feeding movements; domesticated herds are driven from one region to another. Whether the journeys are controlled or not, these are the times when reindeer herds run the gauntlet of predators and scavengers: ravens *Corvus corax* and arctic foxes lie in wait for them along the trails they follow. Reindeer run well, however, and a healthy adult can give a good account of itself by employing its antlers against an attacker.

The rapid growth of vegetation in summer supplies an abundance of food and yet, paradoxically, high summer is a season of wasting for reindeer: mosquitoes and other biting flies are so numerous that the mammals are constantly on the run to avoid their attacks, and burn up body-fuel in their restlessness. In winter, many find shelter along the fringes of the coniferous forests.

Wolf

The timber wolf, grey wolf and white wolf are forms of a single species, *Canis lupus*, which is the immediate ancestor of the domestic dog. White wolves, which tend to retain light-coloured coats throughout the year, live mainly on the tundra. Time was when the wolf was widespread over much of the northern hemisphere, but persecution by man has driven it from many of its strongholds and it now persists only in the most inaccessible parts of its former range. A variety of habitats, from coniferous forests to grassy plains and tundra, still harbour it in Finland and east Europe. It is the largest of the tundra carnivores, except for the polar bear whose incursions inland from the pack ice of the Arctic Ocean are altogether more spasmodic.

The variety of the environments the wolf occupies points to its adaptability, which arises more from its social organization and comparative intelligence than from any metabolic or structural modifications. Essentially a predator which does not hibernate and rarely hides food, it is obliged to hunt all through the year to survive. Its hunting and defensive unit is the pack, an assembly of about ten animals consisting of father, mother, cubs and a few other relatives. The pack defends a territory, the size of which is related to the quantity of prey available within it. In the tundra, where potential victims are scattered, this territory is larger than in the richer environment of the coniferous forest. Pack leaders urinate on boundary land-marks and this marks out the limits of the territory, which is vigorously defended against trespassers. Leadership of the pack is shared between father and mother: the others are subordinate and there is often a single individual which, although constantly driven away when a kill is being made, is tolerated sufficiently for it to move in and scavenge on the left-overs after the rest have had their fill. Cubs are born in June, when food is relatively plentiful; not all the members of a pack reproduce simultaneously, and care of the young is divided among them.

The wolf depends upon herbivores for food and its main hunting seasons are when these are on the move. Hooved mammals, including reindeer, make up at least half the diet, which consists mainly of sick or injured individuals. Wolves are not the fast-moving relentless, powerful killers that they are commonly made out to be: one on its own is no match for a large horned reindeer in good condition and it may take an entire pack to overpower and kill even sickly prey. When a herd has been located, the pack moves in, selects a slow-moving calf or a weak adult and concentrates on this, the wolves taking turns to lead the pursuit until the victim collapses from exhaustion. When no hooved prey is procured, wolves eat anything they find, from lemmings to their own dying brethren.

Far from being wholly destructive, wolves serve a useful function in culling inferior stock from a population, so that healthy survivors are left to perpetuate the species. Compared with losses among calves due to the climate, any influence of wolves upon herds in good condition is virtually negligible.

Polar bear and ringed seal

The world population of the polar bear is probably well under 20,000. Man's hostility is the primary cause of a reduction which has, however, been checked since wiser counsels have prevailed. The species' distribution is circumpolar: probably polar bears visit most of the frozen Arctic Ocean and they may float great distances with the pack ice. They spread along the coasts in summer, becoming tundra animals, but rarely travel more than 50 km inland. A few appear in north Iceland and on the coast of Lapland, although both are outside the southern limit of the pack ice.

Polar bears have several adaptations to their environment: for cold, a heavy coat, small ears, and a low ratio of body surface to large volume; for snow and

Polar bears on Kong Karls Land, Spitsbergen.

ice, a white colour and broad feet like snowshoes. They are huge, heavy animals, up to 3 m long and weighing 700 kg; one standing on its hind legs is big enough to top an elephant. They swim magnificently.

Typically, the polar bear is a lone hunter. When it is on the ice, seals, and especially ringed seals *Pusa hispida*, are essential for its survival.

The ringed is the commonest and smallest seal in the sea adjacent to the tundra of north Europe: it is less than 2 m long and weighs around 50 kg. Its popular name refers to the dark-centred, yellow or white spots forming o's or 8's over its upper surface. It feeds on crustaceans and fish where the ice is land-locked, and it occurs farther north and south than any other arctic seal, penetrating the Baltic and the Gulfs of Bothnia and Riga. But individuals are not great wanderers and rarely do they venture more than 20 km from land; nor are they gregarious. This is essentially an ice seal, which lies close to its breathing hole.

The bear locates the seal by scent and waits at a hole for a head to appear, often after it has stopped up some other holes in the vicinity. With its clawed forepaw it makes a sudden lunge and hauls the victim out on to the surface, during which process the seal's pelvis and other bones may be crushed. Unless it is unusually hungry, the bear devours only the guts and blubber and leaves the rest of the carcase to such scavengers as ravens and arctic foxes.

When it comes ashore for its summer moult, the polar bear will eat almost anything, from lemmings and bilberries *Vaccinium myrtillus* to the offal thrown out from human settlements. At this time its feeding habits closely resemble those of its relative, the brown bear *Ursus arctos*.

Productivity of tundra

Anyone unacquainted with arctic tundra may have gained the impression of a cold, barren and scenically monotonous expanse. That such an environment can provide the necessities of life for large populations of even a few species of warm-blooded animals, some of them big, may have seemed strange. And yet a tundra must be fertile to do so.

Because green plants are the bases of food chains, an important measure of fertility of any ecological system is the weight of the vegetable matter it produces. Such information for tundra is so far rather scanty, but an international scheme operating for a number of years has already yielded sufficient data to suggest general trends.

In polar regions, the greater biological production is in water, not on land. The lakes of arctic tundras contain many species of green algae and aquatic mosses. These support worms, molluscs, small crustaceans and insect larvae which, in turn, provide food for such vertebrates as the char *Salvelinus alpinus*. This is a fish related to the salmon *Salmo salar*; in the arctic, it is similarly anadromous (migrating from salt water into fresh water to spawn) and is so adjusted to cold that it is killed by water exceeding 15°C.

The land vegetation is not homogeneous. Production ranges from 3–10 g of vegetable matter per square metre (g/m²) in the barren higher and drier banks which are dominated by willows and mountain avens *Dryas octopetala*, to 100–250 g/m² at lower levels on wetter sites, where heaths (Ericaceae) and dwarf shrubs produce 50–75 g/m² in new shoots each year. Values for the grasslands and forests of temperate regions are from four to six times as great.

Productivity in alpine tundras appears to vary with exposure: it is about 50–100 g/m² in windswept parts, 100–200 g/m² in alpine meadows, and 250–300 g/m² in communities of heaths with dwarf shrubs. That productivity there tends to be higher than in arctic tundra seems to be a result of the greater amount of light and the longer period during which growth can take place.

This is not the full story. The amount of plant material is often 10–25 times greater below the ground than above it, which points to soil being more favourable than air for growth. In many tundras, the live plants harvested by herbivorous animals form no more than 0·1–2·0 per cent of the total in a year: this indicates that most of the plants are left to die, decay and be broken down by micro-organisms.

Clearly the productivity is there, but low and intermittently scattered over extensive areas. To be successful on tundra, birds and mammals must be able to exploit it by travelling from place to place. Because the species of plants and animals are comparatively few, a food-chain on tundra is short and simple: there are fewer alternatives in the foods available to its component members, thus making it less of a spreading web and more of a linear series. This, in turn, means that fluctuations in the population of only a single component are more likely to affect, directly or indirectly, the lives of all the organisms making up the system.

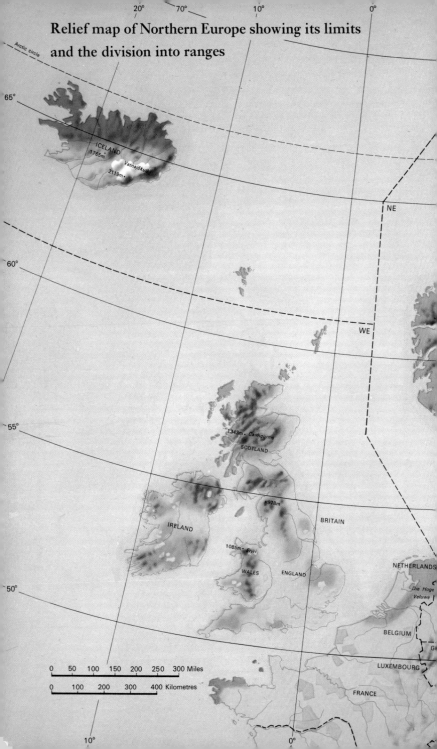

Relief map of Northern Europe showing its limits and the division into ranges

Arctic circle

20°

70°

10°

0°

65°

ICELAND
1765m
Vatnajökull
2119m

NE

60°

WE

55°

1343m • Cairngorms

SCOTLAND

•978m

BRITAIN

IRELAND

1085m • Fryrl

NETHERLANDS

WALES   ENGLAND

Die Hoge
Veluwe

50°

BELGIUM

LUXEMBOURG

0   50   100   150   200   250   300 Miles

0   100   200   300   400 Kilometres

FRANCE

10°

0°

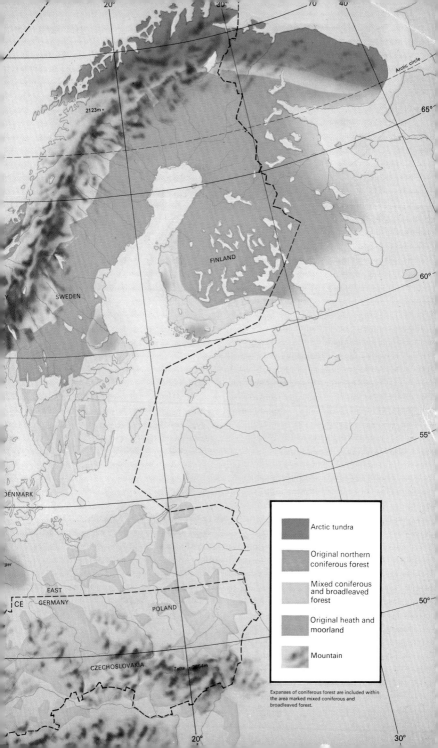

Arctic tundra

Original northern coniferous forest

Mixed coniferous and broadleaved forest

Original heath and moorland

Mountain

Expanses of coniferous forest are included within the area marked mixed coniferous and broadleaved forest.

GLOSSARY

abdomen segments immediately behind thorax (*qv*); esp apparent in insects

acute ending in a point

alternate leaves placed singly at different positions along stem; *cf* opposite

anthers part of stamen producing pollen

apex tip or summit; wing tip in insects

awn long, stiff bristle projecting beyond grain, in grasses

axil angle between leaf and stem

basal at base of stem; in animals, position nearest body

bract modified leaf at base of flower-stalk

bulbil small bulb arising in leaf axil

calyx all the sepals; term often used when sepals are joined to form a tube

carapace in spiders, shield covering cephalothorax (*qv*)

cephalothorax fused head and thorax

cerci long or short projections from posterior of abdomen

ciliate edged with hairs

clavus in bugs, posterior part of forewing

clitellum in earthworms, saddle-like region secreting mucus

corium in bugs, anterior (basal) part of forewing

dextral in snails, shell with right-handed spiral

dioecious having fertile male and female flowers on different plants

elytra in beetles, hardened forewings covering abdomen

gill wing-like structures beneath cap of fungi, producing spores

hemelytra in bugs, forewings with basal halves hardened, remainder membranous; *cf* clavus, corium

inflorescence flower branch including bracts, flower-stalk and flowers

lanceolate spear-shaped

linear long and narrow, almost parallel-sided

mantle skirt of tissue enclosing viscera, lungs; in slugs, visible as a dorsal shield of skin

mesonotum dorsal centre of thorax

metamorphosis change in form; complete: young is totally different from adult, includes a pupal stage, *eg* caterpillar to butterfly; incomplete: young similar to adult, always without pupal stage, *eg* aphid

nerve strand of strengthening or conducting tissue running through leaf

ob- inverted, broadest part being at apex rather than base, *eg* obovate

-oid describing 3-dimensional shape, *eg* ovoid

opposite leaves arising at same level on opposite sides of stem

ovate egg-shaped, broadest part near base

ovipositor egg-laying apparatus of female insects at posterior of body; in ☿ bees and wasps modified into sting

panicle branched inflorescence

pinnate regular arrangement of leaflets in 2 rows on either side of stalk (simply); each leaflet divided again (twice)

perianth term for all floral leaves, petals and sepals

perianth segment one floral leaf, used when petals and sepals are indistinguishable

peristome in snails, outer lip of shell aperture

persistent remaining attached to plant when dead

pronotum dorsal front of thorax

ray-florets elongated florets of composite flower, may form outer ring of 'petals'

rostrum snout or beak, in insects

saprophyte plant deriving its food wholly or partially from dead organic matter

scape leafless flower-stalk

scutellum in bugs, triangular main section of thorax

sepals outer ring of floral leaves, usually green and less conspicuous than petals

simple leaf not divided into segments; unbranched stem or inflorescence

sinistral in snails, shell with left-handed spiral

species group of individuals showing similar features, and which can interbreed to produce viable offspring

spinneret tubes, at tip of abdomen, through which silk for web is extruded

spire shell above most recently formed whorl (*qv*)

sporangium spore-capsule in ferns

spore simple reproductive body

stamen male organ of flower

stigma part of female organ of flower which receives pollen; in Hymenoptera, mark on front edge of forewing near apex

suture in snails, groove between successive shell whorls

thallus plant body undifferentiated into leaf, stem, etc; often flattened

thorax region between head and abdomen bearing legs and wings, esp in insects

umbel cluster of flowers whose stalks (rays) radiate from top of stem, resembling spokes of an umbrella

umbilicus in snails, hollow base of coiling axis of spiral shells

variety group of individuals within a species, possessing one or more distinctive characteristics

viviparous giving birth to live young; in plants, seed germinating while still attached to plant

whorls leaves or flowers arising in circle around stem; in snails, sections of shell

ABBREVIATIONS

The ranges in the order of their listing in the field guide

W	widespread
T	throughout
Br	Britain (England, Scotland, Wales)
Ir	Ireland
Ic	Iceland
Fr	France, north of the Loire
Lu	Luxembourg
Be	Belgium
Ne	Netherlands
De	Denmark
Ge	Germany
Cz	Czechoslovakia
Po	Poland
Fi	Finland
Sw	Sweden
No	Norway
FS	Fenno–Scandia (Norway, Sweden, Finland)
SC	Scandinavia (Norway, Sweden)
NE	Fenno–Scandia, Denmark, north Germany, north Poland
CE	Czechoslovakia, south Germany, south Poland

WE	Britain, Ireland, France, Luxembourg, Belgium, Netherlands

n, s, e, w north, south, east, west

When the species is not native but introduced and naturalized, the countries concerned are put in brackets, eg Fr, Ge, (Br, Ir).

av	average
esp	especially
fl(s)	flower(s)
fl-head	flowerhead
fr(s)	fruit(s)
imm	immature
inflor	inflorescence
juv	juvenile
lf (lvs)	leaf (leaves)
lflet	leaflet
microsp(p)	microspecies
sp	species (singular)
spp	species (plural)
ssp	subspecies
var	variety

MEASUREMENTS

Scale in the plates: the relative sizes of the plants and animals are preserved whenever possible, but the measurements in the entries themselves should be noted.

BL	body length (excludes tail in mammals, includes antennae in insects)
EL	extended length (slugs); ear length (mammals)
FA	forearm length
H	height
HF	hindfoot length
L	total length (includes beak, tail)
SB	shell breadth
SH	shell height (snails); shoulder height (mammals)
TL	tail length
W	number of whorls
WS	wingspan
WT	weight

SYMBOLS

♀	female
♂	male
☿	worker
<	up to
>	more than
?	doubtful
U	underside

moss *Rhacomitrium lanuginosum* GRIMMIACEAE Creeping, much-branched, grey-green, mat-forming. Lvs lanceolate, narrowed from base into long, strongly toothed, silvery hairpoints. Spore capsules egg-shaped on short, rough stalks. Spores ripe early summer. Stone walls, rocks, moorlands, often dominant plant over mountain tops. T. [1]

hair-moss *Polytrichum commune* POLYTRICHACEAE H 15–45 cm. Erect, wiry, deep green, forming large, loose cushions. Lvs lanceolate, <2 cm, narrowed from base with toothed margins, widely spreading from stem. Spore capsules almost cube-shaped, swollen at base, on long stalks <10 cm. Spores ripe summer. Marshy moorland, peat bogs. Used by Lapps for pillows, beds. T. [2]

bog-moss *Sphagnum rubellum* SPHAGNACEAE H 10–30 cm. Soft, erect, much-branched, crimson-red, forming hummocks. Stem lvs with broad, blunt tip; branch lvs shortly pointed, often turned to one side when dry. Spore capsules spherical, chestnut-brown, on short, smooth stalks. Spores ripe Jul–Aug. Tops of hummocks in acid bogs. T. [3]

moss *Pleurozium schreberi* HYPNACEAE H 5–10 cm. Stiff, erect, much-branched, with bright red stems shining through semi-transparent lvs. Lvs broadly oval, concave, clasping stem, with short, double nerves. Spore capsules cylindrical, drooping, on red stalk. Spores ripe autumn. Acid soils of woods, heather moors, mountain grassland. T. [4]

moss *Hylocomium splendens* HYPNACEAE Creeping, regularly and neatly branched, with reddish stems, forming large, loose, glossy yellow or olive-green mats. Lvs broadly oval, concave, toothed, abruptly pointed, with double nerves $\frac{1}{2}$ as long as lf. Spore capsules ovate, on stalks <2·5 cm. Spores ripe spring. Heaths, mountain woods. T. [5]

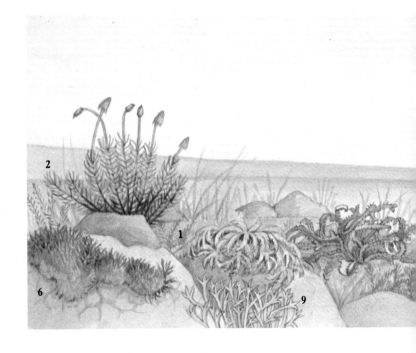

moss *Andreaea rupestris* ANDREAEACEAE H 10–25 mm. Small, tufted, dark red-brown, with erect, forked stems. Lvs ovate or lanceolate, <2 mm, clasping stem, often all turned one way. Spore capsules open into 4 slits held together by lid, unlike any other moss. Spores ripe Jun–Aug. Mountain rocks. T, ex Ic. [6]

liverwort *Diplophyllum albicans* JUNGERMANNIALES H 25–50 mm. Large, densely crowded tufts, <20 cm across, with some erect, usually pale green shoots. Lvs arranged in 2 opposite rows, each with 2 unequal, blunt lobes, toothed at tip. Spore capsules red-brown, stalkless. Spores ripe Mar–Apr. Moist areas. T. [7]

lichen *Cladonia arbuscula* CLADONIACEAE H 4–8 cm. Erect, yellowish-grey, with much-branched, hollow stems. Branches often develop in groups of 4, with tips bending in one direction, and bear small, brown, spore-producing structures. Sandy or stony heaths, moors, bogs. T. [8]

lichen *Cladonia uncialis* CLADONIACEAE H 1–7 cm. Erect, yellowish-grey-green, with once- or twice-forked, hollow, almost inflated stems opening at each fork. Tips sharply pointed, bearing pale brown, spore-producing structures. Peat moors, bogs. T. [9]

Iceland Moss *Cetraria islandica* PARMELIACEAE H 2–6 cm. Erect, chestnut-brown lichen, often red at base, with short, black spines on margins of thallus; lower surface (convex side) often dotted white. Spores produced in circular, brown structures near tips of branches. Mountains, moorlands. T, ex Lu. [10]

Crottle *Parmelia saxatilis* PARMELIACEAE Crust-like lichen, forming flat, grey rosettes of lobes marked by network of fine, white lines; older parts covered in greyish-brown isidia (rod-like outgrowths); lower surface dark. Spore-producing structures rare. Walls, trees, rocks. T. [11]

Fir Clubmoss *Lycopodium selago*
LYCOPODIACEAE H 5–30 cm. Erect,
perennial herb with numerous branches of
equal length. Lvs lanceolate, <8 mm,
clasping stem, arranged in rows.
Sporangia kidney-shaped, in axils of upper
lvs. Spores ripe Jun–Aug. Buds in axils of
lower lvs fall and also form new plants.
Heaths, moors, mountain rocks. T. [1]

Stag's-horn Clubmoss *Lycopodium
clavatum* LYCOPODIACEAE H <15 cm. Far-
creeping, branched, perennial herb with
erect, fertile stems. Lvs bright green,
linear, acute, <5 mm, ending in white
hairpoint. Sporangia in spikes <6 cm, on
stems <15 cm with few, yellowish, scale-
like lvs. Spores ripe Jun–Sep. Heaths,
moors, mountain grassland. T. [2]

Alpine Clubmoss *Lycopodium alpinum*
LYCOPODIACEAE H <7 cm. Far-creeping,
tufted, perennial herb with ascending
branches. Lvs greyish-green, lanceolate,
<5 mm, with short-branched, whitish
points, in 4 rows. Sporangia in spikes
<7 cm, solitary at ends of leafy branches.
Spores ripe Jun–Aug. Heaths, moors,
mountain grassland, mainly arctic and
alpine. T, ex Lu, Ne, extinct Be. [3]

Lesser Clubmoss *Selaginella selaginoides*
SELAGINELLACEAE H 3–15 cm. Perennial
herb with short, sterile and larger, erect,
fertile branches. Lvs lanceolate, 1–4 mm,
spirally arranged, with 1–5 large teeth
each side. Sporangia in axils of
sporophylls (lf-like structures bearing
spores) at ends of leafy branches. Spores
ripe Jun–Aug. Damp mossy or grassy
places, often in mountains. T, ex Lu, Be,
Ne. [4]

Moonwort *Botrychium lunaria*
OPHIOGLOSSACEAE H 5–30 cm. Upright,
perennial herb with short, underground
stems. Lvs solitary, divided into 3–9 pairs

of fan-shaped segments, without midrib.
Sporangia in two rows, on 1–3 times
branched panicle which overtops lf.
Spores ripe Jun–Aug. Dry grassland,
rock-ledges, often in mountains. T. [5]

Royal Fern *Osmunda regalis* OSMUNDACEAE
H 30–150 cm. Upright, perennial herb
with short, stout stems covered in
persistent lf-bases. Lvs lanceolate in
outline, <300 cm, twice-divided into
blunt, oblong segments. Sporangia few,
terminal on lvs, but massed to cover
separate 'fertile' fronds. Spores ripe Jun–
Aug. Damp, peaty places. T, ex Ic, Fi. [6]

Beech Fern *Thelypteris phegopteris*
THELYPTERIDACEAE H 10–20 cm. Perennial
herb with long, creeping, underground
stems. Lvs solitary, triangular in outline,
<50 cm, once-divided into deeply cut
segments; blade at right angles to stem,
sparsely hairy. Sporangia close to edge of
segments, not covered by flap. Spores
ripe Jun–Aug. Woods; shady, lime-free
rocks. T. [7]

Green Spleenwort *Asplenium viride*
ASPLENIACEAE H 5–20 cm. Tufted,
perennial herb. Lvs linear in outline, 20
cm, once-divided into semi-circular, light
green segments <5 mm across, arranged
in pairs along green stalk. Sporangia often
cover entire undersides of mature lvs.
Spores ripe Jun–Sep. Lime-rich rock
crevices, ledges, mainly in mountains. T,
ex Ne, De. [8]

Ostrich Fern *Matteuccia struthiopteris*
ATHYRIACEAE H< 170 cm. Tufted,
perennial herb with short, erect, underground stems producing sterile and fertile
lvs. Sterile lvs bright green, lanceolate in
outline, <170 cm, once-divided into c50
narrow, deeply cut segments; fertile lvs
becoming dark brown. Wet, acid woodlands. T, ex Ic, Ne, (Br, Ir, Fr). [9]

Holly Fern *Polystichum lonchitis*
ASPIDIACEAE H 15–60 cm. Tufted,
perennial herb with short, ascending,
underground stems. Lvs leathery,
lanceolate in outline, <60 cm, once-
divided into 30–100 short-stalked segments
with toothed margins. Sporangia in row
on each side of midrib. Spores ripe Jun–
Aug. Rocks, mainly in mountains. T, ex
Ne, De. [1]

Oak Fern *Gymnocarpium dryopteris*
ASPIDIACEAE H 10–40 cm. Perennial herb
with slender, creeping, underground
stems. Lvs yellow-green, solitary,
triangular in outline, hairless, <40 cm,
2–3 times divided, with lowest pair of
segments often as large as rest of lf.
Sporangia in circular groups (sori). Spores
ripe Jul–Aug. Woods, shady rocks. T. [2]

Hard Fern *Blechnum spicant* BLECHNACEAE
H 10–75 cm. Perennial herb with short,
oblique, underground stems producing
sterile and fertile lvs. Sterile lvs tough,
narrowly lanceolate in outline, <50 cm,
once-divided into 20–60 oblong segments;
fertile lvs <75 cm, with very narrow
segments, undersides covered in sporangia.
Spores ripe Jun–Aug. Acid woods, heaths,
mountains. T. [3]

Parsley Fern *Cryptogramma crispa*
CRYPTOGRAMMACEAE H 15–30 cm. Tufted,
perennial herb with sterile and fertile lvs.
Sterile lvs <2 cm, much-divided into
triangular-ovate segments, lf-stalk twice
as long as blade; fertile lvs with linear
segments covered in sporangia. Spores
ripe Jun–Aug. Acid rocks, screes, in
mountains. T, ex Ne, De. [4]

Bracken *Pteridium aquilinum*
HYPOLEPIDACEAE H <2·5 m. Perennial
herb with far-creeping, underground
stems. Lvs triangular in outline, <400 cm,
with stalk <2 m, 2–3 times divided into
short, pointed or blunt segments.

Sporangia on edges of segments, covered
by rolled lf-margin. Spores ripe Jul–Aug.
Woods, heaths, moors. T, ex Ic. [5]

Lemon-scented Fern *Thelypteris
limbosperma* THELYPTERIDACEAE H 30–100
cm. Tufted, perennial herb with crown
of lanceolate, yellow-green lvs at apex of
short, ascending, underground stems.
Lvs <100 cm, twice-divided into blunt,
toothed segments, lemon-scented when
crushed. Sporangia close to margins of
segments. Spores ripe Jul–Aug. Screes,
woods, esp in mountains. T, ex Ic, Fi.
[6]

Puff-ball *Bovista nigrescens* GASTERO-
MYCETALES H 3–6 cm. Spherical, stalkless
fungus with whitish, fleshy outer layer;
this soon peels off, exposing dark brown,
tough, papery inner layer, which splits at
top to release mass of purplish spores. All
year. Grassland. T. [7]

Dung Roundhead *Stropharia semiglobata*
AGARICINEAE H <12 cm. Fungus with
slimy, straw-yellow, hemispherical cap,
1–4 cm across. Stalk slender, white to
yellow, slimy below narrow ring. Gills
chocolate-coloured when mature. Apr–
Nov. Grassland, usually on old dung.
Poisonous; mealy smell. T. [8]

fungus *Hypholoma elongatum* AGARICINEAE
H 5–9 cm. Cap pale-yellow, somewhat
shiny, pyramidal, 1–2 cm across. Stalk
very slender, similar to cap in colour,
without ring. Gills olive at first, becoming
brown. Aug–Nov. Wet *Sphagnum* bogs.
T, ex Ic. [9]

fungus *Galerina paludosa* AGARICINEAE
H 5–8 cm. Cap dull honey-yellow,
pyramidal, 1–2 cm across. Stalk slender,
wavy and scaly below distinct ring which,
however, soon falls. Gills far apart, broad,
changing from light to dark brown with
age. Wet *Sphagnum* bogs. T, ex Ic. [10]

Juniper *Juniperus communis* CUPRESSACEAE
H 10–60 cm. Dioecious, evergreen tree,
columnar but prostrate in exposed
situations. Lvs in 3s, 1–2 cm, linear,
sharp-pointed with white band above. Fls
May–Jun: ♂ yellow, 8 mm; ♀ green,
ripening in 2–3 yrs into blue-black fleshy
frs. Mountains, woods, moors, heaths. Frs
used to flavour gin; wood-smoke for ham
and cheese. T. [1]

Norway Spruce *Picea abies* PINACEAE
H 30–60 m. Cone-shaped, evergreen tree;
bark reddish, scaly. Lvs dark-green,
4-sided, needle-like, arranged spirally.
Fls May–Jun: ♀ red; ♂ lower and later,
abundant pollen. Cones pendulous.
Mountain forests, plantations elsewhere.
Wood for building, joinery, paper, fuel.
Fr, Ge, Cz, Po, FS, (Br, Ir, Lu, Be, Ne,
De). [2]

Scots Pine *Pinus sylvestris* PINACEAE
H <40 m. Evergreen tree; bark thick,
scaly, dark brown below; papery, pinkish-
brown above. Lvs 3–7 cm by 2 mm, in
pairs, bluish-green, twisted. Fls May–Jun.
Cones 3–6 cm, pendulous, grey to yellow-
brown. Native forests on Continent,
smaller stands in Scotland. Soft wood for
building, poles, paper; source of turpentine,
creosote. Pine looper moths *Bupalus
pinarius* can defoliate. Br, Fr, Ge, Cz, Po,
FS, (Ir, Ic, Lu, Be, Ne, De). [3]

Aspen *Populus tremula* SALICACEAE
H 13–20 m. Dioecious, deciduous tree,
suckering freely. Lvs nearly round, with
bluntly toothed or wavy margin fluttering
in wind. Lf stalks <6 cm, strongly
flattened. Fruiting catkins <12 cm, Mar–
Apr. Woods, <1000 m in C Europe.
Populus from Greek *paipallo* (tremors). T.
[4]

Dwarf Willow *Salix herbacea* SALICACEAE
H 1–2 cm. Prostrate, deciduous, creeping
shrub, with short aerial branches. Lvs
round, toothed, hairless, bright-green,
shining, veins prominent on both sides.
Fls Jun–Aug. Dense carpet on mountains,
rock-ledges, north lowland moors. Br, Ic,
Fr, Ge, Cz, Po, FS. [5]

Eared Willow *Salix aurita* SALICACEAE
H 1–2 m. Deciduous shrub with
spreading, angular branches, raised lines
under bark. Lvs twice as long as broad,
wrinkled, hairy above, grey with matted
hair beneath. Fls Mar–Apr. Damp woods,
heaths, chiefly acid soils. 'Eared' refers to
kidney-shaped pair of stipules below some
leaves. T, ex Ic. [6]

Bog Myrtle *Myrica gale* MYRICACEAE
H <250 cm. Deciduous, dioecious shrub,
strongly suckering; twigs reddish-brown,
hairless after 1st year, shining. Lvs 2–6
cm, oblanceolate, grey-green, deliciously
scented with golden-yellow glands. Fls
Apr–May. Bogs, wet heaths, fens. Bark for
tanning; lvs as insect repellent. Br, Ir, Fr,
Be, Ne, De, Ge, Po, FS. [7]

Silver Birch *Betula pendula* BETULACEAE
H <30 m. Deciduous tree; trunk black,
fissured into rectangular bosses at base,
silvery-white above; twigs hairless, warty.
Lvs narrowly pointed, double-toothed,
hairless. Fls Apr–May. Wings of frs 2–3
times as broad as seeds. Woods, heaths,
esp acid soils. Pioneer after fire. Bark for
tanning; wood for furniture; twigs for
thatching; oil for insect and fungal
repellents. T, ex Ic. [8]

Downy Birch *Betula pubescens*
BETULACEAE H <20 m. Deciduous smooth-
trunked tree; young twigs hairy without
warts. Lvs broadly pointed, irregularly
toothed, usually hairy. Fls Apr–May.
Wings of frs about size of seeds.
Woodland, scrub, often wet, peaty soils.
Uses as *B. pendula*. T. [9]

Dwarf Birch *Betula nana* BETULACEAE
H <1 m. Deciduous, monoecious shrub
with spreading, prostrate branches. Lvs
5–15 mm, thick, almost round; margins
with conspicuous, rounded teeth. Fls
May–Jun. Develops showy reddish colour
in autumn. Common on moorlands, bogs
in north; local and mainly on mountains
in south. Br, Ic, Fr, Ge, Cz, Po, FS.
[10]

Bastard Toadflax *Thesium alpinum*
SANTALACEAE H 10–20 cm. Lvs linear, one-
veined. Fls Jun–Aug, arranged unilaterally
in long, loose terminal clusters, greenish-
white, nearly stalkless in axils of 3 linear
bracts; perianth tubular, 4-lobed and
persistent, 2–3 times length of fr.
Mountain pastures, rocks. Fr, Ge, Cz,
Po, sSw. [1]

Alpine Bistort *Polygonum viviparum*
POLYGONACEAE H 6–40 cm. Slender
perennial. Lvs linear to lanceolate,
tapered both ends, margins inrolled.
Unbranched stems, with terminal spikes
of white or pink fls, Jun–Aug; brownish-
red bulbils replace lower fls. Mountain
grassland, down to sea level in north.
Non-contorted rhizomes edible. Br, Ir, Ic,
Fr, Ge, Cz, Po, FS. [2]

Mountain Sorrel *Oxyria digyna*
POLYGONACEAE H 5–30 cm. Hairless
perennial herb. Lvs fleshy, 1–3 cm, long-
stalked, basal, kidney-shaped. Inflor
leafless, branched spike; fls Jul–Aug,
green, stamens and stigmas red. Frs nuts,
with broad wing turning red. Damp,
rocky places in mountains. Lvs taste acid,
used by Lapps to sour reindeer milk. Br,
Ir, Ic, Fr, Ge, Cz, Po, Sw, No. [3]

Sheep's Sorrel *Rumex acetosella*
POLYGONACEAE H < 30 cm. Slender,
dioecious perennial. Lvs < 4 cm, long and
narrow, often spear-shaped with spreading
or forward-pointing basal lobes, upper lvs
not clasping stem. Inflor erect, branching
from middle or above; fls May–Jul,
reddish. Acid heaths, rough grasslands.
Lvs edible, slightly acid and bitter. T. [4]

Northern Dock *Rumex longifolius*
POLYGONACEAE H 60–120 cm. Stout, erect
perennial. Lvs broadly lanceolate, 3–4
times as long as broad. Inflor dense,
fl-stalk 1½ times as long as broad; fls
greenish, Jun–Jul; fruiting perianth
segments thin, kidney-shaped, and flat.
Roadsides and waste places in uplands.
Once named *R. domesticus* because
frequently found near houses. Br, Ic, Fr,
De, Ge, FS (Cz). [5]

Blinks *Montia fontana* PORTULACACEAE
H 5–50 cm. Perennial or annual herb.
Stems weak, branched in water but short
and tufted on land. Lvs 3–20 mm,
opposite, spoon-shaped, narrowed into
stalk-like base. Fls Apr–Oct, *c*2 mm
across, inconspicuous, in small terminal
clusters. Muddy springs, wet pastures.
T. [6]

Springbeauty *Montia perfoliata*
PORTULACACEAE H < 30 cm. Annual,
hairless herb. Rosette of basal, long-
stalked, fleshy, pale-green lvs, almost
round. Upper lvs fused to form fleshy cup
containing cluster of white fls, May–Jul,
each 5–8 mm across. Arable fields, waste
places on dry, sandy soils. (Br, Fr, Be,
Ne, De, Ge, from NW America.) [7]

Arctic Sandwort *Arenaria norvegica*
CARYOPHYLLACEAE H 3–7 cm. Perennial
herb, loosely tufted. Lvs hairless or
ciliate in lower half, veins obscure. Fls
Jun–Jul, 9–12 mm across, petals 5, white,
longer than hairless sepals; nectaries
green. Base-rich screes, river shingle;
often mineral-rich soils. Annual endemic
with larger flowers (ssp *anglica*) confined
to N England. Br, Ir, Ic, Sw, No. [8]

Spring Sandwort *Minuartia verna*
CARYOPHYLLACEAE H 5–15 cm. Loosely
tufted perennial. Lvs < 20 mm, long,
narrow, sharply pointed, hairless. Inflor
slender, much-branched, erect; fls Jun–
Aug, *c*6 mm across, petals 5, white, up
to 1½ times as long as 3-veined sepals.
Mostly mountains, on base-rich rocks,
screes, open grassland and esp mineral-
rich soils, *eg* old lead-workings. Br, Ir, Fr,
Be, Ge, Cz, Po. [9]

Cyphel *Minuartia sedoides* CARYOPHYL-
LACEAE H 4–8 cm. Perennial herb forming
yellow-green, mossy cushions < 25 cm
across. Lvs linear, 5–15 mm, fleshy,
crowded, overlapping, keeled beneath,
channelled above, margin ciliate, otherwise
hairless. Fls Jun–Aug, scarcely exserted
from cushions, solitary, often lacking
petals, sepals 5, yellowish-green. Exposed
rock-ledges, moraines. Visited for nectar
by small flies. Br, Fr, Ge, Cz, Po. [10]

Lesser Stitchwort *Stellaria graminea*
CARYOPHYLLACEAE H <90 cm. Perennial
herb; stems weak, creeping to ascending,
quadrangular, much-branched. Lvs 15–50
mm, linear, acute, ciliate near base. Fls
May–Aug, 5–12 mm across, petals 5,
white, deeply bilobed, more or less
equalling sepals. Woods, heaths, acid
grasslands. Fls largest in normal, smaller
in ♂-sterile plants. T. [1]

Little Mouse-ear *Cerastium semidecandrum*
CARYOPHYLLACEAE H 1–20 cm. Annual or
overwintering herb; stems erect, branching
from base. Lvs <18 mm, broadly
elliptical. Fls Apr–May, petals 5, white,
notched, shorter than sepals. Fr stalks
turned down from base, later becoming
erect. Whole plant densely covered in
glandular hairs. Dry, open, sandy habitats
including dunes. T, ex Ic. [2]

Alpine Mouse-ear *Cerastium alpinum*
CARYOPHYLLACEAE H 5–20 cm. Loose,
mat-forming, perennial herb. Lvs oval to
elliptical, *c*10 mm; stems and lvs greyish-
green, with long, soft hairs. Fls Jun–Aug,
18–25 mm across, petals white, notched,
twice as long as acute sepals. Rocks,
meadows in arctic, mountains in south.
Br, Ic, Fr, Ge, Cz, Po, FS. [3]

Starwort Mouse-ear *Cerastium
cerastoides* CARYOPHYLLACEAE H 5–10 cm.
Loosely matted, perennial herb. Lvs 6–12
mm, pale-green, narrow, blunt, curving to
one side; lvs and stems hairless except for
line down stem. Fls Jun–Aug, 9–12 mm
across, petals white, deeply notched, twice
as long as narrow sepals. Styles only 3,
other *Cerastium* usually 5. Arctic snowbeds,
springs; mountains elsewhere. Br, Ic, Fr,
Ge, Cz, Po, FS. [4]

Upright Chickweed *Moenchia erecta*
CARYOPHYLLACEAE H 3–12 cm. Erect
hairless annual, branching from base. Lvs
6–20 mm, rigid, narrow, acute, only the
lower stalked. Fls May–Jun, 8 mm across,
petals 4 (5), white. Capsule equalling or

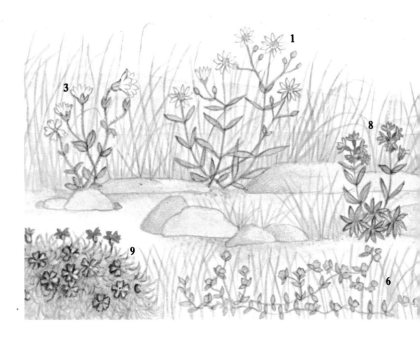

exceeding sepals, which have broad, white margins. Gravelly pastures, heaths, dry slopes. Becoming rare in Low Countries. Br, Fr, Lu, Be, Ne, Ge, Cz. [5]

Smooth Rupturewort *Herniaria glabra* CARYOPHYLLACEAE H < 1 cm. Prostrate, branched, annual or perennial herb, spreading 5–20 cm. Lvs tiny, stalkless, usually hairless. Fls May–Sep, clusters of 10, petals white, 1 mm across, sepals 5 mm, fls look greenish. Open, sandy places. Once supposed to cure hernia. T, ex Ir, Ic. [6]

Sticky Catchfly *Lychnis viscaria* CARYOPHYLLACEAE H 15–90 cm. Erect perennial with hairless stems, sticky below each pair of linear lvs. Fls Jun–Aug, 18–20 mm across, red-purple, short-stalked, petals slightly notched. Cliffs, dry rocks, meadows. Pollinated by butterflies and long-tongued bees. T, ex Ir, Ic. [7]

Alpine Catchfly *Lychnis alpina* CARYOPHYLLACEAE H 5–15 cm. Tufted perennial; stems solitary or several, not sticky. Fls Jun–Jul, bright rose, 6–10 mm across, in compact heads, petals 2-lobed. Exposed heaths, ledges and gravel in mountains, particularly on slag near pyrites mines. Br, Ic, Fr, FS. [8]

Moss Campion *Silene acaulis* CARYOPHYLLACEAE H 2–10 cm. Densely tufted perennial, forming large, moss-like cushions < 25 cm across, covered with short-stalked fls, May–Aug, petals rose, rarely white. Mountains; to sea level in north. Pollinated by butterflies, moths, other insects. Br, Ir, Ic, Fr, Ge, Cz, Po, FS. [9]

Maiden Pink *Dianthus deltoides* CARYOPHYLLACEAE H 15–45 cm. Loosely tufted, creeping perennial. Lvs opposite, narrow, greyish-green, with short hairs on margins. Fls Jun–Sep, *c*18 mm across, scentless, pink or white with dark ring and white spots in centre. Dry fields, sand dunes, rocks, hilly pastures. Petals close when sky overcast. T, ex Ir, Ic, [10]

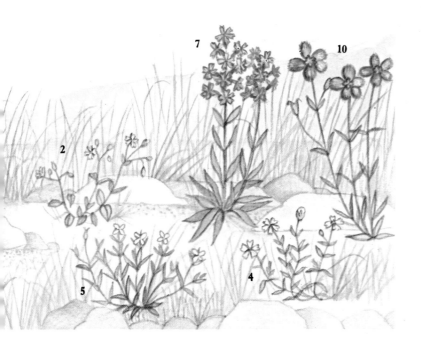

Globeflower *Trollius europaeus*
RANUNCULACEAE H 10–60 cm. Erect,
hairless, perennial herb. Lvs dark-green,
with 3–5 deeply cut lobes. Fls <5 cm
across, spherical, with numerous yellow
sepals, strap-shaped nectaries hidden
between stamens and sepals, May–Aug.
Damp, base-rich meadows and open
woodlands, mainly in mountains.
Poisonous. Br, Ir, Fr, De, Ge, Cz, Po,
FS. [1]

Baneberry *Actaea spicata* RANUNCULACEAE
H 30–65 cm. Nasty-smelling, perennial
herb. Lower lvs large, long-stalked, 1–2
divided into oval lflets; upper lvs smaller.
Fls white, 10 mm across, petals 3–5, in
dense, terminal cluster, May–Jul. Frs
ovoid, green then shining black. Damp,
base-rich woods, mainly in mountains in
south. Poisonous. T, ex Ir, Ic. [2]

Wolf's-bane *Aconitum vulparia*
RANUNCULACEAE H 50–100 cm. Upright,
perennial herb. Lvs dark-green, much
divided into narrow, toothed lobes. Fls in
long spike 20–40 cm, 5 yellow or blue
perianth segments, the posterior forming
characteristic hood, Jun–Aug. Woods,
damp, rocky meadows in mountains.
Poisonous, esp roots; has been used against
lice. Fr, Lu, Be, Ne, Ge, Cz, Po, FS. [3]

Hepatica *Hepatica nobilis* RANUNCULACEAE
H 5–15 cm. Perennial herb. Lvs with 3
broad, rounded lobes, evergreen, often
purplish beneath, distinguished from
closely related *Anemone* by 3 small bracts
below fls instead of lvs, Mar–May. Mountain woods. Fr, De, Ge, Cz, Po, FS. [4]

Spring Anemone *Pulsatilla vernalis*
RANUNCULACEAE H 10–15 cm. Hairy,
evergreen herb. Lvs divided into 3–5
toothed, linear segments. Fls 4–6 cm
across, 6 petals, white inside, flushed pink,
violet or blue outside, solitary, May–Jun.
Fl stems elongate in fr; frs develop
feathery appendages. Alpine meadows.
Fr, De, Ge, Cz, Po, FS. [5]

Alpine Clematis *Clematis alpina*
RANUNCULACEAE H 1–2 m. Scrambling,

deciduous, woody perennial. Lvs divided
into 9 lanceolate, toothed lflets, each 25–50
mm long. Fls <4 cm across, violet or
yellowish-white, 4 petals, solitary, nodding,
May–Jul. Mountains, woods, rocky places.
Fr, Ge, Cz, Po, Fi, No. [6]

Snow Buttercup *Ranunculus nivalis*
RANUNCULACEAE H 5–10 cm. Unbranched,
perennial herb. Basal lvs round, kidney-
shaped, deeply lobed; upper lvs with
lanceolate lobes. Fls yellowish-green, later
pure yellow, <12 mm across, sepals with
reddish-brown hairs, Jun–Jul. Frs ovoid
with beak of equal length. FS. [7]

Glacier Buttercup *Ranunculus glacialis*
RANUNCULACEAE H 4–25 cm. Stout, erect,
hairless, perennial herb. Lvs thick, deeply
divided into elliptical or oblong lobes. Fls
1–3 cm across, change colour from white
to pink to deep purple, sepals with
reddish hairs, Jul–Aug. Fls eaten by
reindeer. Ic, Fr, Ge, Cz, Po, FS. [8]

Columbine *Aquilegia vulgaris*
RANUNCULACEAE H 30–80 cm. Erect,
perennial herb. Lower lvs long-stalked,
divided into 9 irregularly 3-lobed, toothed
segments, hairy below. Fls violet, nodding
with 5 spurred petals, May–Jul. Woods,
mountain pastures; cultivated for ornament.
T, ex De, Fi, Ic, (SC). [9]

Alpine Meadow-Rue *Thalictrum alpinum*
RANUNCULACEAE H 5–20 cm. Slender, wiry,
hairless, perennial herb. Lvs all basal,
divided into 9 rounded, toothed lflets,
dark green above, whitish below. Fls
purplish-green, with 5 petals usually soon
falling, long yellow stamens, Jul–Aug.
Mountain ledges, wet flushes on limy soils;
at sea-level in north. Br, Ir, Fr, FS. [10]

Yellow Adonis *Adonis vernalis*
RANUNCULACEAE H 10–40 cm. Erect,
hairless, perennial herb. Lvs much
divided into fine, linear segments. Fls
yellow, 4–8 cm across, with 10–20 elliptical
petals and 5 hairy sepals, solitary, Apr–
May. Dry pastures and rocks. Poisonous;
cultivated in gardens for ornament. Fr,
Ge, Cz, Po, Sw. [11]

Alpine Bitter-cress *Cardamine bellidifolia* CRUCIFERAE H 1–10 cm. Small, tufted, hairless perennial. Lvs shiny, thick, simple, rarely 2-lobed, in basal rosette. Fls white, <10 mm across, in flat-topped cluster, Jul–Aug. Frs erect pods, <3 cm. Wet gravels, snow beds, exposed summits in mountains. Ic, Fr, Ge, FS. [1]

Northern Rock-cress *Cardaminopsis petraea* CRUCIFERAE H 10–25 cm. Perennial herb with branching rootstock forming rosettes. Lvs of rosettes usually divided into shallow lobes; stem lvs lanceolate, sparsely toothed. Fls white to purple, *c*6 mm across, in clusters of few fls. Frs pods, 12–30 mm, curving upwards. Scree, gravel, rock crevices, sea-level to 1700 m. Br, Ir, Ic, Ge, Cz, Po, Sw, No. [2]

Alpine Rock-cress *Arabis alpina* CRUCIFERAE H 5–40 cm. Loosely tufted, usually hairy, perennial herb. Basal lvs in rosette, coarsely toothed with 4–7 teeth on each side. Fls white, 6–10 mm across, Apr–Jun. Frs pods, <6 cm, on almost horizontal stem. Moist, gravelly snow beds and ledges in mountains, arctic wastes. Br, Ic, Fr, Ge, Cz, Po, Sw. [3]

Mountain Alyssum *Alyssum montanum* CRUCIFERAE H 5–25 cm. Prostrate or erect, hairy, perennial herb. Lvs oblong, green to white, in basal rosette; upper lvs linear. Fls yellow, <15 mm across, in slender clusters, May–Jul. Frs of 2 inflated discs with flattened margins, <5·5 mm. Sandy and snowy places. Fr, Ge, Cz, Po. [4]

Yellow Whitlowgrass *Draba aizoides* CRUCIFERAE H 5–10 cm. Densely tufted, perennial herb with much-branched, hairless stem. Lvs in compact rosettes, linear, <1·5 mm wide. Fls yellow, 8–9 mm across, in loose clusters of 4–18, Mar–Jun. Frs flat, elliptical pods, <12 mm long. Rocks in mountains. Fr, Be, Ge, Cz, Po, Br: in sWales only. [5]

Hoary Whitlowgrass *Draba incana* CRUCIFERAE H 10–35 cm. Robust, hairy, biennial or perennial herb with erect, simple or branched stems. Basal lvs

oblong, stalked, in rosette. Fls white, <5 mm across, in clusters of <40 on leafy stems. Frs <9 mm long, elliptical, twisted. Rocks in mountains; at sea-level in north. Br, Ir, Ic, Fr, De, Fi, No. [6]

Arctic Whitlowgrass *Draba fladnizensis* CRUCIFERAE H 2–10 cm. Dwarf, perennial herb. Basal lvs oblong, usually sparsely covered with hairs; stem lvs 1–2. Fls white, <8 mm across, Jun–Jul. Frs elliptical pods. Dry ridges, plateaux in high mountains. Ic, Fr, Ge, Cz, FS.

Hutchinsia *Hornungia petraea* CRUCIFERAE H 3–15 cm. Slender, slightly leafy annual. Lvs pinnate, divided into 3–15 ovate segments. Fls white, <1·3 mm across, in terminal lfless clusters, Mar–May. Frs pods, <2·5 mm, on horizontal spreading stalks. Rocks and dunes, except far north. Br, Fr, Be, De, Ge, Cz, Sw, No. [7]

Shepherd's Cress *Teesdalia nudicaulis* CRUCIFERAE H 8–45 cm. Erect, often hairless herb with ascending branches. Basal rosette with lvs <5 cm, divided, with 3-lobed terminal segment; stem lvs 1–3. Fls white, *c*2 mm across, petals unequal in length, arranged in terminal cluster, Apr–Jun. Frs 3–4 mm, broadly elliptical and flattened. Sandy heaths, dry banks. T, ex Ic, Fi. [8]

Alpine Penny-cress *Thlaspi alpestre* CRUCIFERAE H 10–50 cm. Erect, hairless, biennial or perennial herb. Basal lvs in rosette, long-stalked; stem lvs ovate, clasping stem. Fls white or lilac, <8 mm across, in compact spike, May–Jul. Frs triangular, winged, 5–7 mm. Often in mineral-rich soils in uplands. Br, Fr, Lu, Be, Ne, Ge, Cz, Po, (Ic, De, FS). [9]

Buckler Mustard *Biscutella laevigata* CRUCIFERAE H 10–50 cm. Very variable, perennial herb. Lvs <13 mm, with basal rosette or not, ovate to linear, toothed or not, sometimes hairy. Fls yellow, <15 mm, in clusters, May–Aug. Frs pairs of rounded, flattened pods like spectacles. Rocks, mainly in mountains. Fr, Be, Ge, Cz, Po. [10]

Round-leaved Sundew *Drosera rotundifolia* DROSERACEAE H 4–8 cm. Perennial, insectivorous herb. Lvs all basal, round, <8 mm, with long stalks 13–15 mm, upper surfaces covered with long, glandular, digestive hairs. Fls white, <5 mm across, in terminal clusters of few flowers on scape, Jun–Aug. Frs smooth capsules. On peat or bog-moss. T. [1]

Great Sundew *Drosera anglica* DROSERACEAE H 10–30 cm. Largest of 3 sundews. Lvs erect, 3 cm, linear, oblong, narrowing into long stalk 5–10 cm. Fls white, in terminal cluster of 3–6 on central scape, 10–18 cm long, Jul–Aug. Among bog-moss in wetter parts of bogs. T, ex Ic. [2]

Oblong-leaved Sundew *Drosera intermedia* DROSERACEAE H 5–10 cm. Similar in size to *D. rotundifolia*, but lvs erect, <1 cm, broadest at tip, narrowing into long hairless stalks. Fls white, in terminal cluster on scape which appears to rise from side of rosette (not centrally as other 2 spp), Jul–Aug. Damp peat on heaths, moors. Br, Ir, Fr, Be, Ne, De, Ge, Cz, Po, FS. [3]

Hairy Stonecrop *Sedum villosum* CRASSULACEAE H 5–15 cm. Reddish, glandular, hairy, perennial herb branching from base. Lvs 6–12 mm, alternate, linear, blunt, yellow-green. Fls lilac or pale pink, <6 mm across, petals with dark central vein, in loose, terminal clusters, Jun–Aug. Reproduces by bulbils in axils of lvs. Moss carpets, streamsides, wet ledges. Br, Ic, Fr, Ge, Cz, Po, FS. [4]

Roseroot *Rhodiola rosea* CRASSULACEAE H 10–30 cm. Erect, hairless, bluish-green, perennial herb arising from thick, fleshy, branched stock. Lvs <4 cm, broad, fleshy, rounded to ovate. Fls ♂ and ♀, greenish-yellow, in terminal clusters, May–Aug. Frs of ♀ fls redden gradually. Mountain rocks, sea-cliffs. Br, Ir, Ic, Fr, Cz, Po, FS. [5]

Mountain Currant *Ribes alpinum*
GROSSULARIACEAE H <2 m. Erect,
deciduous shrub. Lvs <5 cm, as broad
as long, with 3–5 toothed lobes. Fls
yellowish-green, 4–6 mm across, in
separate ♂ and ♀ spikes, ♂ 20–30 fls, ♀
8–15 fls, Apr–May. Frs red berries, 6–8
mm across, insipid. Mountain woods. Br,
Fr, De, Ge, Cz, Po, FS. [6]

Goat's-beard Spiraea *Aruncus dioicus*
ROSACEAE H <2 m. Erect, leafy, perennial
herb. Lvs <1 m, 2–3 times divided into
oval, long-pointed, doubly toothed
segments. Fls white, <5 mm across,
usually unisexual, in large pyramidal
clusters, Jun–Aug. Frs pendant, *c*3 mm
across, poisonous. Damp woods, shady
places in mountains. Fr, Be, Ge, Cz, Po.
[7]

Alpine Lady's-mantle *Alchemilla alpina*
ROSACEAE H 10–20 cm. Stoutly creeping,
perennial herb. Lvs mostly basal, <35 mm
across, divided almost to base into 5–7
oblong segments, green above, silvery and
hairy beneath. Fls yellow-green, 3 mm
across, in dense, terminal clusters, May–
Aug. Rocks, screes in mountains,
descending to sea-level in north, west.
Br, Ir, Ic, Fr, Ne, Ge, FS. [8]

Cloudberry *Rubus chamaemorus*
ROSACEAE H 5–20 cm. Extensively
creeping, underground stems produce
erect, hairy stems. Lvs circular, divided
into 5–7 toothed lobes. Fls white, <2 cm
across, solitary, ♂ and ♀ separate, Jun–
Aug. Frs red then orange, pleasant tasting.
Moors, mountain bogs. Br, Ir, De, Ge,
Cz, Po, FS. [9]

Stone Bramble *Rubus saxatilis* ROSACEAE
H 8–50 cm. Far-creeping, prostrate, non-
woody, perennial herb with branches
rooting at tip. Lvs divided into 3 stalked,
ovate, double-toothed lflets. Fls white,
<8 mm across, in compact terminal
clusters of 2–8, Jun–Aug. Frs scarlet,
translucent. Rocky places, mountain
thickets and woods, mainly in north. T.
[10]

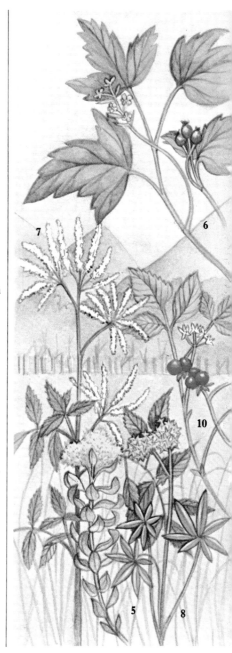

Alpine Rose *Rosa pendulina* ROSACEAE H <2 m. Low, dwarf shrub with yellow-green, occasionally purple bark. Lvs divided into 7–11 oval, double-toothed lflets <6 cm long, usually hairy below. Fls bright carmine, <5 cm across, solitary, Jun–Jul. Frs red, ovoid, pendant, with bottle-like neck. Rocky woods, shady places in mountains. Fr, Be, Ge, Cz, Po. [1]

Rock Cinquefoil *Potentilla rupestris* ROSACEAE H 20–50 cm. Erect, hairy, perennial herb with woody, branched stock. Basal lvs <15 cm, divided into 2–4 pairs of lflets decreasing in size from apex of lf; upper lvs few, less divided. Fls white, <2 cm across, in loose, branching clusters, May–Jun. Frs shiny, hairless. Mountain rocks, woods. Br, Fr, Lu, Be, Ge, Cz, Po, Sw, No. [2]

Ternate-leaved Cinquefoil *Potentilla norvegica* ROSACEAE H 10–70 cm. Erect, hairy, branched, annual or short-lived perennial herb. Lvs divided into 3 elliptical, coarsely toothed segments <7 cm. Fls yellow, <15 mm across, in much-branched, loose clusters, Apr–Jun. Dry, open habitats, waste places. Sometimes naturalized where introduced. De, Ge, Cz, Po, FS, (Br, Fr, Be, Ne). [3]

Grey Cinquefoil *Potentilla cinerea* ROSACEAE H 10–15 cm. Grey-green, mat-forming, prostrate, perennial herb, densely covered in branched, glandular hairs. Lvs 3- or 5-fingered, with toothed, ovate lflets <2 cm. Fls yellow, <15 mm across, longer than sepals, 1–6 per stem, Apr–Jun. Dry, sandy places <1600 m. Fr, Be, De, Ge, Cz, Po, Sw. [4]

Alpine Cinquefoil *Potentilla crantzii* ROSACEAE H 7–20 cm. Softly hairy, prostrate, perennial herb with woody base and few branches, not mat-forming. Lvs 3–5 fingered, lflets <2 cm, widest near top, 2–5 teeth each side, sparsely hairy. Fls yellow, <2 cm across, petals often with orange spot at base, Jun–Jul. Limy rocks, in mountains farther south. Br, Ic, Fr, Ge, Cz, Po, FS. [5]

Shrubby Cinquefoil *Potentilla fruticosa* ROSACEAE H <1 m. Much-branched, hairy, deciduous shrub with peeling bark. Lvs divided into *c*5 elliptical lflets <2 cm, with down-rolled margins. Fls yellow, <25 mm across, solitary or few in terminal cluster, Jun–Aug. Damp, limy rocks in mountains. Br, Ir, Fr, Sw. [6]

Sibbaldia *Sibbaldia procumbens* ROSACEAE H 1–5 cm. Creeping, tufted, perennial herb with branched, woody stock ending in rosette. Lvs of rosette bluish-green, of 3 lflets <2 cm, hairy beneath with 3 apical teeth, the central shorter. Fls yellow, <5 mm across, inconspicuous, petals often absent, Jul–Aug. Willow thickets, mountain grassland. T, ex Ic, Lu, No. [7]

Rowan *Sorbus aucuparia* ROSACEAE H <20 m. Slender tree with ascending branches, silver-grey bark. Lvs divided into *c*15 lanceolate, toothed lflets <6 cm, the terminal similar in size to rest. Fls white, 8–10 mm across, in flat-topped cluster <15 cm, May–Jun. Frs scarlet, <9 mm. Woods, scrub, mountain rocks. T. [8]

Wild Cotoneaster *Cotoneaster integerrimus* ROSACEAE H <2 m. Erect, branched, deciduous shrub with twigs woolly when young. Lvs ovate, <4 cm, short-stalked, hairless above, densely grey and woolly beneath. Fls pink, <5 mm, in small clusters, Apr–Jun. Frs roundish, red, <6 mm. Dry, stony, usually limy slopes, mainly in mountains. T, ex Ir, Ic, Ne. [9]

Purple Saxifrage *Saxifraga oppositifolia*
SAXIFRAGACEAE Mat-forming, perennial
herb with long, creeping, prostrate stems
and short, erect branches. Lvs 2–6 cm,
very dense, in 4 rows, with lime-encrusted
tips. Fls rosy-purple, <1 cm across,
solitary, terminal on short stalks, Mar–
Aug. Rocks, screes throughout arctic,
mountains. Br, Ir, Ic, Fr, Ge, Cz, Po,
FS. [1]

Livelong Saxifrage *Saxifraga paniculata*
SAXIFRAGACEAE H 15–30 cm. Densely
tufted, rosette-forming, perennial herb.
Lvs oblong, tongue-shaped, <4 cm,
curved up at apex, finely toothed, lime-
encrusted. Fls white, sometimes red-
spotted, <1 cm across, in terminal
clusters, Jun–Aug. Rocks and screes in
mountains. Ic, Fr, Ge, Cz, Po, No. [2]

Yellow Saxifrage *Saxifraga aizoides*
SAXIFRAGACEAE H 5–20 cm. Mat-forming,
perennial herb with ascending flowering
stems. Lvs fleshy, linear, oblong, acute,
<2 cm, often with stiff hairs. Fls yellow,
<1 cm across, in loose, terminal clusters
of 1–10, Jun–Aug. Arctic, alpine
streamsides; stony, wet places. Br, Ir, Ic,
Fr, Ge, Cz, Po, FS. [3]

Starry Saxifrage *Saxifraga stellaris*
SAXIFRAGACEAE H 5–20 cm. Rosette-
forming, perennial herb. Lvs fleshy, <3
cm, widest at tip, remotely toothed,
tapering at base. Fls white, <1 cm across,
petals with 2 yellow spots near base,
arranged in open-branched inflor, Jun–
Aug. In springs, by streams, on wet
ledges in mountains, at sea-level in north.
Br, Ir, Ic, Fr, Ge, Cz, Po, FS. [4]

Mossy Saxifrage *Saxifraga hypnoides*
SAXIFRAGACEAE H 5–20 cm. Creeping,
perennial herb with numerous sterile
shoots terminating in rosettes. Stem lvs
lanceolate; rosette lvs with 3–7 bristle-

pointed lobes. Fls white, <15 mm across,
nodding in bud, 3–7 together on slender
stems, Jun–Aug. Rocks, screes from sea-
level to 1600 m. Br, Ir, Ic, Fr, No. [5]

Tufted Saxifrage *Saxifraga cespitosa*
SAXIFRAGACEAE H 4–10 cm. Cushion-
forming, glandular-hairy perennial with
short, densely leafy, sterile shoots. Lvs
<1 cm, with 3–5 lobes, narrowed to
short stalk. Fls off-white, *c*1 cm across,
1–3 per stem, May–Jul. Rocks in
mountains of arctic, sub-arctic. Br, Ic,
FS. [6]

Alpine Saxifrage *Saxifraga nivalis*
SAXIFRAGACEAE H 5–20 cm. Rosette-
forming, perennial herb. Lvs roundish,
coarsely toothed, green above, purple
below, rather thick. Fls greenish-white,
<5 mm across, in dense, head-like inflor
on lfless stem, Jul–Aug. Wet ledges,
crevices in arctic mountains, rare
elsewhere. Br, Ir, Ic, Cz, Po, FS. [7]

Highland Saxifrage *Saxifraga rivularis*
SAXIFRAGACEAE H 2–8 cm. Tufted,
perennial herb not forming basal rosette,
with underground bulbils and often
producing rooting, underground stems.
Lvs <15 mm wide, with 3–7 blunt lobes,
on long stalks. Fls white, <1 cm across,
in small terminal clusters, Jul–Aug.
Wet rocks, flushed snow beds in moss
carpets in arctic, sub-arctic. Br, Ic, FS.
[8]

Drooping Saxifrage *Saxifraga cernua*
SAXIFRAGACEAE H 3–15 cm. Erect, rosette-
forming, perennial herb. Basal lvs kidney-
shaped, with 3–5 acute lobes, on long
stalks <5 cm. Stem lvs simple, oblong or
linear, without stalks. Fls white, <15 mm
across, solitary, often absent, Jul–Aug.
Reproduction by brownish-red bulbils in
axils of stem lvs. Mountains of arctic,
sub-arctic. Br, Ic, Cz, Po, FS. [9]

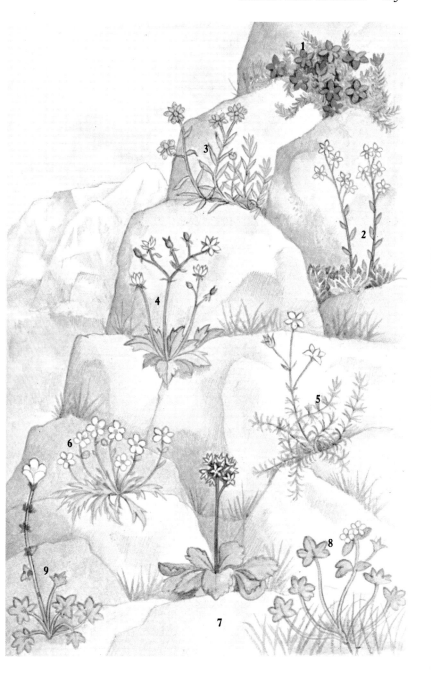

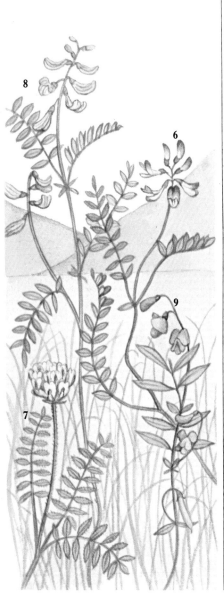

Broom *Sarothamnus scoparius*
LEGUMINOSAE H <2 m. Erect, much-
branched, deciduous shrub with green,
5-angled stem, hairy only when young.
Lvs trifoliate, lflets narrowly elliptical
<2 cm. Fls yellow, <2 cm across,
solitary or in pairs, Apr–Jun. Frs black
pods, <4 cm, with brown hairs on
margins. Heaths, dry sand, except far
north. T, ex Ic, Fi. [1]

Hairy Greenweed *Genista pilosa*
LEGUMINOSAE H <50 cm. Prostrate,
hairy shrub with much-branched, twisted
stems. Lvs ovate, blunt, <5 mm, smooth
above, hairy beneath. Fls yellow, <1 cm
long, in elongated clusters on ascending
branches, Apr–Oct. Frs hairy pods, 15–25
mm. Dry acid heaths, rocks. T, ex Ir, Ic,
FS. [2]

Spiny Furze *Genista germanica*
LEGUMINOSAE H <60 cm. Erect, hairy-
stemmed shrub with branched spines on
old stems. Lvs <2 cm, elliptical, hairy
below. Fls yellow, <1 cm, in short, erect
terminal clusters, May–Sep. Frs hairy
pods, c8 mm. Thickets, acid grassland,
heaths. Fr, Lu, Be, Ne, De, Ge, Cz, Po,
Sw. [3]

Petty Whin *Genista anglica* LEGUMINOSAE
H 10–50 cm. Erect or ascending, spiny
shrub with smooth or hairy stems. Lvs
<8 mm, ovate, pointed. Fls yellow, <8
mm, in short clusters, Apr–Aug. Frs
smooth pods, 12–15 mm, inflated and
pointed at both ends. Dry heaths, moors,
bushy places. Br, Fr, Lu, Be, Ne, De,
Ge, Sw. [4]

Gorse *Ulex europaeus* LEGUMINOSAE
H 60–200 cm. Erect or ascending, densely
spiny shrub. Spines deeply grooved, 15–
25 mm, replacing lvs. Fls yellow, <15
mm, with minutely toothed lips, in loose
clusters, sweet-scented, Feb–Jun. Frs
very hairy, oval, black pods, <15 mm.
Heaths. Used for fodder and bedding,
often naturalized. Br, Ir, Fr, Ne, Ge,
(Lu, Be, De, Cz, Sw, No). [5]

Alpine Milk-vetch *Astragalus alpinus*
LEGUMINOSAE H 10–30 cm. Slender,
prostrate or ascending, perennial herb.
Lvs <8 cm, divided into 17–25 elliptical
lflets, hairy on both surfaces or hairless
above. Fls pale blue, tipped purple, <1
cm long, in spherical, terminal clusters of
5–15 fls, on stems longer than lvs, Jul–
Aug. Frs bluish, hairy pods, <15 mm.
Rocks, screes, mountain grassland. Br, Fr,
Ge, Cz, Po, FS. [6]

Yellow Oxytropis *Oxytropis campestris*
LEGUMINOSAE H <20 cm. Erect, softly
hairy, perennial herb. Lvs <15 cm, with
c10 pairs of elliptical, woolly lflets. Fls
yellow, tinged purple, <2 cm long, in
dense terminal clusters of 6–10 fls, Jun–
Aug. Frs ovoid, hairy pods, <16 mm.
Dry rocks, pastures in mountains. Br, Fr,
Cz, Po, FS. [7]

Hairy Oxytropis *Oxytropis pilosa*
LEGUMINOSAE H 20–50 cm. Erect, very
hairy, perennial herb. Lvs with 9–13 pairs
of oblong to linear lflets, 1–2 cm. Fls
yellow, <14 mm long, in oblong spikes
of many fls, Jun–Aug. Frs short, narrowly
cylindrical pods, <2 cm. Dry, limy rocks,
esp in mountains. Fr, Ge, Cz, Po, Sw.

Wood Bitter-vetch *Vicia orobus*
LEGUMINOSAE H 30–60 cm. Stout, erect,
somewhat hairy, perennial herb. Lvs
divided into 6–9 pairs of elliptical lflets
<2 cm. Fls white with purple veins, <15
mm long, in spikes of 6–20 fls, on stalks
as long as lvs, Jun–Sep. Frs smooth,
yellow pods, <3 cm. Rocks, woody
places. Br, Ir, Fr, Be, De, Ge, No. [8]

Bitter Vetch *Lathyrus montanus*
LEGUMINOSAE H 15–40 cm. Erect,
perennial herb with winged stems,
creeping underground stems and tuberous
roots. Lvs divided into 2–4 pairs of narrow
to elliptical lflets <4 cm. Fls crimson,
turning blue or green, <12 mm long, in
clusters of 2–6 fls, Apr–Jul. Frs smooth,
reddish-brown pods, <4 cm. Woods,
hedges in hilly country. T, ex Ic. [9]

Mountain Clover *Trifolium montanum*
LEGUMINOSAE H 15–60 cm. Erect,
branched, perennial herb. Lflets <7 cm,
lanceolate or elliptical, smooth above,
hairy below, with toothed margins. Fls
white or yellowish, <9 mm long, in dense
heads 15–30 mm across, May–Sep. Frs
1-seeded pods. Dry grassland, mainly in
mountains. Fr, Lu, Be, Ge, Cz, Po, FS. [1]

Bloody Crane's-bill *Geranium*
sanguineum GERANIACEAE H 10–40 cm.
Bushy, perennial herb with stout, creeping,
underground stem. Lvs round, <6 cm,
divided into 5–7 narrow lobes, often
further divided into 3. Fls purple, large,
<3 cm across, solitary, Jun–Aug. Frs
with beak, <3 cm. Rocks, sand, other dry
places. T, ex Ic, Ne. [2]

Wood Crane's-bill *Geranium sylvaticum*
GERANIACEAE H 20–80 cm. Erect, hairy,
perennial herb. Basal lvs <12 cm across,
deeply divided. Fls blue-violet, <3 cm
across, in pairs on stalks, remaining erect
in fr, Jun–Jul. Frs with beak, <25 mm.
Meadows, woods, mainly in mountains.
T, (Ne). [3]

Allseed *Radiola linoides* LINACEAE H 2–8
cm. Delicate, hairless, much-branched,
annual herb. Lvs opposite, elliptical,
<3 mm. Fls white, $c2$ mm across, in
spreading or flat-topped clusters, Jun–Sep.
Frs spherical capsules, $c1$ mm. Sandy or
peaty hollows on heaths. T, ex Ic, Lu,
Fi. [4]

Perennial Flax *Linum perenne* LINACEAE
H 30–100 cm. Erect, hairless, perennial herb
branching from base. Lvs linear, <2 cm
long, 1–3 mm wide. Fls bright-blue, <25
mm across, in loose-branched clusters,
May–Aug. Frs spherical capsules, <7 mm.
Variable sp of meadows, rocks, mainly in
mountains. Br, Fr, Ge, Cz, Po. [5]

Heath Milkwort *Polygala serpyllifolia*
POLYGALACEAE H 6–25 cm. Slender,
creeping, perennial herb, scarcely woody
at base. Lvs 3–15 mm; lower lvs opposite,
elliptical; upper lvs alternate, lanceolate.

Fls 5–6 mm, usually blue, in short, dense
clusters of 3–10, May–Aug. Frs flattened,
oval, 2-lobed capsules, <5 mm. Acid
heaths, grassland. Br, Ir, Fr, Lu, Be, Ne,
De, Ge, Cz, No. [6]

Tufted Milkwort *Polygala comosa*
POLYGALACEAE H 7–20 cm. Erect or
ascending, perennial herb. Lvs <1 cm;
lower lvs narrow, blunt, soon falling;
upper lvs lanceolate, acute. Fls pink,
rarely blue or white, <6 mm, in dense
cylindrical spikes of 15–50, May–Jun. Frs
<5 mm, almost hidden by sepals. Dry
grassland, open woods. Fr, Lu, Be, Ne,
Ge, Cz, Po, Fi, Sw. [7]

Holly *Ilex aquifolium* AQUIFOLIACEAE
H <15 m. Evergreen, dioecious tree or
shrub; grey bark. Lvs hairless, <12 cm,
ovate, spiny, near top of tree may lack
spines. Fls <8 mm across, in clusters,
May–Aug. Frs bright red, spherical,
poisonous. Woods, hedges. Br, Ir, Fr, Lu,
Be, Ne, De, Ge, No. [8]

Mezereon *Daphne mezereum*
THYMELAEACEAE H <2 m. Deciduous
shrub with few, erect, greyish-brown
branches. Lvs <8 cm, light green, hairless. Fls pink-purple, rarely white, <12
mm across, in clusters of 2–4, appearing
before lvs, Feb–May. Frs scarlet, ovoid,
<12 mm. Whole plant poisonous. Woods,
limy soils. T, ex Ir, Ic, (De). [9]

Slender St John's-wort *Hypericum*
pulchrum HYPERICACEAE H 20–60 cm.
Erect or ascending, hairless, perennial
herb with reddish stem. Lvs <1 cm, with
translucent dots. Fls yellow, tinged red,
<15 mm across, in pyramidal clusters,
Jun–Sep. Heaths, open woods on acid
soils. T, ex Ic, Fi. [10]

Trailing St John's-wort *Hypericum*
humifusum HYPERICACEAE H 5–20 cm.
Trailing or ascending, perennial herb.
Lvs lanceolate, <15 mm, without stalks.
Fls yellow, <1 cm across, in clusters,
Jun–Sep. Frs capsules, slightly exceeding
sepals. Open habitats on poor soils. T,
ex Ic, Fi, No. [11]

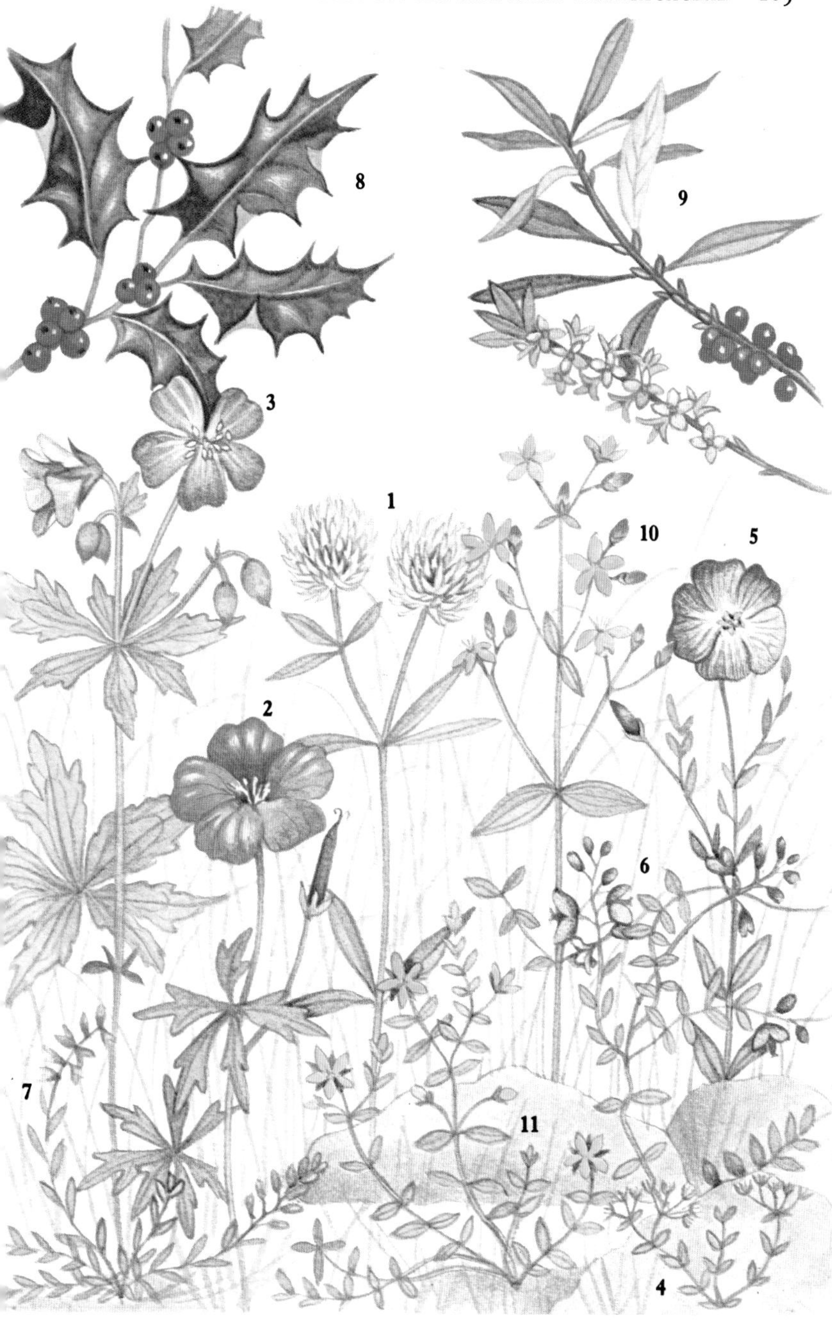
8
9
3
1
10
5
2
6
7
11
4

Teesdale Violet *Viola rupestris* VIOLACEAE
H 2–10 cm. Tufted, hairy, perennial herb
with central rosette, fl-stems in axils. Lvs
<1 cm, kidney- or heart-shaped, with
shallowly toothed margins. Fls pale blue-
violet, <15 mm, with thick, violet spur,
Apr–Jun. Frs hairy capsules, <6 mm.
Open habitats on base-rich rocks, mainly
in mountains. Br, Fr, Lu, Ne, Ge, Cz,
Po, FS. [1]

Yellow Wood-violet *Viola biflora*
VIOLACEAE H 5–20 cm. Slender, erect,
perennial herb with creeping, underground
stem. Lvs kidney-shaped, <4 cm,
broader than long, with rounded teeth.
Fls yellow with brown veins, <15 mm,
solitary or in pairs on leafy stems, not
fragrant, Jun–Aug. Damp or shady places,
mainly in mountains. Fr, Ge, Cz, Po, FS.
[2]

Mountain Pansy *Viola lutea* VIOLACEAE
H 7–20 cm. Perennial herb with creeping,
underground system sending up slender,
solitary stems. Lvs ovate to lanceolate,
<2 cm, becoming narrower upwards,
with short, stiff hairs. Fls yellow, blue,
violet or combination of these, <35 mm
across, with slender spur 3–6 mm, May–
Aug. Mountain grassland, esp on base-
rich soils. Br, Ir, Fr, Be, Ne, Ge, Cz, Po.
[3]

Spotted Rock-rose *Tuberaria guttata*
CISTACEAE H 6–30 cm. Erect, hairy, annual
shrub forming basal rosette. Lower lvs
elliptical, <5 cm; upper lvs lanceolate,
shorter. Fls pale yellow, often with red
spot at base of petals, 8–12 mm across, in
1-sided clusters of 5–12 fls, Apr–Aug.
Open pinewoods, heaths. Br, Ir, Fr, Ne,
Ge. [4]

Heath-rose *Fumana procumbens* CISTACEAE
H <40 cm. Dwarf, hairy, prostrate shrub
with spreading branches. Lvs linear, <18
mm. Fls yellow, <2 cm across, wedge-
shaped petals with dark golden-yellow
spot at base, solitary, May. Frs capsules
with 8–12 seeds. Dry, rocky, stony or
sandy places in low scrub. Fr, Be, Ge,
Cz, Sw. [5]

Alpine Enchanter's-nightshade
Circaea alpina ONAGRACEAE H 10–30 cm.
Creeping, perennial herb with erect or
ascending, almost hairless stems. Lvs in
opposite pairs, ovate, distinctly toothed,
<6 cm. Fls white or pinkish, <3 mm
across, in dense clusters on stems which
do not elongate until petals fall. Frs
1-seeded, covered in hooked bristles.
Mountain woods. T, ex Ir, Ic, Lu. [6]

Three-angled Willowherb *Epilobium
alpestre* ONAGRACEAE H 20–70 cm. Erect,
perennial herb with hairy lines on stems.
Lvs lanceolate, <8 cm, usually arranged
in whorls. Fls pinkish-violet, <2 cm
across, in terminal clusters, Jul–Aug. Frs
long capsules, opening into 4 valves to
release fluffy seeds. Mountains. Fr, Ge,
Cz, Po. [7]

Chickweed Willowherb *Epilobium
alsinifolium* ONAGRACEAE H 5–20 cm.
Slender, ascending, perennial herb with
long, underground stems. Lvs ovate, <4
cm, bluish-green and shiny above, with
short stalk. Fls bluish-red, 8–9 mm across,
in spike of 2–5 fls drooping at top, Jul–
Sep. Frs capsules, <5 mm. By streams,
cold springs in mountains. Br, Ir, Ic, Fr,
Ge, Cz, Po, FS. [8]

Milky-flowered Willowherb *Epilobium
lactiflorum* ONAGRACEAE H 6–25 cm. Erect,
perennial herb with short, underground
stems ending in small rosettes. Lvs
opposite, lanceolate, <25 mm, with few,
small teeth. Fls white, <1 cm across,
Jul–Aug. Frs capsules, <5 cm. Moist
slopes, meadows in arctic, sub-arctic. Ic,
FS.

Alpine Willowherb *Epilobium
anagallidifolium* ONAGRACEAE H 4–10 cm.
Slender, ascending, perennial herb with
numerous prostrate stems, creeping above
ground in summer. Lvs opposite, lanceolate, yellowish-green, <2 cm, hairless,
faintly toothed. Fls rose-red, <5 mm
across, in clusters of 1–3 fls drooping
when young, Jul–Aug. Frs erect, reddish
capsules, <4 cm. Streams, springs in arctic,
mountains. Br, Ic, Fr, Ge, Cz, Po, FS. [9]

Dwarf Cornel *Cornus suecica* CORNACEAE
H 6–20 cm. Dwarf, perennial herb with
creeping, underground system and erect,
annual stems. Lvs ovate, 3- to 5-veined,
hairy above, hairless below. Fls dark
purple, *c*2 mm across, in terminal cluster
of 8–25; surrounded by 4 white, oval,
petal-like bracts. Frs red, spherical, *c*5 mm.
Acid heaths, moors, esp in mountains.
Br, Ic, Ne, De, Ge, Po, FS. [1]

Astrantia *Astrantia major* UMBELLIFERAE
H 30–100 cm. Erect, hairless, perennial
herb. Basal lvs <15 cm across, with 3–7
coarsely toothed lobes. Fls white, tiny, in
convex umbel <5 cm across; surrounded
by coloured bracts, white beneath, pale
greenish-purple above, May–Sep. Frs
ovoid, <8 mm. Woods and meadows;
also naturalized. Fr, Ge, Cz, Po, (Br, De,
Fi). [2]

Bur Chervil *Anthriscus caucalis*
UMBELLIFERAE H 25–80 cm. Wiry,
sparsely hairy, annual herb with hollow
stems. Lvs 2–3 times divided into toothed
lobes <1 cm. Fls white, in umbels 2–4
cm across, of 3–6 rays, May–Jun. Frs
ovoid, covered in hooked spines, <3 mm.
Sandy heaths and dry, open ground. Br,
Ir, Fr, De, Cz, Po, Sw. [3]

Sweet Cicely *Myrrhis odorata*
UMBELLIFERAE H 60–120 cm. Erect,
strongly aromatic, almost hairless, perennial herb with hollow, grooved stems. Lvs
<30 cm, 2–3 times divided into coarsely
toothed, ovate segments. Fls white in
umbels 1–5 cm across, of 4–20 rays, Apr–
Aug. Frs characteristic, ridged pods,
<25 mm long. Cultivated for flowers and
naturalized. Fr, ?Ge, (Br, Ir, Ic, Lu, Be,
Ne, De, Ge, Cz, Po, FS, from mountains
of S Europe). [4]

Spignel *Meum athamanticum* UMBELLIFERAE
H 20–60 cm. Hairless, very aromatic,
perennial herb; stem base covered with
remains of old lvs. Fls white or purple in
umbels 2–6 cm across, of 6–15 rays,

Jun–Aug. Frs ovoid, <10 mm. Alpine meadows. Br, Fr, Be, Ge, Cz, Po, (No). [5]

Lovage *Levisticum officinale* UMBELLIFERAE H 10–250 cm. Stout, aromatic, shiny, perennial herb. Lower lvs <70 cm, 2–3 times divided into irregular, deeply toothed segments. Fls greenish-yellow, in umbels 8–10 cm across, of 12–20 rays, Jun–Aug. Frs ovoid, <7 mm, yellow or brown. Escape from cultivation. (Fr, Be, Ne, De, Ge, Cz, Po, FS, from SW Asia.) [6]

Masterwort *Peucedanum ostruthium* UMBELLIFERAE H 30–100 cm. Erect, almost hairless, perennial herb with hollow, ridged stems. Lvs <30 cm, divided into oval, lobed and toothed segments, downy beneath. Fls white or pinkish, in umbels 5–10 cm across, of 20–50 rays, Jun–Aug. Frs 4–5 mm, rounded, with broad wings. Mountain meadows, woods, stream banks; formerly cultivated as herb and naturalized elsewhere. Fr, Ge, Cz, Po, (Br, Be, De, Sw, No). [7]

Broad-leaved Sermountain *Laserpitium latifolium* UMBELLIFERAE H 60–150 cm. Erect, almost hairless, perennial herb with solid, branched stem. Lvs triangular in outline, divided into oval to heart-shaped, toothed segments, <10 cm. Fls white, in umbels 6–10 cm across, of 25–50 rays, Jun–Aug. Frs 5–10 mm, ovoid, with broad, wavy wings. Woods, rocky places in mountains. Fr, Lu, De, Ge, Cz, Po, FS, (Be). [8]

Diapensia *Diapensia lapponica* DIAPENSIACEAE H <5 cm. Cushion-like, evergreen undershrub forming deep rosettes. Lvs 5–10 mm, leathery, linear, broadest near tip; old lvs often dark-spotted by small, crust-like lichens. Fls white, <2 cm, solitary, on short stalks, May–Jun. Frs capsules. Exposed arctic ridges, dry in summer, little snow in winter. Br, Ic, FS. [9]

Green-flowered Wintergreen *Pyrola chlorantha* PYROLACEAE H 10–30 cm. Hairless, evergreen, perennial herb with creeping, underground stems. Lvs roundish, <25 mm, pale green above, darker beneath. Fls yellowish-green, <12 mm across, bell-shaped, in short clusters of 3–8, Jul–Aug. Frs capsules. Coniferous woods. Fr, De, Ge, Cz, Po, FS. [1]

Serrated Wintergreen *Orthilia secunda* PYROLACEAE H 5–25 cm. Hairless, creeping, evergreen, perennial herb, forming loose, light olive-green rosettes. Lvs ovate, <4 cm, finely toothed. Fls greenish-white, <5 mm across, in 1-sided spikes, Jun–Aug. Woods, rock ledges, in mountains. Br, Ir, Ic, Lu, De, Ge, Cz, Po, FS. [2]

One-flowered Wintergreen *Moneses uniflora* PYROLACEAE H 5–15 cm. Hairless, creeping, evergreen, perennial herb. Lvs light-green, 1–3 cm, round, finely toothed, running down lf-stalk. Fls white, <2 cm across, wide open, drooping, solitary, very fragrant, May–Aug. Damp woods in mountains. Br, Fr, Lu, Ne, De, Ge, Cz, Po, FS. [3]

Umbellate Wintergreen *Chimaphila umbellata* PYROLACEAE H 10–30 cm. Hairless, creeping, dwarf, evergreen shrub. Lvs dark-green, leathery, <7 cm, lanceolate, branched near tip, toothed. Fls pinkish, <12 mm across, in terminal clusters of 3–6, Jun–Jul. Coniferous woods. Fr, De, Ge, Cz, Po, FS. [4]

Yellow Bird's-nest *Monotropa hypopitys* PYROLACEAE H 8–30 cm. Erect, saprophytic herb, lacking chlorophyll. Whole plant creamy-white to yellow, tinged with brown or pink. Lvs scale-like, 5–13 mm, numerous at base of stem. Fls 10–15 mm, in short, drooping clusters, Jun–Sep. Frs roundish capsules. Damp woods, esp conifers or beech. T, ex Ic. [5]

Rhododendron *Rhododendron ponticum* ERICACEAE H 2–5 cm. Erect, hairless, evergreen shrub with spreading branches. Lvs dark, shiny green, like laurel, <25 cm. Fls violet-purple, 4–6 cm, bell-shaped, in terminal clusters c12 cm across, May–Jun. Frs capsules of 7 divisions. Cultivated for ornament; often established in woods. (Br, Ir, Fr, Lu, Be, from S Europe.) [6]

Trailing Azalea *Loiseleuria procumbens* ERICACEAE Creeping, hairless shrub, forming extensive mats. Lvs dense, <8 mm, oval, leathery, with in-rolled margins. Fls pink, 4–5 mm across, short-stalked, in terminal clusters of 2–5, May–Jul. Frs red capsules, <4 mm. Exposed ridges, heaths on acid soils, mainly in mountains. Br, Ic, Fr, Ge, FS. [7]

Blue Heath *Phyllodoce caerulea* ERICACEAE H 10–20 cm. Bushy, evergreen shrub. Lvs linear, <1 cm, densely clustered, with hairy furrow beneath. Fls red in bud, later purple, finally blue, nodding, flask-shaped, 8–10 mm, in terminal clusters of 2–6, Jun–Jul. Frs ovoid capsules. Heathy ground on mountains. Br, Ic, Fr, FS. [8]

Mossy Mountain-heather *Cassiope hypnoides* ERICACEAE H 5–15 cm. Creeping, mat-forming, evergreen shrub with moss-like branches. Lvs linear, acute, <4 mm, spreading, almost hairless. Fls white, <5 mm, solitary, bell-shaped, Jul–Aug. By streams, in damp moss, throughout arctic mountains. Ic, FS. [9]

White Arctic Bell-heather *Cassiope tetragona* ERICACEAE H 10–30 cm. Erect, evergreen shrub. Lvs scale-like, blunt, hairy, <5 mm, arranged in 4 rows pressed against hard stems. Fls creamy-white with pink lobes to petals, <8 mm, solitary, bell-shaped, Jul. Dry, stony, calcareous soils in arctic mountains. FS. [10]

Bearberry *Arctostaphylos uva-ursi*
ERICACEAE H <5 cm. Prostrate, hairless,
evergreen, mat-forming shrub. Lvs
leathery, ovate, <30 mm, dark-green
above, paler beneath. Fls greenish-white
to pink, <6 mm, flask-shaped, May–Jul.
Frs spherical, c10 mm, bright red,
tasteless. Dry heaths, open woods,
moorland. T, ex Lu, Be. [1]

Alpine Bearberry *Arctostaphylos alpina*
ERICACEAE H <2 cm. Prostrate, deciduous
shrub with hairless twigs. Lvs <50 mm,
ovate, broadest near tip, saw-toothed,
withering in autumn but persisting till
spring. Fls white, <4 mm, flask-shaped,
May–Jun as soon as snow goes. Frs juicy
black when ripe. Exposed heaths, ridges
on mountains, except far north. Br, Fr,
Ge, Cz, FS.

Heather *Calluna vulgaris* ERICACEAE
H 15–80 cm. Much-branched, evergreen
shrub with twisted, prostrate or ascending
branches. Lvs linear, 1–2 mm, with 2
short projections at base, in 4 rows
pressed to stem. Fls purple, <4 mm,
bell-shaped, in loose spikes 3–15 cm long,
Jul–Oct. Frs few-seeded capsules. Moors,
heaths, open woods, dunes. T. [2]

Cross-leaved Heath *Erica tetralix*
ERICACEAE H 20–70 cm. Much-branched,
evergreen shrub with straggling, ascending
branches. Lvs linear, 2–4 mm, 4 in whorl,
covered in glands and long hairs. Fls
rose-pink, <7 mm, flask-shaped, nodding,
in terminal clusters of 4–12, Jun–Oct.
Frs hairy capsules. Bogs, wet heaths,
coniferous woods. T, ex Ic, (Cz). [3]

Bell Heather *Erica cinerea* ERICACEAE
H 15–75 cm. Branched, evergreen shrub
with ascending stems and numerous,
short, leafy shoots. Lvs linear, <7 mm, 3
in whorl, hairless. Fls crimson-purple,
<6 mm, flask-shaped, in elongated
terminal clusters 1–7 cm, Jun–Sep. Frs
hairless capsules. Dry heaths, moors, open
woods. Br, Ir, Fr, Be, Ne, Ge, No. [4]

Cowberry *Vaccinium vitis-idaea* ERICACEAE
H <30 cm. Prostrate or ascending, much-branched, evergreen shrub. Lvs oval, broadest near tip, <3 cm, leathery, dark green above, paler beneath. Fls white tinged with pink, <6 mm, bell-shaped, in drooping terminal clusters, May–Jul. Frs red berries, <1 cm, edible but acid. Moors, heaths, coniferous woods. T. [5]

Bilberry *Vaccinium myrtillus* ERICACEAE
H 15–60 cm. Erect, deciduous shrub with creeping, underground stems and angled, green twigs. Lvs bright green, ovate, acute, <3 cm, with fine teeth. Fls greenish-pink, <6 mm, spherical, solitary, drooping, May–Jul. Frs black berries with bluish bloom, sweet, edible. Heaths, moors, woods. T. [6]

Bog Bilberry *Vaccinium uliginosum*
ERICACEAE H <75 cm. Erect, deciduous shrub with creeping, underground stems and smooth, brown twigs. Lvs ovate, blunt, <25 mm, without teeth. Fls pale pink, <4 mm, in terminal clusters of 1–4, May–Jun. Frs black berries with bluish bloom, sweet, edible in small quantities. Moors, heaths, pinewoods. T, ex Ir. [7]

Cranberry *Vaccinium oxycoccos* ERICACEAE
Prostrate, evergreen shrublet with slender stems extending <80 cm. Lvs ovate to oblong, <8 mm long, 5 mm broad, dark green above, whitish beneath, widely separated. Fls pink, <6 mm, on hairy stalks, in terminal clusters of 1–4, May–Jul. Frs round, white berries spotted with red or brown, <8 mm, edible. Bogs, wet heaths. T, ex Ic. [8]

Crowberry *Empetrum nigrum*
EMPETRACEAE H 15–45 cm. Low, dioecious, evergreen shrub with prostrate to ascending stems. Lvs oblong to linear, <6 mm, blunt, with down-turned margins. Fls pinkish, 1–2 mm across, solitary, inconspicuous amongst lvs, Apr–Jun. Frs black, fleshy berries, <5 mm, with 2–9 stones. Moors, bogs. T. [9]

Bird's-eye Primrose *Primula farinosa*
PRIMULACEAE H 3–30 cm. Perennial herb
with basal rosettes. Lvs elliptical, blunt,
<10 cm, finely toothed, dusty-looking
on underside. Fls pink, <16 mm across,
in terminal clusters of 2 or more on
leafless stalks, May–Jul. Frs cylindrical
capsules, much longer than calyx.
Marshes, damp grassland, mainly in
mountains. Br, Fr, De, Ge, Cz, Po, Fi,
Sw. [1]

Northern Androsace *Androsace
septentrionalis* PRIMULACEAE H 8–30 cm.
Annual or biennial, rosette-forming,
somewhat hairy herb with one or more
erect, leafless stems. Lvs elliptical, <35
mm, toothed, with short stalks. Fls white
or pink, <5 mm, in umbels of 5–30,
May–Jul. Frs spherical, many-seeded
capsules. Dry meadows, sandy fields in
mountains. Fr, De, Ge, Cz, Po, FS. [2]

Chickweed Wintergreen *Trientalis
europaea* PRIMULACEAE H 5–30 cm. Erect,
hairless, perennial herb with slender,
creeping, underground stems and whorl of
lvs at top of stem. Lvs lanceolate, <9 cm,
stiff, shining. Fls white, <18 mm across,
usually solitary, on stalks <7 cm, May–
Aug. Heaths, coniferous woods. T, ex Ir.
[3]

Alpine Gentian *Gentiana nivalis*
GENTIANACEAE H 3–15 cm. Slender, erect,
annual herb, usually with few branches.
Lvs ovate, blunt, <5 mm, lower
sometimes forming rosette. Fls brilliant,
deep blue, <1 cm across, terminal on
stems and branches, Jul–Aug, open only
above 10°C. Frs elliptical capsules.
Meadows, birch woods, river banks,
damp alpine or arctic ledges. Br, Ic, Fr,
Ge, Cz, Po, FS. [4]

Spring Gentian *Gentiana verna*
GENTIANACEAE H 2–20 cm. Tufted,
perennial herb with underground stems
ending in rosette of elliptical lvs <15 mm.
Stems lvs few, smaller. Fls brilliant, deep
blue, <25 mm, solitary, on short stems,
Apr–Jul. Frs oblong capsules. Stony turf
on limy soils in mountains; at sea-level in
wIr. Br, Ir, Fr, Ge, Cz, Po. [5]

Slender Gentian *Gentianella tenella*
GENTIANACEAE H 2–10 cm. Slender, annual
or biennial herb, branching from base.
Lvs elliptical, <12 mm, few, basal, but
1–4 pairs on each stem. Fls sky blue or
dirty violet, <6 mm across, solitary, on
stalks much longer than fls,. Jul–Aug.
Exposed ridges, dry heaths, usually
limy rocks in mountains. Ic, Fr, Ge, Cz,
Po, FS.

Fringed Gentian *Gentianella ciliata*
GENTIANACEAE H 8–30 cm. Slender,
biennial herb, not forming rosette. Lower
lvs tongue-shaped; upper lvs <3 cm,
lanceolate. Fls blue, <5 cm across, in
clusters of 2–5, on long stalks, petal lobes
fringed with long, blue hairs, Aug–Oct.
Dry, rocky meadows and woods. Fr, Lu,
Be, Ne, Ge, Cz, Po. [6]

Northern Bedstraw *Galium boreale*
RUBIACEAE H 20–45 cm. Creeping,
perennial herb with erect, 4-angled stems.
Lvs lanceolate to elliptical, <4 cm, bright
green, in whorls of 4. Fls white, <3 mm
across, in pyramidal, leafy, terminal spike,
May–Aug. Frs 2-celled, olive-brown,
densely covered in hooked bristles.
Damp meadows and rocks, stream banks.
T. [7]

Round-leaved Bedstraw *Galium
rotundifolium* RUBIACEAE H 10–30 cm.
Slender, leafy, perennial herb. Lvs almost
circular, <15 mm, with bristly-haired
margins, in whorls of 4. Fls white or
greenish-white, <3 mm across, in loose
terminal clusters, May–Jul. Frs 2-celled,
covered in hooked bristles. Bushy places
in mountains. Fr, Ge, Cz, Po, Sw, (Ne,
De, No).

Heath Bedstraw *Galium saxatile*
RUBIACEAE H 10–20 cm. Mat-forming,
perennial herb with many prostrate, non-
flowering stems and ascending, flowering
shoots. Lvs ovate, broadest near tip, <10
mm, 6–8 in whorl, with marginal prickles
pointing forwards. Fls white, <3 mm
across, in terminal clusters, Jun–Aug.
Heaths, moors, dry grassland, woods. T,
ex Ic, ?Fi. [8]

Jacob's-ladder *Polemonium caeruleum*
POLEMONIACEAE H 30–90 cm. Erect, leafy,
perennial herb. Lvs <40 cm, lower with
winged stalks, divided into 6–12 pairs of
lateral lflets 2–4 cm. Fls fragrant, blue or
white, <3 cm across, drooping, in loose,
terminal clusters, May–Aug. Frs erect
capsules. Rocks, damp meadows, mainly
in mountains. Br, Ir, De, Ge, Cz, Po, Sw,
No. [1]

Dodder *Cuscuta epithymum* CONVOLVU-
LACEAE Slender, twining, red-stemmed,
annual parasite attached to host plant by
suckers. Lvs small, scale-like. Fls pinkish,
fragrant, in dense, spherical clusters
<1 cm across, Jun–Oct. Frs 2-celled
capsules. Parasitic on heather, gorse,
clover. T. [2]

Wood Forget-me-not *Myosotis sylvatica*
BORAGINACEAE H 15–45 cm. Erect, hairy,
perennial herb with much-branched, very
leafy stems. Lvs ovate or elliptical, <8
cm. Fls bright blue, <10 mm across, in
terminal clusters much elongated after
flowering, May–Jul. Frs developing 4 dark
brown, shining nutlets. Damp meadows,
mountain woods. T, ex Ir, Ic, Fi, ?No.
[3]

Alpine Forget-me-not *Myosotis alpestris*
BORAGINACEAE H 5–20 cm. Very variable,
erect, hairy, perennial herb with creeping,
underground stems. Basal lvs lanceolate,
<10 cm; upper lvs oval, elliptical or
linear. Fls blue, <8 mm across, in short,
terminal clusters, Apr–Sep. Frs black
nutlets. Basic rocks in mountains. Br, Fr,
Ge, Cz, Po. [4]

Pyramidal Bugle *Ajuga pyramidalis*
LABIATAE H 10–30 cm. Perennial herb
with erect, all-round hairy stems, also
creeping, underground stems. Lower lvs
ovate, blunt, <10 cm decreasing upwards,
with leafy bracts tinged blue or violet
longer than fls. Fls pale violet-blue, in
terminal spikes, <18 mm, May–Jul.
Mountain meadows. T, ex Ne. [5]

Wood Sage *Teucrium scorodonia* LABIATAE
H 15–50 cm. Erect, hairy, branched,
perennial herb with creeping, underground
stems. Lvs opposite, ovate, <7 cm,
heart-shaped at base, with rounded teeth
and wrinkled surface. Fls yellowish-green,
<9 mm, in loose, leafless spike <15 cm,
Jun–Sep. Open woods, dry rocks, heaths,
dunes. T, ex Ic, Fi, (De, Sw). [6]

Limestone Woundwort *Stachys alpina*
LABIATAE H 30–100 cm. Very hairy, erect,
perennial herb. Lvs purplish, ovate, <16
cm, heart-shaped at base, with rounded
teeth. Fls variable, dull purple to red,
may have yellow eye, <22 mm, in whorls
in axils of lanceolate bracts, Jun–Sep.
Shady places, mainly in mountains. Br,
Fr, Be, Ge, Cz, Po. [7]

Jupiter's-distaff *Salvia glutinosa*
LABIATAE H 50–100 cm. Erect, hairy,
usually branched, perennial herb. Lvs
opposite, ovate, heart-shaped at base,
toothed, very sticky, strong-smelling. Fls
yellow with reddish-brown markings, <4
cm, in whorls of 2–6 forming loose spike,
Jun–Sep. Mountain woods. Fr, Ge, Cz,
Po. [8]

Deadly Nightshade *Atropa belladonna*
SOLANACEAE H 50–150 cm. Erect, hairy,
branched, perennial herb. Lvs ovate,
pointed, <20 cm, narrowed into stalk.
Fls violet or green, <3 cm, solitary,
drooping, Jun–Aug. Frs black berries,
<20 mm across, poisonous. Woods, scrub,
mainly in mountains; naturalized
elsewhere. Long cultivated for medicine.
T, ex Ic, Fi, No, (Ir, De, Sw). [9]

White Mullein *Verbascum lychnitis*
SCROPHULARIACEAE H 50–150 cm. Erect,
greyish, hairy, biennial herb with winged
stems. Lvs ovate to oblong, <30 cm,
slightly toothed, green above, whitish and
hairy beneath. Fls white or yellow, <2
cm across, in branching, pyramidal spike,
Jun–Sep. Frs egg-shaped capsules. Dry,
open, often sandy woodland. T, ex Ir, Ic,
(FS). [10]

Spiked Speedwell *Veronica spicata*
SCROPHULARIACEAE H 5–60 cm. Erect,
hairy, perennial herb. Lvs opposite, <4
cm, lower oval, upper lanceolate, toothed.
Fls blue, <8 mm across, in terminal
spikes <30 cm, Jul–Oct. Frs flattened,
2-celled capsules, <4 mm. Dry grassland,
rocks. Br, Fr, De, Ge, Cz, Po, FS, (Ne). [1]

Alpine Speedwell *Veronica alpina*
SCROPHULARIACEAE H 5–15 cm. Creeping,
perennial herb. Lvs opposite, ovate to
elliptical, <25 mm. Fls deep blue, <7
mm across, in dense clusters of 4–12, Jul–
Aug. Frs bluish-green capsules. Streamsides, damp rocks in arctic, alpine
mountains. Br, Ic, Fr, Ge, Cz, Po, FS. [2]

Rock Speedwell *Veronica fruticans*
SCROPHULARIACEAE H 5–15 cm. Creeping,
perennial herb with woody base. Lvs
opposite, oblong, <20 mm. Fls deep blue,
purplish in centre, <15 mm across, Jul–
Aug. Frs capsules, <8 mm. Rocky
slopes, ledges, in arctic, mountains. Br,
Ic, Fr, Ge, Cz, Po, FS. [3]

Heath Speedwell *Veronica officinalis*
SCROPHULARIACEAE H 10–40 cm. Creeping,
hairy, perennial herb, rooting and forming
mats. Lvs opposite, elliptical, <3 cm,
toothed, and hairy on both sides. Fls blue,
<6 mm across, in spikes of 15–25 fls
arising in leaf axils, May–Aug. Dry soils
in grassland, heath, woods. T. [4]

Large Yellow Foxglove *Digitalis
grandiflora* SCROPHULARIACEAE H 40–100
cm. Erect, biennial or perennial herb with
hairy stems. Lvs lanceolate, <25 cm,
finely toothed. Fls yellow, <5 cm, bell-
shaped, brown-veined within, in long,
slender spike, Jun–Sep. Very poisonous.
Mountain woods, clearings. Fr, Lu, Be,
Ge, Cz, Po. [5]

Alpine Bartsia *Bartsia alpina* SCROPHU-
LARIACEAE H 10–30 cm. Creeping,
perennial herb. Lvs opposite, ovate, <25
mm, toothed. Fls dull purple, <2 cm, in
terminal clusters, Jun–Aug. Frs broad
capsules longer than calyx. Semi-parasite
of grasses. Arctic, alpine meadows.
Br, Ic, Fr, Ge, Cz, Po, FS. [6]

Irish Eyebright *Euphrasia salisburgensis*
SCROPHULARIACEAE H 2–20 cm. Slender,
much-branched, annual herb. Lvs
opposite, lanceolate, <7 mm, purple-
tinged, with 1–4 pairs of bristle-pointed
teeth. Fls white veined with violet, <8
mm, lower lip with 3 notched lobes,
Jun–Aug. Semi-parasite, grassland
and rocks in mountains. Ir, Fr, Ge, Cz,
Po, FS, ?Br. [7]

Moor-king *Pedicularis sceptrum-carolinum*
SCROPHULARIACEAE H 30–80 cm. Erect,
perennial herb, forming rosette. Basal lvs
lanceolate, <20 cm. Fls yellow, closed,
with red margin to lower lip, <3 cm,
Jun–Aug. Damp meadows, thickets, in
mountains. De, Ge, Cz, Po, FS. [8]

Marsh Lousewort *Pedicularis palustris*
SCROPHULARIACEAE H 5–70 cm. Almost
hairless, annual or biennial herb with erect,
branching stem. Lvs oblong, <4 cm, with
toothed lobes. Fls red-pink, <25 mm,
calyx hairy, in terminal spike, May–Aug.
Marshes, damp meadows. T, ex Ic. [9]

Common Lousewort *Pedicularis
sylvatica* SCROPHULARIACEAE H 5–25 cm.
Almost hairless, biennial or perennial herb
with single, erect stem; many basal
branches. Lvs lanceolate, <2 cm, twice
divided into segments. Fls pink, <25 mm,
in terminal spikes of 3–10, Apr–Jul. Bogs,
heaths, moors. T, ex Ic. [10]

Woodland Cow-wheat *Melampyrum
nemorosum* SCROPHULARIACEAE H 15–50 cm.
Erect, hairy, semi-parasitic, annual herb.
Lvs opposite, <4 cm wide, giving way to
violet-blue, lf-like, toothed bracts. Fls
bright yellow, <2 cm, Jun–Aug. Woods
in mountains. De, Ge, Cz, Po, Fi, Sw.
[11]

Small Cow-wheat *Melampyrum
sylvaticum* SCROPHULARIACEAE H 10–40 cm.
Erect, hairy, annual herb. Lvs opposite,
elliptical-lanceolate, <12 mm wide, giving
way to greenish, lf-like, bracts. Fls
brownish-yellow, <1 cm, Jun–Aug.
Woods in mountains. Br, Ir, Ic, Fr, De,
Ge, Cz, Po, FS. [12]

Greater Broomrape *Orobanche rapum-genistae* OROBANCHACEAE H 20–80 cm.
Stout, hairy, perennial root-parasite on shrubby Leguminosae, esp gorse and broom. Stem erect, yellowish, with scales near base. Fls yellowish tinged with purple, <25 mm, in long, dense spike <35 cm, May–Jul. Heaths. Br, Ir, Fr, Lu, Be, Ne, Ge. [1]

Red-berried Elder *Sambucus racemosa* CAPRIFOLIACEAE H <4 m. Small, deciduous shrub with arching stems and grey bark. Lvs divided into 5–7 ovate or elliptical, toothed segments. Fls greenish-white, in dense, ovoid clusters <6 cm across, Apr–May. Frs red, spherical berries, <5 mm. Woods, scrub in mountains. Frs used for wine-making. Fr, Lu, Be, Ne, Ge, Cz, Po, (Br, De, FS). [2]

Blue Honeysuckle *Lonicera caerulea* CAPRIFOLIACEAE H <2 m. Erect, deciduous shrub with yellowish-brown to reddish, flaking bark. Lvs elliptical, <7 mm. Fls yellowish-white, <16 mm, bell-shaped, in pairs in axils of lvs, May–Jul. Frs dark blue, succulent berries, <1 cm across. Mountains. Fr, Ge, Cz, Fi, Sw, (No). [3]

Twinflower *Linnaea borealis* CAPRIFOLIACEAE H 8–15 cm. Dwarf, creeping, evergreen shrub. Lvs roundish, <16 mm, toothed in upper half. Fls pinkish-white, sweet-scented, <8 mm, bell-shaped and drooping, hairy within, in pairs on long, slender stems, Jun–Aug. Frs densely hairy nutlets, <3 mm. Coniferous woods, heaths. Br, Fr, Ne, De, Ge, Cz, Po, FS. [4]

Moschatel *Adoxa moschatellina* ADOXACEAE H 5–10 cm. Hairless, perennial herb with long, slender, underground stems. Lvs divided into oval segments, <3 cm, dull green above, shining below. Fls green, *c*5 together in terminal head somewhat like town-hall clock (another name), Mar–May. Frs green, spherical, <5 mm. Woods, only in mountains farther south. T, ex Ic. [5]

Teasel-leaved Scabious *Knautia dipsacifolia* DIPSACACEAE H 40–150 cm. Very variable, erect, perennial herb with stem often softly hairy below. Lvs in opposite pairs, elliptical to narrowly lanceolate; upper lvs toothed. Fls bluish-violet to lilac, in heads <4 cm across, Jun–Sep. Woodland margins in mountains. Fr, Be Ge, Cz, Po.

Woolly Bellflower *Campanula bononiensis* CAMPANULACEAE H 30–100 cm. Erect, hairy, somewhat branched, perennial herb with swollen roots. Lvs ovate, pointed, <8 cm, finely hairy above, white and woolly beneath. Fls blue-lilac, <19 mm, drooping in dense, long, often 1-sided spikes, Jun–Aug. Woods, thickets, forest margins in mountains. Fr, Ge, Cz, Po. [6]

Giant Bellflower *Campanula latifolia* CAMPANULACEAE H 50–100 cm. Stout, erect, softly hairy, perennial herb with bluntly angled stems. Lvs ovate-lanceolate, rounded at base, <12 cm; lower lvs shortly stalked. Fls blue (rarely white), <5 cm, hairy inside, solitary, in axils of lvs, Jun–Sep. Woods, river banks, mountain meadows. Br, Fr, De, Ge, Cz, Po, FS, (Be, Ne). [7]

Spiked Rampion *Phyteuma spicatum* CAMPANULACEAE H 30–80 cm. Erect, hairless, perennial herb with swollen, fleshy roots. Basal lvs long-stalked, <5 cm, ovate, blunt, with heart-shaped base and coarse teeth. Fls yellowish-white, in spherical heads <8 cm, becoming cylindrical in fr, May–Jul. Mountain woods and meadows. Br, Fr, Lu, Be, Ne, De, Ge, Cz, Po, No, (Fi, Sw). [8]

Goldenrod *Solidago virgaurea* COMPOSITAE H 5–100 cm. Very variable, stout, erect, perennial herb. Basal lvs <10 cm, ovate to lanceolate, broadest near tip; upper lvs elliptical, all somewhat toothed. Fl-heads yellow, <1 cm, on straight, erect branches in leafy, terminal clusters, Jul–Sep. Woods, grassland, cliffs. Source of yellow dye. T, ex Ic. [9]

Blue Fleabane *Erigeron acer* COMPOSITAE
H 10–60 cm. Erect, slender, hairy, annual
or biennial herb, usually branched above.
Lvs lanceolate, broadest near tip, <10 cm.
Fl-heads <15 mm across, with pale purple
ray-florets and yellow central florets in
long-stalked, loose clusters, Jun–Sep. Dry
grassland, rocks, walls, banks, dunes. T,
ex Ic. [1]

Mountain Fleabane *Erigeron alpinus*
COMPOSITAE H 2–30 cm. Erect, hairy,
perennial herb. Basal lvs narrowly
elliptical, <8 cm, short-stalked. Fl-heads
<3 cm across, violet or pink ray-florets
and yellow central florets, usually solitary,
Jul–Sep. Grassland, open woodland, rocky
places, in mountains. Fr, Ge, Cz, Po. [2]

One-headed Fleabane *Erigeron uniflorus*
COMPOSITAE H 3–15 cm. Erect, downy,
perennial herb. Lvs narrow, <5 cm,
rounded at tip, hairy when young. Fl-
heads densely hairy, <15 mm across,
white or lilac ray-florets and yellow
central florets, always solitary, Jul–Aug.
Snow patches, pastures, in arctic, alpine
mountains. Ic, Fr, Ge, Cz, Po, FS. [3]

Small Cudweed *Filago minima*
COMPOSITAE H 5–15 cm. Erect, woolly,
annual herb, branching above middle. Lvs
narrow, lanceolate, <1 cm, without stalks.
Fl-heads inconspicuous, <3 mm, in small
clusters of 3–6, terminal or in forks of
stem, May–Sep. Sandy heaths, fields, on
acid soils. T, ex Ic, Fi. [4]

Mountain Everlasting *Antennaria dioica*
COMPOSITAE H <20 cm. Mat-forming,
hairy, perennial herb with erect flowering
shoots. Lvs <4 cm, in rosettes, narrow,
blunt, broadest near tip, green above,
white and woolly beneath. Fl-heads on ♀
plants <12 mm across, on ♂ <6 mm
across, rose-pink or white, in dense,

terminal clusters of 2–8, May–Jul. Heaths, dry grassland, only in mountains farther south. T, ex Ic. [5]

Jersey Cudweed *Gnaphalium luteoalbum* COMPOSITAE H 10–40 cm. Hairy, annual herb with erect or ascending stems branched above. Lvs <3 cm, lanceolate, broadest near tip, white and hairy on both sides, upper lvs clasping stem. Fl-heads yellow, <5 mm, in dense, lfless, terminal clusters of 4–12, Jun–Sep. Damp, sandy heaths, waste places. Br, Fr, Be, Ne, De, Ge, Cz, Po, Sw. [6]

Heath Cudweed *Gnaphalium sylvaticum* COMPOSITAE H 20–50 cm. Erect or ascending, perennial herb, covered in whitish, woolly hairs. Lvs <8 cm, lanceolate, 1-veined, green above, hairy below, diminishing in size up stem. Fl-heads dark brown, <6 mm, solitary or in clusters of 2–8 in top ½ of stem, Jun–Sep. Open woods, heaths, on acid soils. T. [7]

Highland Cudweed *Gnaphalium norvegicum* COMPOSITAE H 15–30 cm. Like *G. sylvaticum* but smaller, with broader, 3-veined lvs <10 cm, hairy on both sides, diminishing in size only at tip of stem. Fl-heads dark brown, <7 mm, solitary or in clusters of 2–3 in top ¼ of stem, Jul–Aug. Mountain heaths, woods. Br, Ic, Fr, Ge, Cz, Po, FS. [8] Dwarf cudweed *G. supinum* also on mountain tops. [9]

Field Wormwood *Artemisia campestris* COMPOSITAE H 20–80 cm. Very variable, scentless, perennial herb with erect and ascending stems, woody below, branched above. Lvs much divided into linear segments only $c1$ mm wide, hairy when young. Fl-heads spherical, yellow or reddish, <4 mm, in narrow, elongated clusters. Dry sand and rocks, absent from north. T, ex Ir, Ic. [10]

White Butterbur *Petasites albus*
COMPOSITAE H 10–70 cm. Creeping,
perennial herb with very large lvs. Lvs
<30 cm across, long-stalked, roundish
heart-shaped, green above, white and
woolly-hairy beneath, margin strongly
toothed. Fl-heads white, in dense spikes
on stout stems, appearing before lvs,
Mar–May. Stems lengthen <70 cm
in fr. Damp woods, streamsides, in
mountains. Fr, Lu, De, Ge, Cz, Po, Sw,
No, (Br). [1]

Purple Colt's-foot *Homogyne alpina*
COMPOSITAE H 10–40 cm. Perennial herb
with creeping, underground stems. Lvs
<4 cm, round with heart-shaped base,
shining dark green above, with toothed
margin and long, hairy stalks <10 cm.
Fl-heads purple, solitary, <15 mm,
terminal on stems with scale-like lvs, Jun–
Sep. Damp pastures, open woods in
mountains. Fr, Ge, Cz, Po, (Br). [2]

Arnica *Arnica montana* COMPOSITAE
H 25–60 cm. Creeping, perennial herb
with erect stems and basal rosette. Lvs
elliptical, <17 cm, hairy above. Fl-heads
orange-yellow, <8 cm across, usually
solitary, on hairy stalks, May–Jul. Acid
grassland, heaths, mainly in mountains.
Used as cure for sprains, bruises. Fr,
Lu, Be, Ne, De, Ge, Cz, Po, Sw, No.
[3]

Heath Groundsel *Senecio sylvaticus*
COMPOSITAE H 30–70 cm. Erect, annual
herb with slender, furrowed stem. Lvs
yellowish-green, deeply divided into
irregularly shaped segments, upper
clasping stem, cottony at first, becoming
hairless. Fl-heads yellow, <9 mm, with
8–14 ray-florets, Jul–Sep. Woods, heaths,
except far north. T, ex Ic. [4]

Woodland Groundsel *Senecio nemorensis*
COMPOSITAE H 50–200 cm. Erect, very
leafy, perennial herb, branched above. Lvs
elliptical, <20 cm, all heads yellow, <35
mm across, with 5–6 ray-florets, Jul–Aug.
Damp meadows, woods. Strong-smelling
when dry. Fr, Be, Ne, Ge, Cz, Po, (Sw).

Stemless Carline Thistle *Carlina acaulis*
COMPOSITAE H <30 cm. Rosette-forming,
perennial herb. Lvs <30 cm, elliptical,
divided into toothed and spiny segments,
sparsely woolly-hairy below. Fl-heads
large, <13 cm across, stemless, appearing
white due to silvery, spreading bracts;
central florets yellow or pinkish, May–
Sep. Rocky slopes, poor pastures, in
mountains. Fr, Ge, Cz, Po. [5]

Alpine Saw-wort *Saussurea alpina*
COMPOSITAE H 10–50 cm. Very variable,
rosette-forming, perennial herb with stout,
erect, cottony stems. Lvs ovate to
lanceolate, <18 cm, sharp-toothed, white
and cottony below. Fl-heads purple, <2
cm, stalkless, in small, dense, terminal
clusters, vanilla-scented, Jul–Sep. Woods,
meadows, cliffs, in mountains; at sea-level
in north. Br, Ir, Fr, Ge, Cz, Po, FS. [6]

Great Marsh Thistle *Carduus personata*
COMPOSITAE H 80–200 cm. Erect,
perennial herb with narrow, spiny, winged
stems. Lvs lanceolate, basal lvs divided
into 8–12 segments; upper undivided but
with large teeth <3 mm, each with spine
<2 mm. Fl-heads purple, <2 cm across,
stalkless, in small, dense, terminal clusters,
Jul–Aug. Mountain woods, meadows,
streamsides. Fr, Ge, Cz, Po.

Melancholy Thistle *Cirsium heterophyllum*
COMPOSITAE H 50–150 cm. Erect,
perennial herb with cottony, unwinged
stems. Lvs lanceolate, <40 cm, green
above, white-felted below, with softly
prickled margins; upper clasping stem.
Fl-heads purple, <5 cm across, usually
solitary, on long stems, Jul–Aug. Damp
woods, meadows, streamsides, mainly in
mountains but lowlands in north. Br, Ir,
Fr, De, Ge, Cz, Po, FS, (Ic). [7]

Spotted Cat's-ear *Hypochoeris maculata*
COMPOSITAE H 15–75 cm. Erect, perennial
herb, forming basal rosette. Lvs elliptical,
<15 cm, often spotted with dark purple,
toothed. Fl-heads lemon-yellow, <45 mm
across, solitary or in small clusters, on
leafy stems, May–Aug. Heaths, cliffs,
open woodland. T, ex Ir, Ic. [8]

Rough Hawkbit *Leontodon hispidus*
COMPOSITAE H 10–60 cm. Erect, perennial
herb, forming rosette. Lvs lanceolate,
<30 cm, variously toothed. Fl-heads
yellow, <4 cm, solitary, on densely hairy
stems, May–Sep. Grassland, rocky places.
May be eaten as salad. T, ex Ic. [1]

Alpine Sow-thistle *Cicerbita alpina*
COMPOSITAE H 50–200 cm. Erect,
perennial herb with furrowed stem. Lower
lvs divided, upper lanceolate. Fl-heads
pale blue, <2 cm across, in terminal
cluster, Jul–Sep. Moist rocks, open woods,
in mountains. Br, Fr, Ge, Cz, Po, FS. [2]

Alpine Hawkweed *Hieracium alpinum*
COMPOSITAE H 10–15 cm. Erect or
ascending, hairy, perennial herb, forming
rosettes. Fl-heads yellow, on 1–3 leaved
stems, Jul–Aug. Meadows, cliffs, screes, in
mountains. Br, Ic, Fr, Ge, Cz, Po, FS. [3]

Chives *Allium schoenoprasum* LILIACEAE
H 15–40 cm. Perennial herb. Lvs basal,
cylindrical, bluish-green, <25 cm. Fls
pink or purple, <12 mm, in globular
clusters <35 mm across, Jun–Jul.
Meadows, damp rocks. Br, Fr, Lu, Be,
Ge, Cz, Po, Fi, Sw, (Ic, No). [4]

Martagon Lily *Lilium martagon*
LILIACEAE H 50–100 cm. Erect, bulbous,
perennial herb. Lvs lanceolate, with rough
margin, <20 cm, lower in whorls, upper
alternate. Fls dull purple, <4 cm across,
Jun–Sep. Frs 6-angled capsules, <3 cm.
Woods, pastures, in mountains. Fr, Lu,
Be, Ne, Ge, Cz, Po, (Br, De, Sw, No). [5]

Snowdon Lily *Lloydia serotina* LILIACEAE
H 5–15 cm. Bulbous, perennial herb.
Basal lvs narrow, <25 cm; stem lvs 2–4,
lanceolate, shorter. Fls white with
purplish veins, <1 cm, funnel-shaped,
usually erect and solitary, Jun–Aug.
Mountain rocks, pastures. Br, Fr, Ge, Cz,
Po. [6]

Alpine Squill *Scilla bifolia* LILIACEAE
H 10–20 cm. Bulbous, perennial herb with
lfless stem. Lvs usually 2, lanceolate, <10
cm, shining, with basal sheaths. Fls bright

blue (pink or white), <9 mm, in cluster
of 2–8, Mar–May. Woods, meadows. Fr,
Lu, Be, Ne, Ge, Po. [7]

Spiked Star-of-Bethlehem *Ornithogalum
pyrenaicum* LILIACEAE H 50–100 cm.
Hairless, bulbous, perennial herb. Lvs
linear, <60 cm, withered before fls
appear. Fls greenish-white, <10 mm, in
cylindrical, terminal cluster, May–Jul. Frs
ovoid capsules, <8 mm. Woodland margins,
meadows. Br, Fr, Lu, Be, (Ge). [8]

Whorled Solomon's-seal *Polygonatum
verticillatum* LILIACEAE H 30–80 cm.
Erect, perennial herb. Lvs linear-lanceolate,
<12 cm, in whorls. Fls greenish-white,
<8 mm, in short-stalked clusters of 1–4
in axils of lvs, May–Jul. Frs red berries,
<6 mm. Woods in mountains. Br, Fr, Lu,
Be, De, Ge, Cz, Po, FS. [9]

Purple Crocus *Crocus albiflorus* LILIACEAE
H 5–10 cm. Perennial herb. Lvs long,
narrow, 2–4, appearing with fls. Fls
purple or white, <5 cm, solitary, hairy on
throat, Feb–May. Meadows and pastures
in mountains. Fr, Ge, Cz, (Br, Ir). [10]

Heath Rush *Juncus squarrosus* JUNCACEAE
H 15–50 cm. Wiry, erect, rosette-forming,
perennial herb. Lvs grass-like, deeply
channelled, <15 cm, with broad, sheathing
bases. Fls dark chestnut-brown, <7 mm,
in terminal clusters, Jun–Sep. Moors,
bogs, heaths, mainly acid soils. T. [11]

Three-leafed Rush *Juncus trifidus*
JUNCACEAE H 10–20 cm. Tufted, grass-like,
perennial herb, forming circular patches.
Lvs mainly basal but stem has 2–4 bracts,
<8 cm. Fls chestnut-brown, <4 mm, in
axils of bracts, Jun–Sep. Rocks, slopes, in
arctic and alpine mountains. Br, Ic, Fr
Ge, Cz, Po, FS. [12]

Spiked Wood-rush *Luzula spicata*
JUNCACEAE H 10–20 cm. Erect, tufted,
perennial herb, surrounded by dead lf-
sheaths. Lvs grass-like, <8 cm, channelled,
hairy. Fls chestnut-brown, <5 mm, in
drooping, terminal clusters, Jun–Aug.
Heaths, plateaux, in arctic and alpine
mountains. Br, Ic, Fr, Ge, FS [13]

Blue Moor-grass *Sesleria caerulea*
GRAMINEAE H 10–50 cm. Erect perennial.
Lvs flat, bluish-green. Fls in dense, erect
panicles. Mar–Aug. Dry rocks, meadows.
T, ex Ne, De, (No). [1]

Purple Moor-grass *Molinia caerulea*
GRAMINEAE H 20–120 cm. Erect, wiry,
deciduous perennial. Lvs flat, hairy above.
Fls in purplish spikes, Jun–Sep. Damp
places on moors, heaths, mountains. T. [2]

Alpine Meadow-grass *Poa alpina*
GRAMINEAE H 10–40 cm. Tufted perennial;
persistent, basal lf-sheaths. Lvs flat, green,
contracted at tip. Fls in loose panicles,
Jun–Aug. Stony, rocky places in mountains.
Br, Ir, Ic, Fr, Ge, Cz, Po, FS. [3]

Mat-grass *Nardus stricta* GRAMINEAE
H 10–40 cm. Wiry, tufted perennial. Lvs
needle-like, whitish, persistent. Fls in
erect, 1-sided spikes, May–Aug. Heaths,
moors, mountains. T. [4]

Heath-grass *Sieglingia decumbens*
GRAMINEAE H 10–50 cm. Tufted perennial.
Lvs stiff, flat or inrolled, sparsely hairy.
Fls in spikelets of 3–12 in terminal
clusters, Jun–Aug. Damp grassland in
mountains. T. [5]

Silver Hair-grass *Aira caryophyllea*
GRAMINEAE H 10–30 cm. Slender, hairless,
annual. Lvs thread-like. Fls tiny, silvery
or purple-tinged, in loose panicles, Apr–
Jul. Dry, acid heaths, open woodland. T,
ex Ic, Fi, No. [6] The closely related sp
Deschampsia flexuosa also on heaths. [7]

Early Hair-grass *Aira praecox*
GRAMINEAE H 2–20 cm. Slender, hairless
annual. Lvs blunt, inrolled. Fls tiny,
silvery or purple-tinged, in compact
panicles, Apr–Jun. Dry, acid heaths,
moors. T, ex Ic, Fi. [8]

Brown Bent *Agrostis canina* GRAMINEAE
H 10–60 cm. Hairless perennial. Lvs
pointed, flat or rolled. Fls awned, on
panicles, Jun–Jul. Acid grassland or
heaths, mountains. T. [9]

Purple-stem Cat's-tail *Phleum phleoides*
GRAMINEAE H 10–50 cm. Erect perennial;

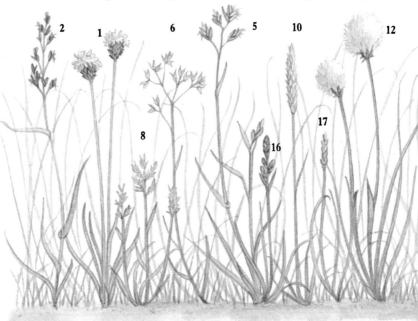

slender, purplish stems. Lvs with fine, blunt tip, rough margins. Fls in spike-like cylinders, Jun–Jul. Dry heaths, hills. T. [10]

Holy-grass *Hierochloe odorata* GRAMINEAE H 20–50 cm. Slender, creeping perennial. Lvs finely pointed, flat, with rough margins. Fls in loose panicles, Apr–Aug. Wet arctic and mountain grassland, rocks. T, ex Lu, Be, Ne. [11]

Hare's-tail Cottongrass *Eriophorum vaginatum* CYPERACEAE H 30–50 cm. Erect perennial. Basal lvs thread-like, stem lvs short, clasping stem. Fls in rounded spike; develop white, 'cottony' bristles in fr, Apr–Jun. Peat bogs. T, ex Ic. [12]

Deergrass *Scirpus cespitosus* CYPERACEAE H 5–35 cm. Erect perennial. Lf-sheaths light brown, shining. Fls in solitary spikelets, May–Aug. Bogs; wet, acid heaths. T. [13]

Pill Sedge *Carex pilulifera* CYPERACEAE H 10–30 cm. Perennial with arching, 3-angled stems. Lvs yellow-green, tapering. Fls in terminal clusters, May–Jun. Frs hairy, spherical. Acid, peaty or sandy heaths, grassland. T. [14]

Black Alpine-sedge *Carex atrata* CYPERACEAE H 30–50 cm. Hairless perennial with rigid stems. Lvs flat, persistent, dark-brown bases. Fls in black spikes, Jun–Aug. Arctic and mountain meadows, wet rock ledges. Br, Ic, Fr, Ge, Cz, Po, FS. [15]

Stiff Sedge *Carex bigelowii* CYPERACEAE H 5–25 cm. Creeping perennial with rigid stems, rough above. Lvs stiff, arching, with persistent bases. Fls in purplish spikes, Jun–Aug. Damp, stony places in mountains. Br, Ir, Ic, Ge, Cz, FS. [16]

Rock Sedge *Carex rupestris* CYPERACEAE H 5–15 cm. Creeping perennial. Lvs often twisted, with persistent bases. Fls in single spike, Jun–Jul. Ledges, exposed ridges. Br, Ic, Fr, Ge, Cz, Po, FS. [17]

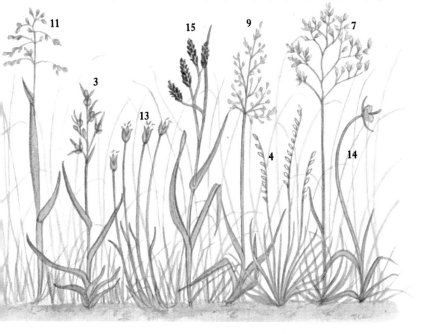

Lady's-slipper *Cypripedium calceolus*
ORCHIDACEAE H 15–45 cm. Erect,
somewhat hairy, perennial herb with
creeping, underground stems. Lvs 3–5,
ovate, with prominent veins below. Fls
solitary, 6–9 cm, with reddish-maroon
segments and large, pale yellow, slipper-
shaped lip with faintly darker veins, May–
Jul. Survival of this beautiful orchid is
threatened by collectors. Br, Fr, Lu, Ge,
Cz, Po, FS. [1]

Heath Spotted-orchid *Dactylorhiza*
maculata ORCHIDACEAE H 15–50 cm.
Erect, hairless, perennial herb, arising
from palmately divided root-tubers. Lvs
linear, folded upwards, often marked with
dark, circular spots. Fls pale pink or
white, dotted or lined, lip has small
central tooth, and wavy edge, in dense
terminal spike, May–Jul. Bogs, heaths,
moors. T. [2]

False Musk Orchid *Chamorchis alpina*
ORCHIDACEAE H 5–12 cm. Erect, perennial
herb, arising from tuberous base. Lvs
numerous, narrow, channelled. Fls
greenish-yellow, few, on loose spike, like
musk orchid *Herminium monorchis*, but
scentless, though rich in nectar, Jul–Aug.
Damp heaths, on calcareous soils in
mountains. Fr, Ge, Cz, Po, FS. [3]

Small White Orchid *Leucorchis albida*
ORCHIDACEAE H 10–30 cm. Erect, hairless,
perennial herb. Lower lvs $c4$, oblong, <8
cm, glossy above, with pronounced keel
below; upper lvs 1–2, narrow. Fls
greenish-white, $<2\cdot5$ mm, half drooping,
in dense, 1-sided, narrow, cylindrical
spike <6 cm, faintly vanilla-scented, Jun–
Aug. Mountain grassland. Br, Ir, Fr, Be,
De, Ge, Cz, FS. [4]

Lesser Butterfly-orchid *Platanthera*
bifolia ORCHIDACEAE H 15–45 cm. Erect,
hairless, perennial herb. Lower lvs 2–3,
elliptical, <9 cm; upper lvs smaller,
bract-like. Fls whitish, 18 mm across,
with long, slender, almost horizontal spur
and parallel anthers <2 mm, in loose spike
<20 cm, sweet-scented, May–Jul. Open
woods, grassland. T, ex Ic. [5]

White Helleborine *Cephalanthera*
damasonium ORCHIDACEAE H 15–50 cm.
Erect, hairless, perennial herb with angled
stems. Lvs $c4$, bract-like. Fls cream to
white, <2 cm, 3–12 in leafy spike, the
lower separated, the upper pressed together
and scarcely opening, Apr–Jul. Woods,
woodland margins, calcareous soils. Br,
Fr, Lu, Be, Ne, De, Ge, Cz, Sw.
[6]

Limodore *Limodorum abortivum*
ORCHIDACEAE H 30–80 cm. Stout, erect,
perennial herb with livid-violet stems and
tuberous roots. No lvs, but stem covered
with thick purplish scales. Fls <4 cm
across, violet soon fading to yellow, widely
spaced on loose spike, May–Jul. Woods in
hills; saprophytic on dead plants. Fr, Lu,
Be, Ge, Cz. [7]

Bog Orchid *Hammarbya paludosa*
ORCHIDACEAE H 3–12·5 cm. Slender, erect,
hairless, perennial herb with stem
angled above. Lvs small, stout, concave,
with broad, rounded apex. Fls tiny,
greenish-yellow, with lip at top, no spur,
in loose spikes <5 cm. Edges of pools,
or wet, acid bogs where water moves
among bog-moss. T, ex Ic, Lu.
[8]

Lesser Twayblade *Listera cordata*
ORCHIDACEAE H 3–20 cm. Slender,
perennial herb, slightly hairy above, with
creeping, underground stem. Lvs 2,
opposite, <25 mm, heart-shaped, near
base of stem. Fls reddish-green, <4 mm
across, in short, few-flowered spike, May–
Aug. Wet, boggy slopes among heather
and bog-moss. Difficult to see, even in
flower. T, ex Lu, Be. [9]

Creeping Lady's-tresses *Goodyera*
repens ORCHIDACEAE H 10–25 cm. Erect,
hairy, perennial herb with creeping,
underground stems ending in rosettes.
Basal lvs <25 mm, ovate-lanceolate,
narrowed into stalk, conspicuously veined.
Fls fragrant, white, <4 mm, in twisted,
1-sided spike <5 cm, Jul–Aug. Mossy,
acid woodland, esp in mountains. T, ex
Ir, Ic. [10]

Rounded Snail *Discus rotundatus*
ENDODONTIDAE SH 2·5–3 mm, SB 6–7 mm,
W 6–7. Shell dextral, spire slightly raised;
whorls cylindrical; slight, peripheral keel;
numerous, transverse ridges; umbilicus
large, $c\frac{1}{3}$ SB. Shell yellow-brown with
transverse, reddish blotches; animal grey-
brown, with dark dots. Woodlands; rocky
areas, even on acid soils. Breeds
throughout year. Feeds on dead wood,
algae. T, ex Ic, nFS. [1]

Ash-black Slug *Limax cinereoniger*
LIMACIDAE EL 10–20 cm. Very large;
variable, usually dark brown or black with
prominent, paler keel on back; tentacles
dark, spotted with brown and black; sole
dark, with pale central stripe. Old woods,
sometimes lichen-covered rocks in open.
Breeds summer; mates suspended from
vertical surface on short, mucous thread.
Feeds on fungi, lichens, decaying
vegetation. T, ex Ic, nFS. [2]

Slender Slug *Limax tenellus* LIMACIDAE
EL 25–35 mm. Slightly keeled on back;
pale yellow, sometimes red-brown, with
blackish head and tentacles. Mucus yellow.
Old woods; rather local. Eggs Nov–Mar.
Feeds on fungi. T, ex Ir, Ic, nFS.
[3]

Tree Slug *Lehmannia marginata*
LIMACIDAE EL 75 mm. Slight keel on back;
pale or dark grey; lyre-shaped dark bands
on mantle, 2 dark bands on sides; sole
paler. Exudes copious, watery mucus
when irritated. Trees, sometimes
descending by hanging from mucous
thread; rocks. Breeds winter. Feeds on
fungi, lichens. T. [4]

Spotted Kerry Slug *Geomalacus
maculosus* ARIONIDAE EL 90 mm. Medium-
sized, with no keel on back; mantle $c\frac{1}{3}$ BL;
grey, black or brown, with numerous,
conspicuous, yellow or white spots; sole
pale. Mucus pale yellow. Open moorland,
occasionally woods, often on lichen-
covered rocks. Breeds Jul–Aug. Feeds on
lichens, moss. Rolls up like woodlouse
when touched. swIr, nwFr. [5]

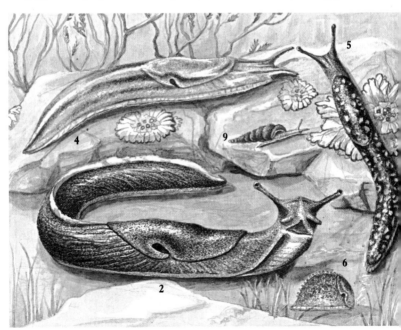

Hedgehog Slug *Arion intermedius*
ARIONIDAE EL 15–20 mm. Very small,
no keel on back; yellowish-grey, with
darker head and back; when body
contracted, tubercles become conical; sole
pale. Mucus yellow. Woods, grassland.
Breeds autumn. Herbivorous. T, ex Ic,
Fi. [6]

Large Black Slug *Arion ater* var *ater*
ARIONIDAE EL *c*14 cm. No keel on back;
prominent mantle, respiratory orifice, body
tubercles. Normally black (red-brown in
var *rufus*); sole greyish; foot fringe grey,
yellow or orange. Juv straw-yellow with
faint grey bands. Mucus sticky, colourless
to orange. Woods, grassland, moors, even
at high altitudes. Breeds most of the year.
Omnivorous. T, ex Fi. [7]

Dusky Slug *Arion subfuscus* ARIONIDAE
EL 5–7 cm. No keel on back; yellow-
brown, darker on back, with darker bands;
sole pale yellow; foot fringe yellow, with
black lines. Mucus yellow or orange.

Woodlands, under logs, in litter. Breeds
autumn. Feeds on algae, fungi, esp large
fungi. T. [8]

Craven Door Snail *Clausilia dubia*
CLAUSILIIDAE SH 11–15 mm, SB 3–3·5 mm,
W 13. Shell sinistral, club-shaped, with
tapering spire; transverse striations;
aperture pear-shaped, with 2 folds on
shell wall. Shell and animal grey-brown.
Rocks, esp limestone. Feeds on fungi,
lichens. WE, CE. [9]

White-lipped Snail *Cepaea hortensis*
HELICIDAE SH 15 mm, SB 18 mm, W 5.
Shell dextral, spherical, glossy; aperture
large, rounded; peristome curved with
internal thickening, almost always pale;
umbilicus closed. Shell normally yellow,
may be pink or brown, with 0–5 dark
bands; animal yellowish-grey. Woods,
grassland, gardens, in mountains <2000 m.
In colonies; breeds spring-autumn.
Herbivorous. Eaten by birds, esp thrushes,
small mammals. T, ex nFS. [10]

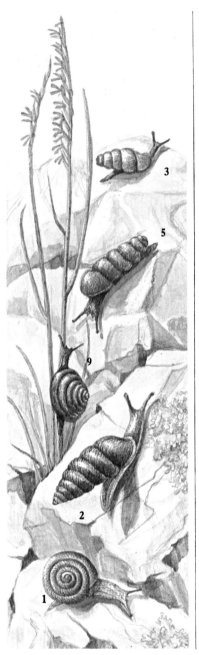

Rock Snail *Pyramidula rupestris*
PYRAMIDULIDAE SH 1·5–2 mm, SB 2·5–3 mm, W 4–4½. Shell dextral, conical, with deep suture; regular, oblique striations; aperture rounded with sharp peristome; umbilicus deep, wide. Shell dark brown, paler when dry; animal grey. Dry places on rocks, walls, occasionally on vegetation or ground, esp in limestone areas. Young born alive. Feeds on lichens. WE, CE. [1]

Large Chrysalis Snail *Abida secale*
CHONDRINIDAE SH 6–8 mm, SB 3 mm, W 9–10. Shell dextral, cylindrical with conical apex, suture moderate; striated; aperture dilated with thickened, pale peristome and 9 teeth within; umbilicus small. Shell and animal brown or grey-brown. Dry rocks on limestone and chalk uplands. WE, CE. [2]

Mountain Whorl Snail *Vertigo alpestris*
VERTIGINIDAE SH 2 mm, SB 1 mm, W 5. Shell dextral, cylindrical, whorls rounded with strong, transverse striations; apex blunt; 4 teeth in aperture (1 on upper wall, 1 on inner, 2 on outer); umbilicus small. Shell yellow-brown, transparent, glossy; animal dark grey. Stone walls, fields, woods on limestone uplands < 1200 m, but local. Br, Ge, Cz, Po, FS. [3]

snail *Columella aspera* VERTIGINIDAE
SH 1·5–2 mm, SB *c*1·5 mm, W 5–6. Shell dextral, cylindrical with blunt apex, whorls rounded, sutures fairly deep; fine, regular striations; aperture rounded, peristome sharp; umbilicus narrow, deep. Shell silky olive-brown to greyish; animal grey, darker above. Acid areas, including peat bogs, moors, pinewoods. Br, Ir, Ne, Ge, Po, FS. [4]

snail *Columella columella* VERTIGINIDAE
SH 2·5–3·25 mm, SB *c*1·5 mm, W 7–8. Similar to *C. aspera*, but larger, taller, with more whorls, less regular striations, shinier surface. High, exposed, calcareous areas above tree-line, < 1000 m. Ge, Cz, Po, nFS. [5]

Pellucid Glass Snail *Vitrina pellucida*
VITRINIDAE SH 3–3·5 mm, SB 5–6 mm,
W 3–4. Shell dextral, depressed with
low, blunt, conical spire; whorls increase
rapidly; no umbilicus. Shell very thin-
walled and transparent, slight greenish
tinge; animal pale grey, with head and
tentacles darker, mantle partly covering
front of shell. Widespread, including
coniferous woodland, mountains,
moorland. Breeds autumn–spring,
normally annually but biennially at higher
altitudes. Feeds on decaying vegetation,
animal matter. T. [6]

Rayed Glass Snail *Nesovitrea hammonis*
ZONITIDAE SH 2 mm, SB 4–4·5 mm, W 4½.
Shell dextral, slightly convex above
and below; glossy with deep, regular,
transverse striations, minute spiral
striations on upper surface; umbilicus
narrow, deep. Shell rich horn-brown,
paler below; animal grey, with darker
head and back. Woods, including
coniferous, and grassland; prefers wet
habitats, tolerates dry. Breeds throughout year. T. [7] (*N. petronella* very
similar, but prefers more montane
habitats.)

Garlic Glass Snail *Oxychilus alliarius*
ZONITIDAE SH 2·5 mm, SB 6–6·5 mm,
W 4–4½. Shell dextral, depressed convex
above, flattened below, thin, smooth, very
shiny; umbilicus small. Shell rich horn-
brown, paler below; animal bluish-black.
Woodland, in leaf litter, on fallen wood;
also more open habitats, even very acid
soils. Breeds most of year. Feeds on
animal, vegetable matter. Smells strongly
of garlic when irritated. T. [8]

Tawny Glass Snail *Euconulus fulvus*
EUCONULIDAE SH 2·4–3 mm, SB 2·5–3 mm,
W 5–6. Shell dextral, conical with blunt
apex; surface glossy with fine, irregular
striations; umbilicus minute. Shell thin,
transparent, rich horn-brown; animal
grey-black. Coniferous, broad-leaved
woodland, in moss, leaf litter, fallen
wood, also grassland, rocks; prefers moist
situations. Breeds autumn. T. [9]

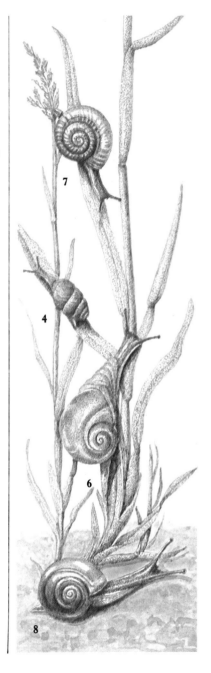

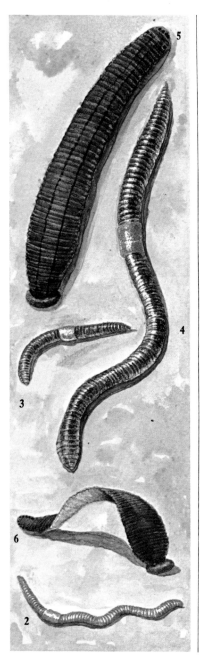

Grey Worm *Allolobophora caliginosa*
LUMBRICIDAE L 40-100 mm. Body
cylindrical; pale grey, with anterior
segments flesh-pink; clitellum on
segments 28, 29-34. Most habitats, but
not in very acid, peaty soils. Feeds mainly
on humus. T. [1]

Eisen's Worm *Bimastos eiseni* LUMBRICIDAE
L 30-65 mm. Body cylindrical; violet or
reddish above, yellow below; clitellum
red, on segments 24-33. Moorland, bogs,
in moss, under stones, decaying leaves. T,
ex Ic, Fi, No. [2]

Octagonal Worm *Dendrobaena octaedra*
LUMBRICIDAE L 17-40 mm. Body
cylindrical, tail octagonal; red, yellowish,
violet-brown or copper; clitellum on segments 27, 28, 29-33, 34. Wet moorland, in
moss, under stones, decaying leaves. T. [3]

Red Worm *Lumbricus rubellus*
LUMBRICIDAE L 25-150 mm. Body
cylindrical, tail usually flattened;
iridescent ruddy-brown or reddish-violet
above, pale yellow below; clitellum on
segments 26, 27-31, 32. Esp damp, highly
organic soil, in surface litter, or burrows
in soil. Feeds on humus. T. [4]

Dutrochet's Leech *Trocheta subviridis*
ERPOBDELLIDAE L 80-215 mm. Greyish-
green or reddish, generally with 2
longitudinal, brown lines on back. In
burrows in soil; breeds in water. Feeds
on earthworms, insect larvae. Only
terrestrial sp in Europe. T, ex Ic, FS. [5]

Horse Leech *Haemopis sanguisuga*
HIRUDIDAE L 50-100 mm. Similar to *T.
subviridis*, but smaller, black or dark green.
Aquatic, in moorland pools; also under
stones, in grass, just above water-level in
summer. Feeds on invertebrates. T, ex Ic.
[6]

millipede *Proteroiulus fuscus* BLANIULIDAE
L ♂ 7-11 mm, ♀ 7-15 mm. Small, slender,
cylindrical; dark brown, with darker,
lateral blotches; 1st row of 8-10 eyes and
2nd row of 2-3 distinctive. Esp woods,
coniferous or broadleaved, in litter, soil,

dead wood; also in bogs, on wet, pine-
peat moors. Herbivorous. ♂s rare:
reproduction by unmated ♀s. T. [7]

millipede *Schizophyllum sabulosum*
IULIDAE L ♂ 15–28 mm, ♀ 21–47 mm. 2
orange-red stripes on back distinctive; var
rubripes has broken stripes, blood red legs.
Sandy soils, old dune slacks, also
coniferous, broadleaved woods; rare on
farmland. T, ex Ic. [8]

centipede *Geophilus carpophagus*
GEOPHILIDAE L 35–60 mm. Red-brown,
darker, more sombre than other spp in
this family. Nocturnal; eats insects;
uncultivated areas, generally open or
upland, under stones, bark, in litter, soil;
also in houses. Sometimes phosphorescent
if disturbed. T, ex Ic. [9]

centipede *Lithobius variegatus* LITHOBIIDAE
L 16–24 mm. Handsome, pale brown
marbled with dark violet; underside and
jaws yellow; back legs banded. Nocturnal;
moorland, mountains, also undisturbed
lowlands; uncommon gardens, greenhouses.
Only sp known to climb trees. Br, Ir. [10]

centipede *Lithobius crassipes* LITHOBIIDAE
L 9–14 mm. Chestnut-brown; small
number of antennal segments (*c*20)
distinctive. Nocturnal; open moors,
mountains, also grassland, woods. T,
ex Ic. [11] (*L. curtipes* very similar,
distinguished by protective habit of
curling up; moorland, mountains. T, ex
nBr, Ir, Ic.)

woodlouse *Porcellio scaber* PORCELLIONIDAE
BL 11–18 mm. Body tuberculate; usually
grey, sometimes (esp ♀) yellow or orange
speckled with black; base of antennae
orange. Ubiquitous: gardens, walls, tree
trunks, grassland, sand-dunes, occasionally
dry heaths, moors. Does not roll into ball.
T. [12] (Few woodlice on mountains,
moors, heaths: only wide-ranging spp, *eg*
*P. scaber, Oniscus asellus, Trichoniscus
pusillus*; occasionally chalk-loving spp on
limestone outcrops, screes, *eg*
Armadillidium pulchellum, A. pictum.)

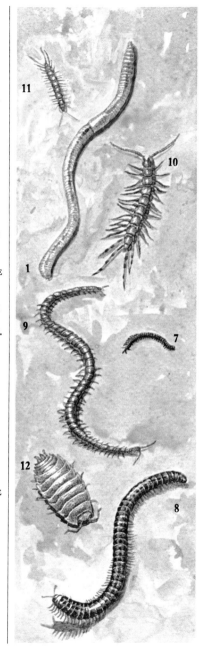

Mayflies (Ephemeroptera). Small to large, with short antennae, 2–3 long cerci; 1–2 pairs of wings. Weak fliers. Metamorphosis incomplete. Nymphs aquatic, mainly herbivorous. Mayflies unique in having 2 winged stages: dull-coloured sub-imagos (anglers' 'duns') emerge from nymphal skins, soon moult to more iridescent adults (known as 'spinners', imitated for fishing flies). Brief life of adult spent dancing over water.

mayfly *Baetis muticus* BAETIDAE BL 5–6 mm + 2 cerci 9–10 mm, WS 12–13 mm. Hindwings very small; body brown-black, wings smoky. Summer; near rivers >500 m. Nymph lives in running water. T, ex Ic. [1]

Dragonflies (Odonata). Mostly large, with long, slender bodies, short antennae; 2 pairs of membraneous wings, usually with black mark on front margin; large eyes. Prey on other insects, catching them in flight. Metamorphosis incomplete. Nymphs aquatic, predatory, head with specialized mask for catching prey.

Blue Aeshna *Aeshna caerulea* AESHNIIDAE WS 76–80 mm. Wings right-angled to body at rest; abdomen very bright blue; thorax brown with narrow, blue, zigzag stripe. Flies Jun–early Aug; moors, clearings in woods, esp pines. Nymph in acid, boggy pools. T, ex Ic, but only nBr. [2]

Brilliant Emerald Hawker Dragonfly *Somatochlora metallica* CORDULIIDAE WS 60–80 mm. Wings right-angled to body at rest. ♂ brilliant emerald green; abdomen constricted at 3rd segment, small yellow spot on 2nd and 3rd segments; wing-bases yellowish. ♀ body bronze-green, wing-bases deeper yellow. Flies Jun–Aug; mountains, woodlands. Nymph in slow or rapid streams. T, ex Ic. [3]

Northern Emerald Hawker Dragonfly *Somatochlora arctica* CORDULIIDAE WS 60–80 mm. Similar to *S. metallica*, but dull metallic green. Jun–Aug; moorlands, coniferous and birch woods. Nymph in peaty pools. T, ex Ic, ?De, but only nBr. [4]

Keeled Orthetrum *Orthetrum caerulescens* LIBELLULIDAE WS 56–66 mm. Wings right-angled to body at rest; brown stripes across thorax; abdomen blue, unmarked, strongly keeled on back. Rapid flight. Jun–Sep; marshy heathlands. Nymph in stagnant pools. T, ex Ic. [5]

Black Sympetrum *Sympetrum danae* LIBELLULIDAE WS 54–60 mm. Wings right-angled to body at rest; ♂ body all black, ♀ and imm ♂ bodies black and yellow. Short, darting flights. Jul–Oct; heaths, moors, clearings in pinewoods. Nymph in peaty bog pools. T, ex Ic. [6] Closely related Common Sympetrum, *S. striolatum* [7]

Scarce Ischnura *Ischnura pumilio* COENAGRIIDAE WS 28–36 mm. Wings folded along slender body at rest; ♂ wing-veins diagnostic red-brown; body generally dark greenish-blue, blue tip to abdomen, dark mark on top of 8th segment; ♀ orange-brown with black top to 8th. Weak flight. Jun–Aug; moorland, wetter heaths. Nymph in boggy pools. T, ex Ic, Fi, No, but rare Br, Sw. [8]

Northern Coenagrion *Coenagrion hastulatum* COENAGRIIDAE WS 34–38 mm. Wings folded along body at rest; ♂ thorax black with blue stripes, abdomen blue with black marks; ♀ thorax green or grey-green, abdomen black. Jun–Aug; marshy areas, moorlands. Nymph in boggy pools. T, ex Ic. [9]

Caddisflies (Trichoptera). Dull-coloured, hairy, rather moth-like, with long antennae; 2 pairs of wings, usually held roof-like over body at rest. Metamorphosis complete. Larvae caterpillar-like (but with only three pairs of legs), aquatic, some free-living, others making cases of sticks or leaves.

caddisfly *Rhyacophila obliterata* RHYACOPHILIDAE WS 25–28 mm. Antennae long, but shorter than wings; first 2 segments of palps (sensory feelers on mouth) short, thick; hairy wings yellow-brown. Jun–Sep; fast-flowing mountain streams. Aquatic larva greenish with yellower head, free-living. T, ex Ic, Ne. [10]

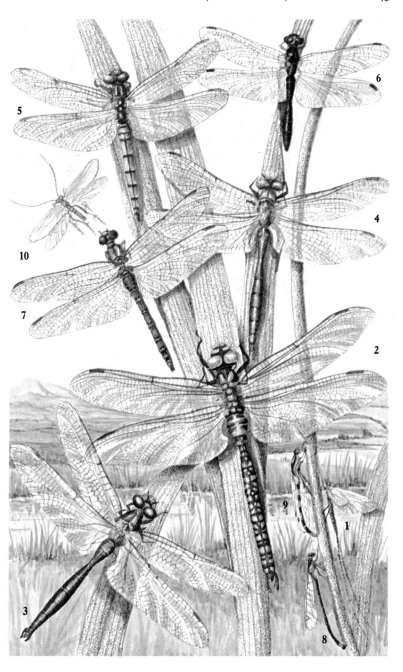

springtails COLLEMBOLA BL <5 mm (many <1 mm). Wingless, often white or grey. Common everywhere, including mountains, glaciers; live in litter at soil surface, mostly feeding on plant debris. Many jump actively and are thus seen when disturbed. T. [1]

Crickets, grasshoppers (Orthoptera). Medium to large, stout-bodied, with short to very long antennae, large blunt head, saddle-shaped pronotum; long hindlegs modified for jumping; usually 2 pairs of wings held along back. Active in warmer weather, sounds produced by stridulation: ♂ bush-crickets rubbing wings together, ♂ and many ♀ grasshoppers rubbing hindlegs on wings. Metamorphosis incomplete. Nymphs like small, wingless adults.

Bog Bush-cricket *Metrioptera brachy-ptera* TETTIGONIIDAE BL ♂ 11–18 mm, ♀ 13–20 mm + sword-like ovipositor 8–10 mm. Antennae very long, wings usually short; underside of abdomen bright green. ♂ shrill, repeated chirping. Active in sunshine, Jul–Sep; moister heaths, moorlands, esp where cross-leaved heath. Insectivorous. T, ex Ir, Ic. [2]

Large Marsh Grasshopper *Stethophyma grossum* ACRIDIDAE BL ♂ 21–29 mm, ♀ 29–35 mm. Antennae short; creamy line along front edge of forewings; body greenish-yellow; hindlegs: tibiae black and yellow, femora with red underside. Ticking noise. Active in sunshine, Aug–Sep; wet peat bogs on moorlands, often where cottongrass. Herbivorous. T, ex Ic. [3]

Heath Grasshopper *Chorthippus vagans* ACRIDIDAE BL ♂ 13–16 mm, ♀ 16–20 mm. Side keels of pronotum strongly angled. Wings smoky-brown or blackish-brown; legs striped with black. Short chirps grouped in rapid succession, interspersed with short pauses. Active in warm weather, Aug; dry, sandy heaths with heather. Herbivorous. T, ex Ic. [4]

Mottled Grasshopper *Myrmeleotettix maculatus* ACRIDIDAE BL ♂ 13–15 mm,

♀ 11–15 mm. ♂ antennae clubbed, ♀ thickened; sides of pronotum angled; forewings dark, never green; body varies from dark mottled grey-green to purplish-brown, well camouflaged. Isolated bursts of repeated chirps. Flies in sunshine, Jun–Oct; drier moorlands, heaths. Herbivorous. T, ex Ic. [5]

Blue-winged Grasshopper *Oedipoda caerulescens* ACRIDIDAE BL 15–30 mm. Body yellow-brown; forewings yellow-brown with 2 dark bars, but hindwings blue with dark bands below apex: thus, camouflaged at rest, conspicuous in flight. Summer; heaths, drier parts of moorlands. Herbivorous. Fr, Ge, Cz, Po, sSw. [6]

Red-winged Grasshopper *Oedipoda germanica* ACRIDIDAE BL 15–31 mm. Similar to *O. caerulescens*, with darker bands across forewings, but hindwings red with darker margins: thus, camouflaged at rest, conspicuous in flight. Summer; dry, stony hillsides. Herbivorous. CE. [7]

Cockroaches (Dictyoptera). Small to large, flattened, with long, spiky legs and very long, slender antennae; 2 cerci at rear of abdomen; usually 2 pairs of heavily veined wings held flat over back; front of thorax extends forward and almost covers head. Omnivorous. Metamorphosis incomplete. Nymphs like small, wingless adults.

Tawny Cockroach *Ectobius pallidus* BLATTIDAE BL 6–9 mm. Wings fully developed in both sexes; long legs roughly equal in length. Nocturnal, but will fly by day, May–Oct; heaths, downs. Eggs laid in ootheca (purse-like case) 3–4 mm long. Searches for food on ground; very active. CE, WE, not Ic, FS. [8]

Snow Scorpion-fly *Boreus hyemalis* MECOPTERA BL 3–6 mm. Like small, wingless grasshopper with long antennae; head elongate, extended below into beak. Autumn–winter; mountains, glaciers, sometimes pine forests. Crawls on snow, can jump; scavenges, preys on snow-trapped insects on calm days. Caterpillar-like larvae develop in spring, pupate Sep, adults emerge Oct. Br, NE, CE. [9]

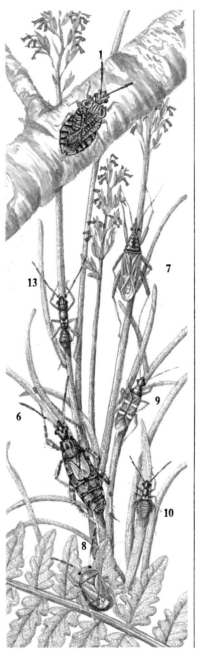

Land and water bugs (Hemiptera–
Heteroptera). Minute to large, sometimes
colourful, generally flattened, wings folded
flat over body at rest. Mouthparts form
rostrum for sucking juices of plants
or animals. Hemelytra divided into
corium and clavus. Metamorphosis
incomplete.

Birch Flatbug *Aradus betulae* ARADIDAE
BL 8–9 mm. Rostrum short; head elongate,
rounded, with pointed protuberance each
side; whole body flat. Jul–Aug; birches,
moorland edges, mountains. Feeds on
fungi. T, ex Ir, Ic, but only nBr. [1]

Mountain Shieldbug *Elasmucha
ferrugata* ACANTHOSOMIDAE BL 8–11 mm.
Thorax sharply pointed at sides; forward-
pointing spine on top of 2nd visible
abdominal segment. Hibernates, lays eggs
on bilberries May onwards; moorlands,
heaths, forests. ♀ remains with eggs and
1st stage nymphs. T, ex Ic, Lu, Be, De.
[2]

Blue Bug *Zicrona caerulea* PENTATOMIDAE
BL 6–7 mm. Overwinters, lays eggs May–
Jun, new adults Jul onwards; dry
moorlands, heaths, chalk downs. Feeds
on beetles, larvae, often attacks resting
butterflies. 1st stage nymphs gregarious.
T, ex Ir, Ic, De. [3]

Heath Bug *Rhagognathus punctatus*
PENTATOMIDAE BL 7–9 mm. Head flat at
front; thorax with pointed edges.
Overwinters, lays eggs May onwards, new
adults Aug; moors, heaths. Feeds on
larvae of heather leaf-beetle, other insects.
T, ex Ic, rare Ir. [4]

Pine-cone Bug *Gastrodes grossipes*
LYGAEIDAE BL 6–7 mm. Oval; pointed
head. Overwinters in pine cones, active
on warmer days, lays eggs Apr–Jun, new
adults Jul–Sep; pinewoods, heaths. Eggs
laid on pine needles. Hiding by day in
cones, adult and nymph feed nocturnally
on sap from needles, seeds in cones. T, ex
Ic. [5] (Spruce-cone bug *G. abietum*,
similar, but paler.)

Heath Assassin Bug *Coranus subapterus*
REDUVIIDAE BL 9–12 mm. Elongate, but
stoutly built; spine on scutellum almost
upright; usually short-winged, non-flying.
Jul–Oct; heaths, sand-dunes. Hunts
insects, spiders. Eggs laid in moss, leaf
litter; overwinter, hatch Apr–May.
Stridulates loudly if handled. T, ex Ir,
Ic. [6]

Heath Damsel Bug *Nabis ericetorum*
NABIIDAE BL 6·5–7 mm. Rostrum
prominent; generally short-winged.
Overwinters, lays eggs in grass stems,
May–Jun, new adults Aug; moorlands,
heaths. Preys on bugs, other insects,
caterpillars. T, ex Ic. [7]

Bracken Bug *Monalocoris filicis* MIRIDAE
BL 2·5–3 mm. Adult hibernates, lays eggs
May–Jun, new adults Jul–Aug; moorlands,
heaths, woods. Feeds on sporangia of
ferns. T, ex Ic. [8]

capsid bug *Systellonotus triguttatus*
MIRIDAE BL ♂ 4·5–5 mm, ♀ 3–4 mm. ♂
winged; ♀ usually wingless, rather ant-
like with swollen abdomen (but long
antennae not elbowed, or angled, like ant's).
May–Aug; open, sandy heaths, often with
ants. Eggs laid in creeping willow. Herbivorous, predatory. T, ex Ic. [♂ 9] [♀ 10]

capsid bug *Globiceps cruciatus* MIRIDAE
BL ♂ 5–6 mm, ♀ 4·5–5·5 mm. ♂ full-
winged, ♀ usually short-winged. Jul–Sep;
sandy heaths, sand dunes, moorland,
roadsides. Feeds on insects, also
herbivorous. T, ex Ic, ?Ir. [11]

capsid bug *Orthotylus ericetorum* MIRIDAE
BL 3–4 mm. Adult, Jun–Oct; heaths,
moors. Feeds on heathers. Eggs laid on
shoots, overwinter. T, ex Ic. [12] (Many
rather similar spp.)

capsid bug *Myrmecoris gracilis* MIRIDAE
BL 4–6·5 mm. Ant-like, antennae long (but
not elbowed, or angled, like ant's); wings
small; forelegs strong. Jun–Aug; dry, sandy
heaths. Feeds on aphids and honeydew,
eggs of grass bugs, small invertebrates;
occasionally in ant nests.Eggs laid in
grass stems, overwinter. T, ex Ir, Ic. [13]

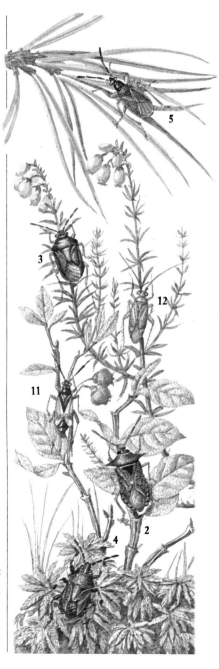

Spittlebugs, leafhoppers, plant lice, aphids (Hemiptera–Homoptera). Minute to large; antennae short and bristly or long and thread-like; 2 pairs of wings, often membraneous, held roof-like over body at rest (*cf* Heteroptera); sucking mouthparts for plant-feeding. Metamorphosis incomplete. Nymphs wingless.

spittlebug, froghopper *Neophilaenus lineatus* CERCOPIDAE BL 4·5–6 mm. Sides parallel at rest; body colour variable, but finely downy all over; pale yellow stripe on front margin of forewings; hind tibiae with few spines. Summer; widespread, moors, heaths. Nymph produces 'spittle' of anal froth on plant and lives inside it. T, ex Ic. [1] [cuckoo-spit 2]

leafhopper *Notus flavipennis* TYPHLOCYBIDAE BL 3·5–4 mm. Slender, with pointed head; all pale yellow except for black abdomen, showing through wings; legs with rows of spines. Very active, summer; moorlands, bogs, watersides, on sedges. T, ex Ic. [3]

leafhopper *Cicadella viridis* CICADELLIDAE BL 5·5–9 mm, ♂ smaller than ♀. Yellow head with 2 black spots; ♂ wings dark blue, ♀ green. Jun–Oct; widespread in marshy ground, bogs. Eggs laid in rushes, other plants. T, ex Ic. [♀ 4]

leafhopper *Ulopa reticulatus* CICADELLIDAE BL 3–4 mm. Front of head rounded, swollen; body brown with reddish tinge; black punctures on head, thorax; dark marks on pronotum; wings transparent, black. Summer; moorlands, on heaths. T, ex Ic. [5]

leafhopper *Psammotettix striatus* CICADELLIDAE BL 3–3·5 mm. Front of head brown, top and thorax yellow, with black lines across 2nd segment of thorax; forewings longer than abdomen, greenish-yellow. Summer; moorlands, heaths, on grasses. T, ex Ic. [6]

cixiid *Cixius cambricus* CIXIIDAE BL 4–6 mm. Head squat; pronotum light brown; wings large, membranous, with

conspicuous, spotted veins. Jun–Jul; very local in heather. nwBr, Cz, Ge, Po, Fr. [7]

Spruce-gall Aphid *Adelges abietis* ADELGIDAE BL 1–5 mm. Greenish or brownish, with 3 oblique veins on transparent forewings; usually covered in white, waxy threads. May–Aug; some have 1-year cycle wholly in spruce woods; others with 2-year cycle, lay eggs on larches in 1st year. Eggs cause 'pineapple' galls, in which nymphs live. T, ex Ic, [8] [gall 9]

Lacewings (Neuroptera). Small to large; long antennae, and soft, slender bodies; generally brown or green. 2 pairs of gauzy wings held roof-like over body at rest; slow fliers; biting mouthparts, feed on aphids, plant-lice, other insects. Metamorphosis complete.

Brown Pine Lacewing *Hemerobius pini* HEMEROBIIDAE WS 14–17 mm. Head and body brown; wings translucent, black marks on forewings. Crepuscular, 2

broods, May–Aug; pine-forests. Larva broader in middle, with pointed abdomen, 3 pairs of legs, sickle-shaped jaws; sucks juices from pine insects. T, ex Ir, Ic. [10]

Green Pine Lacewing *Chrysopa dorsalis* CHRYSOPIDAE WS 28–34 mm. Head and body yellow-green; wings transparent, with prominent, greenish net-veins and dark marks near apex of each. Nocturnal, but flies by day if disturbed, Jul–Aug; pinewoods. Eggs attached to needles by long stalks. Larva hairy, rather pointed at each end, often covered with debris for camouflage; sucks pine insects. T, ex Ic, but only sBr. [11]

ant-lion *Myrmeleon formicarius* MYRMELEONTIDAE WS 6–8 cm. Body long, brown, like dragonfly, but with short, stout antennae; wings gauzy, slightly pointed, with clear, brown veins and, often, blotches. Slow, rather flappy flight. Summer; sandy heathlands. Larva lives in small pit in sand, catches insects that fall in. WE, CE, Sw, but not Br, Ir. [12]

Butterflies, moths (Lepidoptera). Small to large, easily distinguished by covering of fine scales which give colour and pattern; usually proboscis for sucking nectar. Butterflies mostly day-fliers, with clubbed antennae; chrysalis without cocoon. Moths mostly night-fliers, with thin, pointed or feathery antennae; cocoon or chamber formed round pupa. Caterpillars feed mostly on plants: those listed are often only examples from a wider range.

Apollo *Parnassius apollo* PAPILIONIDAE ws 70–80 mm. White with large, rounded, black spots on forewings; red rings edged with black on hindwings. Jul–Aug; mountains, 750–1800 m. Caterpillar red and black-spotted, conspicuous; feeds on stonecrops. Fr, Ge, Po, sFS, accidental Br. [1]

Clouded Apollo *Parnassius mnemosyne* PAPILIONIDAE WS 53–63 mm. ♂ white with black veins, 2 black marks on forewings, small mark near middle of hindwings, black body; ♀ greyer-white, with hindwings more blackish, spot not clear. May–June; hills, mountains, to 1500 m, damp lowland meadows in north. Caterpillar feeds on corydalis. Fr, De, Ge, Cz, Po, sFS. [2]

Bath White *Pontia daplidice* PIERIDAE WS 43–49 mm. White with greenish-black apex to forewings and spot in middle; hindwings grey-white with few marks; underside of forewings with greenish apex, of hindwings mostly greenish with white patches. Strongly migratory. Several broods, Feb–Mar, May–Sep; meadows, rocky valleys, to 1800 m. Caterpillar feeds on rock-cresses, mignonettes, mustards. Fr, Ge, Cz, Po; migrant T, ex Ir, Ic, nFS. [3]

Pale Arctic Clouded Yellow *Colias nastes* PIERIDAE WS 45–49 mm. Pale yellow-white with darker margins, brown veins, open spot at apex cell on forewings; underside of hindwings greenish-yellow with orange central spot. Jun; hill, rough ground over 300 m. Caterpillar feeds on alpine milk-vetch. nSC. [4]

Moorland Clouded Yellow *Colias palaeno* PIERIDAE WS 52–55 mm. Similar to *C. nastes*, but wings yellower with still darker, broader margins; underside of forewings with larger dark margin. Jun–Jul; moorlands, bogs. Caterpillar feeds on bilberries. Fr, De, Ge, Cz, Po, FS. [5]

Northern Clouded Yellow *Colias hecla* PIERIDAE WS 42–48 mm. Similar to *C. nastes*, but darker with orange-yellow wings, prominent dark borders; underside of hindwings darker greyish-yellow with orange-red spot in middle. Jun–Jul; mountain slopes, rough grassland to 1000 m. Caterpillar feeds on alpine milk-vetch. nFS. [6]

Grizzled Skipper *Pyrgus malvae* HESPERIIDAE WS 23–27 mm. Brown with white spots; underside similar, but brown paler, often yellowish. Rapid, 'whirring' flight. 2 broods, Apr–Aug; mountains, wet heaths, meadows, to 1800 m. Caterpillar feeds on cinquefoils, mallows, agrimonies, strawberries. T, ex nBr, Ir, Ic, nFS. [7]

Large Grizzled Skipper *Pyrgus alveus* HESPERIIDAE WS 29–37 mm. Similar to *P. malvae*, but larger; and northern ssp less spotted, esp on hindwings; underside of hindwings greener. Jun–Aug, mountains, hills, grasslands, 900–1800 m. Caterpillar feeds on cinquefoils, rock-roses, brambles. T, ex Br, Ir, Ic, Ne, De, nFS. [8]

Olive Skipper *Pyrgus serratulae* HESPERIIDAE WS 25–29 mm. Dark brown, with white marks on forewings; underside of forewings paler, of hindwings olive-brown, both with white spots. Jun–Aug; mountains, hills, to 2500 m. Caterpillar feeds on cinquefoils, lady's-mantles. Fr, Ge, Cz, Po. [9]

Camberwell Beauty *Nymphalis antiopa*
NYMPHALIDAE WS 62–70 mm. Dark purple
with broad, cream margin, bordered by
mauve spots; underside browner, with less
distinct, bluer marks. Jun–Jul, spring
(after hibernation), autumn (after
migration); hills, mountains, but almost
anywhere on migration. Caterpillar feeds
on willow, birch. T, ex Ir, Ic, but rare
Br, Ne, De, No. [1]

Painted Lady *Cynthia cardui*
NYMPHALIDAE WS 55–61 mm. Orange-red
and black, with white spots on blackish
apex of forewings; underside similar, but
paler. Rapid flier, may appear anywhere;
some years more abundant. Apr–autumn
(latterly as migrant); lowlands to 1800 m
in mountains. Caterpillar feeds on nettles,
also thistles. T, but only migrant nBr, Ic,
nFS. [2]

Niobe Fritillary *Argynnis niobe*
NYMPHALIDAE WS 50–62 mm. Orange-
brown, patterned with black; underside of
hindwings often greenish-based, with
silvery spots, silver-centred reddish spots
near margin and small, silvery spot, often
with black centre, in middle of cell. Rapid
flier. Jun–Jul; moorlands to tree-line.
Caterpillar feeds on violets, more rarely
plantains. T, ex Br, Ir, Ic, nFS, but rare
Ne. [3]

Dark Green Fritillary *Argynnis aglaja*
NYMPHALIDAE WS 50–62 mm. Orange-
brown, heavily patterned with black;
underside of forewings paler, of hindwings
greenish with silvery spots, yellow band
near margin. Rapid flier. Jun–Jul;
meadows, heaths, moorlands to tree-line.
Caterpillar feeds on violets, also bistorts.
T, ex Ic. [4]

Mountain Fritillary *Boloria napaea*
NYMPHALIDAE WS 36–44 mm. Red-brown
patterned with black, darker wing-base;
undersides of forewings more uniform, of
hindwings with complicated pattern of
yellow and orange-brown, some silvery
spots. Jul–Aug; mountains around tree-
line. Caterpillar feeds on alpine bistort.
Fr, nwFS. [5]

Bog Fritillary *Boloria eunomia*
NYMPHALIDAE WS 42–48 mm. Orange-
brown patterned with black, including
irregular black lines in middle of both
wings; underside yellower, with 6 yellow,
white or silver spots round margin of
hindwings. Jun–Jul; marshy areas,
moorlands, to 1500 m. Caterpillar feeds
on common bistort, bilberries. Fr, Ge,
Cz, Po, FS. [6]

Frejya's Fritillary *Boloria freija*
NYMPHALIDAE WS 38–46 mm. Similar to
B. eunomia, but paler; prominent, dark,
zigzag band across forewings; underside
of hindwings with bold, black, zigzag
line. May–Jun; tundra, moorlands,
mountains. Caterpillar feeds on northern
bilberry, cloudberry. FS, ?Po. [7]

Heath Fritillary *Mellicta athalia*
NYMPHALIDAE WS 38–42 mm. Variable,
but dark orange-brown, strongly and
regularly patterned with black; underside
paler, of hindwings distinctly yellow with
patterned bands across wing. 2 broods,
May–Jun, Aug–Sep; meadows, heaths,
moors to 1500 m. Caterpillar feeds on
plantains, cow-wheats. T, ex Ir, Ic, but
only sBr. [8]

Marbled White *Melanargia galathea*
SATYRIDAE WS 47–53 mm. White or
yellowish with heavy, strongly contrasting,
black markings; underside paler, esp
hindwings (♀ markings yellow-brown).
Jun–Jul; lowlands to 1500 m in mountain
valleys. Caterpillar feeds on grasses (*eg*
cat's-tails), wheat. sBr, Fr, Lu, Be, Ge,
Cz, Po. [♂ 9]

Rock Grayling *Hipparchia alcyone*
SATYRIDAE WS 55–66 mm. Grey-brown
with yellow-brown band and white-
centred, black spot below apex on
forewings; broad, white or yellow-white
band on hindwings; underside of forewings similar but paler, of hindwings
greyer in parts and crossed by white,
sinuate band. Rapid flier. Jun–Jul;
mountains to 1800 m, among rocks.
Caterpillar feeds on grasses, esp false
bromes. Fr, Ge, Cz, Po, sNo. [10]

Grayling *Hipparchia semele* SATYRIDAE
WS 40–52 mm. Brown with yellow-orange
band and 2 white-centred, black spots on
forewings; hindwings similar, but less
orange and usually 1 spot; underside of
forewings similar to upperside, only 1
spot visible when resting, of hindwings
grey-brown. Often rests at angle to sun to
reduce shadow, improve camouflage. Jul–
Aug; heaths, rough pastures. Caterpillar
feeds on grasses (*eg* hair-grasses). T, ex Ic,
but only sFS. [1]

Baltic Grayling *Oeneis jutta* SATYRIDAE
WS 55–58 mm. Pale brown with yellow-
ringed, black spots along margins of both
wings; underside of forewings similar but
paler, of hindwings mottled darker brown
and grey with paler centre. May–Jul;
scattered pines, esp on wet moors,
settling on trunks. Food of caterpillar
unknown. Po, FS, but rare No, ?Ge. [2]

Arran Brown *Erebia ligea* SATYRIDAE
WS 49–56 mm. Dark chocolate- or red-
brown with black-spotted, orange-brown
band near margins of both wings;
underside of forewings more orange-
brown with white-centred, black spots; of
hindwings brown with orange-ringed,
black spots variably bordered on inside by
white streak. Jun–Aug; hills, mountain
valleys to 1500 m, often among spruce.
Caterpillar feeds on grasses, *eg* wood
millet. Fr, Ge, Cz, Po, FS. [3]

Large Ringlet *Erebia euryale* SATYRIDAE
WS 43–48 mm. Similar to *E. ligea*, but
smaller. Jul–Aug; mountains, 900–1800 m,
often among spruce. Caterpillar feeds on
grasses. Fr, Ge, Cz, Po. [4]

Mountain Ringlet *Erebia epiphron*
SATYRIDAE WS 35–40 mm. Variable, but
forewings generally dark chocolate-brown
with orange-red band (often in form of
large spots) marked by row of small, black
spots (sometimes white-centred); hindwings similar, but less distinct pattern;
underside paler. Jul–Aug; mountains,
moorlands, often among conifers, 600–
1200 m. Caterpillar feeds on grasses, esp
tufted hair-grass. Br, Fr, Ge, Cz, Po. [5]

Scotch Argus *Erebia aethiops* SATYRIDAE
WS 43–53 mm. Similar to *E. epiphron*,
but white-centred, black spots on
forewings larger, pale grey band on
underside of hindwings. Aug–Sep;
mountains, moorlands, among conifers,
to 1800 m. Caterpillar feeds on grasses,
eg cock's-foot, annual meadow-grass. Br,
Fr, Lu, Be, Ne, Ge, Cz, Po. [6]

Dusky Meadow Brown *Hyponephele
lycaon* SATYRIDAE WS 41–50 mm. Pale
brown with orange-brown centre to
forewings and black spot near apex in ♂,
♀ has 2 black spots; underside of
forewings orange-yellow with brown edges
and larger, white-centred, black spot
near apex, of hindwings still paler brown
near margin. Jul–Aug; rocky moorlands
mountains, drier areas up to 1800 m.
Caterpillar feeds on grasses, esp meadow-
grasses. Ge, Cz, Po, sFi. [♀ 7]

Large Heath *Coenonympha tullia*
SATYRIDAE WS 39–42 mm. Variable, but
forewings orange-brown with dusky
edges; hindwings brown-black with lighter
spots near margin; underside of forewings
with white-centred, black spot near apex
and adjacent white mark, of hindwings
with row of pale-edged, black spots near
margin. Jun–Jul; boggy moors, wet
heaths. Caterpillar feeds on cottongrass,
white beak-sedge. T, ex Ic, ?De. [8]

Small Heath *Coenonympha pamphilus*
SATYRIDAE WS 29–33 mm. Variable, but
generally orange-brown with narrow,
brown margins. May–Oct; grassy
moorlands, meadows, to 1800 m.
Caterpillar feeds on grasses, *eg* mat-grass,
annual meadow-grass. T, ex Ic. [U 9]

Scarce Heath *Coenonympha hero*
SATYRIDAE WS 31–35 mm. Dark grey-
brown with unmarked forewings and
orange-edged, black spots on margin of
hindwings; underside of forewings grey-
brown, of hindwings with white and
orange markings. May–Jun; moorlands,
damp meadows. Caterpillar feeds on
grasses, esp *Elymus arenarius*. Fr, Be, Ne,
De, Ge, Po, sFS. [10]

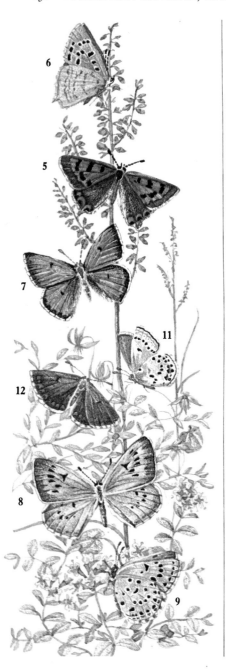

Large Wall Brown *Lasiommata maera*
SATYRIDAE WS 52–58 mm. Underside of
forewings with larger spot and yellow
surround, of hindwings grey with row of
small spots near margin. 2 broods, May–
Jun, Aug–Sep; rocky hills, mountains to
1800 m. Caterpillar feeds on grasses. T,
ex Br, Ir, Ic, Ne, nFi. [♀ 1]

Northern Wall Brown *Lasiommata
petropolitana* SATYRIDAE WS 37–43 mm.
Upperside darker brown with orange-
edged, white-centred, black spot near
apex of forewings; ♂, less orange on
forewings, underside greyer. Jul–Aug;
rocky hills, dry moorlands, often among
conifers. Caterpillar feeds on grasses,
esp fescues. FS, ?Ge, ?Cz. [♀ U 2]

Green Hairstreak *Callophrys rubi*
LYCAENIDAE WS 27–31 mm. Upperside
brown or grey-brown, usually unmarked;
underside green, with line of small, white
spots across hindwings. Mar–Jun; rough
ground, moors, to 2250 m. Caterpillar
feeds on bird's-foot-trefoils, gorse, broom,
bilberries. T, ex Ic. [3] [U 4]

Small Copper *Lycaena phlaeas*
LYCAENIDAE WS 25–32 mm. Variable, but
forewings coppery-red, edged and spotted
with black; hindwings dark black-brown
with coppery-orange band on margin;
underside of forewings like upperside but
with grey margin, of hindwings grey or
brown and usually spotted. Several broods,
Feb–Sep; heathland, hill slopes to 1800 m.
Caterpillar feeds on docks, sorrels,
knotgrass. T, ex Ic. [5] [U 6]

Purple-edged Copper *Palaeochrysophanus
hippothoe* LYCAENIDAE WS 33–35 mm.
♀ forewings paler orange-red, spotted or
suffused with blackish, and hindwings
black with black-spotted, orange band
near margin; undersides greyish with
black spots, some copper-orange on both
wings. Jun–Jul; moorlands, meadows,
usually boggy areas, to 1500 m. Caterpillar
feeds on docks, common bistort. T, ex
Ir, Ic, Ne, extinct Br. [♂ 7]

Large Blue *Maculinea arion* LYCAENIDAE

WS 35–43 mm. Adult, Jun–Jul; heaths, rough grassland, to 1800 m. Caterpillar first feeds on thyme; later wanders until meets ant (usually *Myrmica scabrinodis*) which, attracted by caterpillar's secretion, carries it to nest where it then feeds on ant larvae, pupates, and eventually emerges as adult butterfly. T, ex Ir, Ic, Ne, nFi, nSw, No, but rare Br. [8] [U **9**]

Silver-studded Blue *Plebejus argus*
LYCAENIDAE WS 25–31 mm. Variable, but
♂ upperside purplish-blue with dark margin, and underside grey with black spots, orange margin. ♀ upperside much browner, often blue on basal halves of both wings, and underside also browner, with white band inside orange margin. 2 broods in south, May–Sep; heaths, hill slopes. Caterpillar feeds on bird's-foot-trefoils, other Leguminosae. T, ex nBr, Ir, Ic, nFS. [♂ U **10**]

Cranberry Blue *Vacciniina optilete*
LYCAENIDAE WS 27–31 mm. Violet-blue with narrow, black margin; underside grey with black spots near black-lined margin, and some black-edged, orange spots on hindwings. Jul; mountains, moorlands, to 2250 m. Caterpillar feeds on *Vaccinium*, esp cranberry. De, Ge, Cz, Po, FS. [**11**]

Brown Argus *Aricia agestis* LYCAENIDAE
WS 25–29 mm. Underside grey with white-edged, black spots and margin of orange-red spots. Several broods, Apr–Sep; heaths, mountain slopes, to 1000 m. Caterpillar feeds on rock-roses, crane's-bills, stork's-bill. T, ex nBr, Ir, Ic, Fi, No, but only sSw. [**12**]

Common Blue *Polyommatus icarus*
LYCAENIDAE WS 29–37 mm. ♀ upperside brown, often washed blue, with orange spots along margins (black-centred on hindwings), and underside browner than in ♂, more strongly marked. 2 broods, Apr–Aug; moorlands, mountains, meadows, to 1800 m. Caterpillar feeds on Leguminosae, esp clovers, trefoils, vetches. T, ex Ic. [♂ **13**] [♂ U **14**]

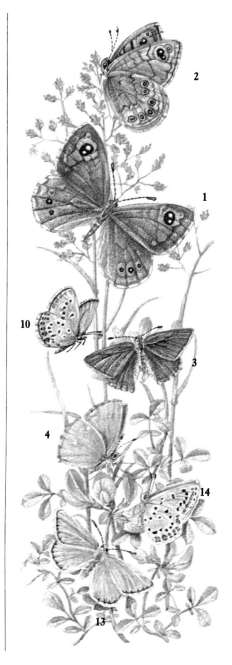

Plume moths (Pterophoridae): delicate, long-legged, with forewings divided into 2 lobes and hindwings into 3; weak fliers; usually rest with wings at right angles to body, looking like capital T.

plume moth *Buckleria paludum*
PTEROPHORIDAE WS 12–13 mm. Light brown, with white marks near apex of forewings. Nocturnal, but will fly by day; 2 broods, Jun, Aug; bogs, moors where wet. Caterpillar feeds on leaves of sundews, avoiding insect-catching hairs. T, ex Ic, No. [1]

plume moth *Amblyptilia acanthodactyla*
PTEROPHORIDAE WS 18–21 mm. Purplish-brown, with black marks and white spots on forewings, giving marbled effect; apex of forewings pointed. Nocturnal, hiding by day; 2 broods, Jul, Sep–Nov; heaths, moorlands. Caterpillar feeds on buds, flowers, of woundworts, restharrows, heathers. T, ex Ic. [2]

Pyralid moths (Pyralidae): rather long-legged; wings often translucent; 2 pairs of palps (sensory feelers on mouth), 1 pair usually projecting well in front of head.

grass moth *Crambus ericellus* PYRALIDAE WS 19–25 mm. Forewings brown with white line along middle and black spots edged with bluish line near margin; hindwings pale brown; at rest, sits with wings rolled round body. Nocturnal, though readily flies by day, Jun–Jul; mountains, moorlands. Caterpillar unknown. T, ex sBr, Ir, Ic, Lu, Be. [3]

grass moth *Agriphila latistria* PYRALIDAE WS 21–25 mm. Forewings brown with white stripe from base to margin; wings rolled round body at rest. Nocturnal, but will fly by day, Jul; moorlands, heaths, coastal dunes. Caterpillar feeds on grasses. T. [4]

grass moth *Catoptria furcatella*
PYRALIDAE WS 19–21 mm. Forewings dark brown, crossed by narrow, white line; hindwings grey-brown. Flies in afternoon,

resting on ground, Jul–Aug; grassy slopes of mountains. Caterpillar feeds on grasses, *eg* sheep's-fescue. Br, Fr, Ge, Cz, Po, FS. [5]

pyralid moth *Oncocera palumbella* PYRALIDAE WS 20–26 mm. Forewings slender, grey with 2 brown transverse bands, black spot near middle; hindwings pale brown. Rapid flight. Nocturnal, but readily flies by day, Jul–Aug; heaths, moorlands. Caterpillar lives in web, feeds on heathers. T, ex Ic. [6]

Pine Moth *Dioryctria abietella* PYRALIDAE WS 24–29 mm. Variable, but forewings slender, grey with dark brown transverse lines; hindwings pale. Generally dusk or night flier, camouflaged at rest by day, Jun–Jul; pinewoods, esp Scots pine. Caterpillar feeds in pine cones, will also burrow into shoots in spring. T, ex Ic. [7]

pyralid moth *Eudonia alpina* PYRALIDAE WS 19–23 mm. Forewings pale grey with darker markings; hindwings pale brown, unmarked. Flies in afternoon, Jun; mountains, moorland. Caterpillar believed to feed on lichens or mosses. T, ex Ic, De. [8]

Case-bearing Rush Moth *Coleophora caespititiella* COLEOPHORIDAE WS 10–12 mm. Wings narrow, pointed, with large fringe scales all round; forewings grey-brown, powdered with white; hindwings grey. Jun–Jul; moorland bogs, on rushes. Caterpillar lives in tiny, cylindrical, white case on rushes, esp soft rush, heath rush, Aug–Oct. T, ex Ic. [9]

Swift moths (Hepialidae): forewings and hindwings broadly similar in shape and venation; rapid fliers.

Map-winged Swift *Hepialus fusconebulosa* HEPIALIDAE WS 30–43 mm. Variable, but forewings orange-brown with darker marks, and narrow, white lines below margin; hindwings smoky grey. Very rapid flight. Crepuscular, Jun–Jul; hills, moorlands. Caterpillar feeds on roots of bracken, taking 2 years to develop. T, ex Ic. [10]

tortricid moth *Expate congelatella*
TORTRICIDAE WS ♂ 19–23 mm, ♀ 8–11
mm. ♂ has normal wings: forewings grey-
brown with lighter centre containing
dark, squarish mark, another mark below
apex; hindwings brown. ♀ only vestigial
wings. ♂ flies before dusk, comes to light,
Oct–Dec; moors, heaths. Caterpillar feeds
on bilberries, heathers. T, ex Ic. [♂ 1]

Pine-shoot Moth *Rhyacionia buoliana*
TORTRICIDAE WS 17–22 mm. Forewings
distinctive, rather squarish, reddish-orange
with several grey-white transverse lines,
white fringe; hindwings pale grey.
Nocturnal, Jul–Aug; pinewoods, esp
Scots pine. Caterpillar feeds on pine
shoots, can cause serious damage in
plantations. T, ex Ic. [2]

tortricid moth *Hedya atropunctana*
TORTRICIDAE WS 14–15 mm. Forewings
pinkish-white with brown central mark;
hindwings grey. Nocturnal, but will fly
readily by day, Jun; moorlands.
Caterpillar feeds on bog myrtle, forming
webbing tent. T, ex Ic. [3] Similar sp,
Olethrartus mygindianus, distinct brown
pattern on forewings. CE, NE. [4]

Mountain Burnet *Zygaena exulans*
ZYGAENIDAE WS 26–32 mm. Body fat,
black; antennae slightly swollen, angled,
pointed; forewings semi-transparent, with
red patches, green-grey margin; hindwings
red with thin, black margin. Day flier,
esp in sunshine, Jul; mountains, moorlands.
Caterpillar green and black; feeds on
moss campion. nBr, sFr, FS, ?Ge. [5]

Pine Hawk-moth *Hyloicus pinastri*
SPHINGIDAE WS 70–75 mm. Body stout;
abdomen striped white; forewings
pointed, dark grey with some black marks;
hindwings smaller, grey-brown. Nocturnal,
May–Jul, clinging to tree trunks by day,
well camouflaged, wings folded roof-like
over body; among conifers, esp Scots pine,
Norway spruce. Caterpillar large, green
with creamy lines, single blunt spine on
posterior; feeds on pine and spruce needles,
can be destructive to trees. T, ex Ic. [6]

Emperor Moth *Saturnia pavonia*
SATURNIIDAE WS 50–80 mm. Antennae
very feathery, wing-pattern conspicuous;
♀ grey-brown and delicately patterned.
♂ flies in sunshine, ♀ mostly nocturnal,
Apr–May; moorlands, heaths. Caterpillar
large, bright green with black marks
between rows of black-bristled, yellow
warts round body, interspersed with
orange rings; feeds on heathers, spinning
large cocoon. T, ex Ic. [♂ 7]

Eggar and lackey moths (Lasiocampidae):
generally large, stout-bodied, hairy, with
broad wings of varying shades of brown;
antennae of ♂ markedly feathery, of ♀
simpler.

Drinker *Philudoria potatoria* LASIO-
CAMPIDAE WS 46–64 mm. ♀ fatter-bodied,
than ♂, yellow-brown, also with dark line
diagonally across forewings, white spot
near centre; hindwings with similar line,
but no white spot. Rapid flight. ♂
diurnal, ♀ nocturnal, Jul; moorlands,
damp heaths. Caterpillar slate-grey with
yellow marks along back and sides, long
tufts of hairs; feeds on grasses; overwinters. T, ex Ic. [♂ 8]

Oak Eggar *Lasiocampa quercus*
LASIOCAMPIDAE WS 52–74 mm. Northern
ssp *L. q. callunae*: ♂ dark chocolate-
brown with broad, pale band across both
wings, pale spot near middle of forewings;
♀ larger. Rapid flight. Diurnal, ♂ locating
♀ by scent, May–Jun; moorlands, heaths.
Caterpillar brown with purple marks on
sides, long tufts of brown hairs; feeds on
heathers; 2-year life-cycle, pupating in
strong, oval cocoon near ground. T, ex
Ic. [♀ 9] Southern ssp *L. q. quercus*: paler,
1-year life-cycle. T, ex Ic, Fi.

Fox *Macrothylacia rubi* LASIOCAMPIDAE
WS 44–46 mm. ♂ red-brown. ♂ diurnal,
♀ crepuscular or nocturnal, May–Jun;
moorlands, heaths. Caterpillar chocolate-
brown, long hairs causing skin-rash if
handled; feeds on heathers, brambles,
later hibernating. T, ex Ic. [♀ 10]

Looper moths (Geometridae): often rather fluttery; many sit with wings over back, like butterflies; name from characteristic looping movement of caterpillars, also called 'inch-worms', 'earth-measurers'.

Black Mountain *Psodos coracina*
GEOMETRIDAE WS 22–24 mm. Smoky grey-black, speckled with white. Diurnal, esp in sunshine, Jul; mountains, over 650 m. Caterpillar feeds on bistorts. nBr, Fr, Ge, Cz, Fi. [1]

Netted Mountain *Semiothisa carbonaria*
GEOMETRIDAE WS 20–21 mm. Blackish-brown with white zigzags across both wings. Diurnal, esp in sunshine, Apr–May; mountains, high moorlands. Caterpillar feeds on bilberries, heathers, alpine bearberry. T, ex Ic, No. [2]

Smoky Wave *Scopula ternata*
GEOMETRIDAE WS 23–26 mm. White or creamy-white with delicate, narrow, brown or reddish lines across wings. Diurnal and nocturnal, Jun–Jul; moorlands, heaths. Caterpillar feeds on bilberries, willows, heathers, later hibernating. T, ex Ic. [3]

Grey Mountain Carpet *Entephria caesiata* GEOMETRIDAE WS 31–34 mm. Well camouflaged: forewings grey-brown with prominent, wavy, white, transverse lines and broader, brown, median band; hindwings grey, but variable. Nocturnal, but flies readily by day, Jul–Aug; moorlands, heaths. Caterpillar feeds on bilberries, heathers. T. [4]

Common Heath *Ematurga atomaria*
GEOMETRIDAE WS 24–29 mm. ♂ has long, feathery antennae; strongly patterned, but variable: grey-brown with orange-brown, wavy, transverse lines. Diurnal; 2 broods, May–Jun, Aug; moorlands.

Caterpillar feeds on heathers, bird's-foot trefoils. T, ex Ic. [5]

Small Argent and Sable *Eulype subhastata* GEOMETRIDAE WS 23–25 mm. Black with broken, white bands across wings, often more white than black. Diurnal; sometimes 2 broods, May–Jul; moorlands. Caterpillar feeds on bilberries, bog myrtle, spinning tips of plants together. T, ex Ic. [6] Similar Argent and Sable *E. hastata* larger, usually still whiter, caterpillar feeds on birches. T, ex Ic.

Northern Spinach *Eulithis populata* GEOMETRIDAE WS 29–33 mm, ♀ smaller than ♂. Forewings yellow-brown with darker, orange-yellow, median and basal bands, outer margin often with dark patch; hindwings yellowish-white, but variable. Usually nocturnal, Jul–Aug; mountains, moorlands. Caterpillar feeds on bilberries. T, ex Ic. [7]

Narrow-winged or **Heath Pug** *Eupithecia nanata* GEOMETRIDAE WS 19–21 mm. Forewings rather sharply angled, grey-brown delicately patterned with blackish; hindwings smoky-grey with barred marginal scales. Crepuscular, but easily disturbed by day; 2 broods, May–Jun, Jul–Aug; moorlands. Caterpillar feeds on heathers. T. [8]

Tiger moths (Arctiidae): usually colourful, often flying by day; caterpillars hairy.

Clouded Buff *Diacrisia sannio* ARCTIIDAE WS 35–46 mm. Forewings of ♂ yellowish with large, red-brown spot; hindwings whitish with darker edges and central S-shaped mark; both wings of ♀ red-brown, mostly covered with black scales. ♂ diurnal, ♀ crepuscular, Jun–Jul; moorlands, heaths. Caterpillar feeds on heather, plantains, dandelions. Makes flimsy cocoon on ground. T, ex Ic. [♀ 9]

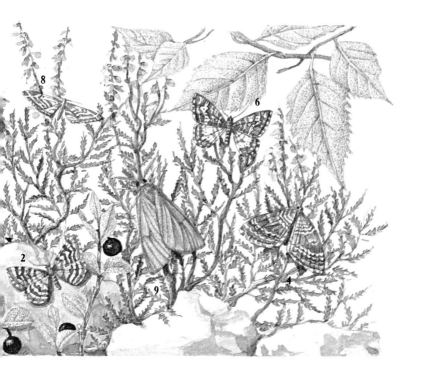

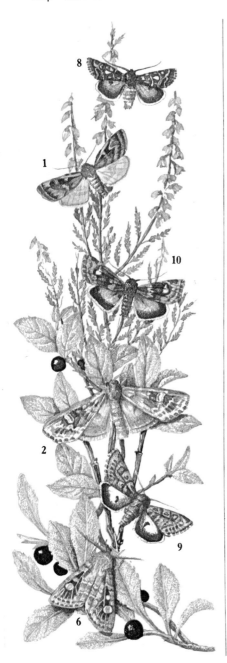

Owlet or underwing moths (Noctuidae): rather stout-bodied, often soberly coloured, well camouflaged, wings at rest folded roof-like over body; caterpillars, called 'cutworms', crawl in contrast to looping Geometridae.

Heath Rustic *Xestia agathina* NOCTUIDAE WS 27–35 mm. Forewings brown or grey with white marks near base, faint cross lines (sometimes more heavily patterned); hindwings mostly white. Nocturnal, Aug–Sep; heaths, moorlands. Caterpillar feeds on heathers. T, ex Ic, FS, but rare Be. [1]

Golden Rod Brindle *Lithomoia solidaginis* NOCTUIDAE WS 40–44 mm. Stout body; hindwings brownish, camouflaged at rest on lichen-covered rocks. Rapid flight. Nocturnal, Aug–Sep; moors, mountains. Caterpillar feeds on bilberries, alpine bearberry. T, ex Ic. [2]

Small Wainscot *Photedes pygmina* NOCTUIDAE WS 22–29 mm. Fat body; squarish wings, forewings nondescript, brown; hindwings grey-white. Nocturnal Aug–Sep; wet moorlands, marshy ground. Caterpillar mines in stems of sedges. T, ex Ic. [3]

Small Dotted Buff *Photedes minima* NOCTUIDAE WS 20–26 mm. Pale grey-brown, forewings spotted. Nocturnal, Jul–Aug; moorlands. Caterpillar feeds on grasses, esp tufted hair-grass. T, ex Ic. [4]

Marbled Minor *Oligia strigilis* NOCTUIDAE WS 24–27 mm. Hindwings grey to white. Very well camouflaged at rest. Rapid flight. Nocturnal, Jun–Jul; moors, rough grassland. Caterpillar feeds on grass stems. T, ex Ic. [5] (Several similar spp.)

Northern Dart *Xestia alpicola* NOCTUIDAE WS 35–40 mm. Stout body; forewings dingy brown-grey, strongly patterned with black apical and subapical spots, transverse zigzag, and paler patches; hindwings smoky-brown. Nocturnal, Jul–Aug; mountains, uplands. Caterpillar

feeds on crowberry, bilberries, alpine
bearberry. T, ex Ic. [6]

Antler *Cerapteryx graminis* NOCTUIDAE
WS 29–37 mm. Hindwings smoky-brown.
Nocturnal, strongly attracted to light, but
will fly by day, Jul–Sep; moors, heathland.
Caterpillar feeds on grasses; often
abundant, can be very destructive. T. [7]

Beautiful Yellow Underwing *Anarta
myrilli* NOCTUIDAE WS 22–25 mm.
Forewings patterned dark reddish or
purplish, with white spot in centre, dark
submarginal line; hindwings yellow with
broad, brown border. Diurnal, esp in
sunshine, Apr–Aug; moorlands.
Caterpillar feeds on heathers. T, ex Ic. [8]

Broad-bordered White Underwing
Anarta melanopa NOCTUIDAE WS 25–31
mm. Forewings dark blackish, speckled
with white; hindwings white with darker
margins and black-brown central mark.
Diurnal, flying even on dull days (if
warm), May–Jun; mountains, moorlands.
Caterpillar feeds on bilberries. T, ex Ir,
Ic, De, but only nBr, nFi. [9]

Small Dark Yellow Underwing *Anarta
cordigera* NOCTUIDAE WS 22–25 mm.
Forewings dark grey with large, white
spot; hindwings orange-yellow, edged
with brown. Camouflaged at rest on
lichen-covered rocks. Diurnal in sunshine,
resting if overcast, May; mountains,
moorlands. Caterpillar feeds on alpine
bearberry, bilberries. T, ex Ir, Ic, but
only nBr. [10]

Haworth's Minor *Celaena haworthii*
NOCTUIDAE WS 25–29 mm. Hindwings
greyish. Nocturnal, Aug–Sep; moorlands,
wet areas. Caterpillar feeds on stems of
cottongrass, may burrow into roots. T,
ex Ic. [11]

Ashworth's Rustic *Xestia ashworthii*
NOCTUIDAE WS 35–40 mm. Squarish
wings, hindwings grey-brown. Nocturnal,
Jul–Aug; mountains, among rocks.
Caterpillar feeds on rock-roses. wBr, Fr,
Ge, Cz, Po. [12]

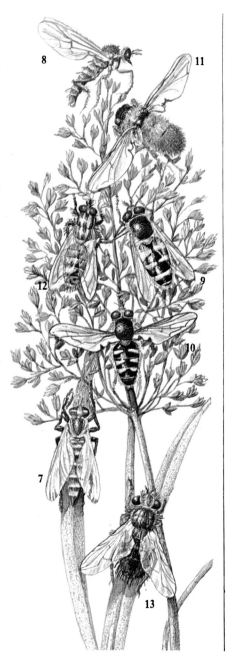

Flies (Diptera). Tiny to large, slender to stout, usually large-headed. 1 pair of transparent wings and small, knob-like halteres (balancers) in place of hindwings; mouthparts for sucking and often also for piercing. Metamorphosis complete. Larvae, or maggots, legless.

daddy-long-legs *Tipula alpinum*
TIPULIDAE BL 12–17 mm, WS *c*30 mm.
Brown line near apex of transparent wings; ♀ with orange-brown tip to abdomen. Summer; moorlands, mountains. Larva ('leatherjacket') in soil. WE, CE. [♀ 1]

Snowfly *Chinonea araneoides* TIPULIDAE
BL 4–5 mm. Wingless crane-fly. Summer; mountains above snow-line. Larva in rotting leaves or nests of wasps, small mammals. Fr, Ge, FS. [2]

winter gnat *Trichocera saltator*
TRICHOCERIDAE WS *c*16 mm. Winter gnats do not bite man, resemble small, slender crane-flies. All year; caves, gorges; swarms dance on sunny, winter days. Larva in decaying vegetation. T, ex Ic. [3]

biting midge *Culicoides obsoletus*
CERATOPOGONIDAE BL 2–3 mm. ♂ antennae plumed. ♀ bites man, esp at sunset, causing small, red spots on exposed skin. Swarms, summer; widespread, moorlands, mountains, forests. Larva in damp litter. Br, Ir, Fr, Ge, No. [♂ 4]

black flies, buffalo gnats *Simulium* spp
SIMULIIDAE BL 2 mm. Short, stout bodies, rather broad wings, thick legs; ♂ antennae feathery; ♀ with vicious bite. Active in sunshine, summer; northern moorlands, hills. Larvae 1·5 mm long, maggot-like; fan-like bristles at front; in running streams, attached to stones; sieve food out of water. Several similar spp. T. [♀ 5]

March-fly *Bibio reticulatus* BIBIONIDAE
BL 5–7 mm. Thick-bodied; short, broad wings, short antennae below eyes; tibiae with circlet of spines at apex. Swarms, spring; moorlands, heaths, rough grassland. Larva in humus. WE, CE. [6]

robber-fly *Epitriptus cingulatus* ASILIDAE
BL 11–12 mm. Hairy with bristly legs,
pale hairs at top of face and prominent
'beard'. Catches insects in flight. Diurnal,
Jun–Sep; widespread, including heaths,
moorlands. Larva in decaying vegetation.
T, ex Ic. [7]

dance-fly *Rhamphomyia sulcata*
EMPIDIDAE BL 6–8 mm. Head almost
spherical, thorax humped; grey, bristly.
Preys on other flies. Early spring;
moorlands. ♂s in erratic dances over water.
Larva in decaying wood. WE, CE. [8]

Hoverflies (Syrphidae): generally bright-
coloured, often mimicking wasps and
bees; eyes large. Hover continually on
rapidly beating wings.

hoverfly *Sericomyia silentis* SYRPHIDAE
WS 19–28 mm. But for large eyes, rather
wasp-like. Hovers freely. May–Sep;
moorlands, wetter parts of heaths, also
lowlands. Larva, 'rat-tailed maggot', with
breathing tube, in decaying peat bogs,
stagnant pools. T, ex Ic. [9] *S. lappona*,
widespread, Apr–Aug. T, ex Ic. [10]

Reindeer Warble-fly *Oedmagena tarandi*
OESTRIDAE BL 13–25 mm. Stout; abdomen
hairy, yellow-brown. Buzzes in flight.
Summer; tundra, mountains, open forest.
♀ lays eggs on reindeer. Larva burrows
under skin, producing large swelling
(warble); when fully grown, breaks out,
pupates in soil. FS. [11] (Related warble-
flies parasitize cattle, sheep.)

flesh-fly *Brachicoma devia* CALLIPHORIDAE
BL 6–8 mm. Eyes bright red; antennae
with short, downy outgrowth. 2
generations, Apr–Sep, 2nd overwintering;
heathlands. ♀ keeps egg in body until it
hatches, deposits larva in bumblebee nest.
T, ex Ic. [12] (Many other spp, mostly
carrion-feeders).

tachinid fly *Gonia picea* TACHINIDAE
BL 8–12 mm, WS *c*20 mm. Bristly, reddish;
thorax black. Flies low, Mar–Apr;
heathlands. Eggs scattered by ♀ in flight.
Larva parasitic inside caterpillar. WE. [13]

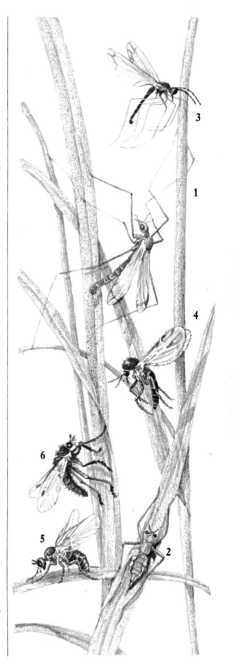

Bees, wasps, ants, ichneumons, sawflies (Hymenoptera). Usually 2 pairs of wings, with stigma, but many wingless; some have stings; mouthparts for biting (wasps, ants, ichneumons, sawflies) or sucking (bees). Except sawflies, all have narrow 'wasp-waists' (sub-order Apocrita); sawflies are 'waistless' and ♀s also have saw-like ovipositors (sub-order Symphyta). Metamorphosis complete. Larvae usually legless maggots, but those of sawflies have legs.

Girdled Colletes, Plasterer Bee *Colletes succincta* COLLETIDAE BL 8–10 mm. Head and thorax brown, hairy; ♀ abdomen shiny, each segment fringed with whitish hairs; ♂ abdomen dull, 1st segment with pale brown hairs. Feeds at flowers of heather, Jul–Aug; sandy heaths, moorlands. Solitary; nest tunnel in ground, 20–25 cm long, coated with sticky material which sets: cells filled with honey and pollen, 1 egg in each. WE, CE, Sw. [1]

White-zoned Mining-bee *Lasioglossum leucozonium* HALICTIDAE BL 7–9 mm. Black, 3 bands of whitish hairs on abdomen; ♂ slimmer, with white facial hairs. Spring–autumn; heaths. Nest at end of tunnel, often several in close proximity forming small colonies. ♀ overwinters in tunnel to start new nest. WE, CE. [2]

Grey-haired Mining-bee *Andrena cineraria* ANDRENIDAE BL 13–15 mm. Head, thorax, base of abdomen blue-black with whitish-grey hairs; ♂ with white hairs on face; brush on hindlegs to collect pollen. If handled, emits smell reminiscent of burnt sugar. Feeds at flowers of heather, spring; heathlands. Nest sloping tunnel in ground, esp sandy soil of banks, path edges, 10–30 cm long, with branches to chambers where eggs laid on stored pollen. WE, CE. [3]

homeless-bee *Nomada lathburiana* ANDRENIDAE BL 9–13 mm. Brightly coloured, wasp-like, not hairy; no pollen-collecting brush on hindlegs. Heathlands. Makes no nest; instead ♀ waits by nest of grey-haired mining-bee, lays eggs in its cells. WE, CE. [4]

Bilberry Bumblebee or **Humblebee** *Bombus lapponicus* BOMBICIDAE BL 12–18 mm, ♂ smaller than ♀. Thorax and abdomen both very round, black with yellow band at front of thorax and red 'tail'; pale yellow hairs on top of head; venation clear on transparent wings. Feeds at flowers, esp bilberries, summer; mountains, moorlands. Nests socially in hole in ground, often under stone; larvae feed on pollen in cells; ♀s hatch first in spring. NE, WE, but ?Ir. [5]

Heath Bumblebee or **Humblebee** *Bombus jonellus* BOMBICIDAE BL 12–16 mm, ♂ smaller than ♀. Mostly black, but thorax with yellow bands at front and rear, abdomen with 1st segment yellow and 'tail' white; fringe of pollen-basket reddish; faces of ♀ and ♀ black, but of ♂ yellow. Feeds at flowers of heathers, bilberries, spring; heaths, moorlands. Nest colonies vary in size; larvae develop on pollen in cells. T. [6]

Red-banded Sand-wasp *Ammophila sabulosa* SPHECIDAE BL 20–23 mm. Elongated, with very long, narrow waist, club-like abdomen, long legs; all black except red waist and front of abdomen. May–Sep; mountains, heaths, dry areas. Solitary; ♀ stings and immobilizes caterpillar, carries it to excavated burrow in sandy soil, lays egg on it; larva then feeds on paralysed but living caterpillar. T, ex Ic. [7] Heath Sand-wasp *A. pubescens* similar. T, ex Ic, No. [8]

Heath Potter-wasp *Eumenes coarctata* VESPIDAE BL 11–14 mm. Thorax rounded, abdomen with narrower front-section; shiny black with yellow markings, including yellow bands on rear and 2 half-bands on front of mainly black abdomen, yellow tibiae. May–Sep; heaths, moorlands, often with scattered pines. Solitary; ♀ builds thin-walled, flask-like, 'clay' nest about 15 mm long, using sand cemented with saliva, attached to plant (*eg* heather), pine needles, wood or wall; method of providing paralysed caterpillar as food for larva same as *A. sabulosa*. T, ex Ic. [9]

sawfly *Pontania crassipes* TENTHREDINIDAE BL 3–4·5 mm. Antennae ⅔ length of forewings; wings translucent with yellow or whitish-yellow stigma; thorax dark, abdomen black. Summer; moorlands, mountains. Larva in pea-shaped gall on leaf, usually near midrib, of willow. Br, NE. [**1**]

sawfly *Pontania dolichura* TENTHREDINIDAE BL 2·5–4·5 mm. Shape similar to *P. crassipes*; abdomen also black, but stigma on forewings mostly white. Jun–Jul; mountains, usually over 350 m. Larvae in paired, sausage-shaped galls on each side of midrib of willow leaves. Br, Ir, CE, NE. [**2**]

Pine Sawfly *Diprion pini* DIPRIONIDAE BL 7–10 mm, ♂ smaller than ♀. Antennae: ♂ feathery, ♀ slightly toothed; stigma on forewings yellow-brown with large, open cell beneath; ♂ black, ♀ yellow-brown and black. Rather slow flight. May–Jul, often swarming in autumn; among pines. Larva caterpillar-like, with 8 pairs of abdominal legs; when disturbed, sits up in S-shaped defensive posture, moves body actively; feeds on pine needles, often in vast numbers, and spins brown cocoon on them. T, ex Ic. [♀ **3**]

sawfly *Pristophora mollis* TENTHREDINIDAE BL 6–7·5 mm. Underside of thorax with sculptured surface, head with keel round front area; black or brown. May–Jul; mountains, moorlands. Larva caterpillar-like; feeds on bilberries. T, ex Ic. [**4**] (Many other mountain spp broadly similar.)

sawfly *Amauronematus abnormis* TENTHREDINIDAE BL 5–6 mm. Wings shorter than abdomen; body surface dull, sculptured; black, with yellow head and mesonotum. Apr–Jul; mountains. Larva undescribed, possibly on dwarf willow. nBr, NE. [**5**]

ichneumon fly *Ophion undulatus* ICHNEUMONIDAE BL 11–14 mm, ♀ with long ovipositor. Long body with long slender waist; red-brown. Moorlands, heaths. Egg laid in moth caterpillar, esp oak eggar; larva develops inside caterpillar, eventually killing it. T, ex Ic, Fi [♀ **6**]

Persuasive Burglar *Rhyssa persuasoria* ICHNEUMONIDAE BL ♂ 20 mm, ♀ 30 mm + ovipositor 40 mm. Antennae as long as forewings; body blue-black with white spots. Summer; pinewoods. Name from not being kept out by thick walls: ♀ drills thin ovipositor through pine trunk to lay egg by larva of wood-wasp; parasitic larva then develops inside wood-wasp larva. T, ex Ic. [♀ **7**]

Red Ant, Wood Ant *Formica rufa* FORMICIDAE BL ♂ ♀ 9–10 mm, ☿ 5–7 mm. ♂ and ♀ winged, ☿ wingless; ♂ abdomen pointed, ♀ oval, ☿ rounded; ♂ black, ♀ black with red middle of body and 1st abdominal segment, ☿ reddish with mostly black abdomen. Bites fiercely, squirts formic acid; wide range of foods include other insects, larvae, worms. Mating flight May–Jun; various dry habitats, but esp among pines. Strongly social. Large nest <1·5 m high, 3 m across, built of pine needles; in sites other than pinewoods, often less conspicuous. T, ex Ic. [☿ **8**]

Negro Ant *Formica fusca* FORMICIDAE BL 5–7 mm, ☿ smaller than ♂ ♀. ♂ and ♀ winged, ☿ wingless; brown-black with reddish legs. Predatory, but also feeds on honeydew. Heathlands, in shady, damper areas. Colonies on ground. WE, CE. [☿ **9**]

ant *Myrmica scabrinodis* FORMICIDAE BL 3·5–6·5 mm, ☿ smaller than ♂ ♀. ♂ and ♀ winged, ☿ wingless; light reddish-yellow to dark red, with dark brown head and middle of body. Heathlands. Nest in ground; host of caterpillar of large blue butterfly. T, ex Ic. [☿ **10**]

Beetles (Coleoptera). Mostly compact, with tough skins, varied antennae, biting mouth parts, usually strong legs, no cerci; forewings hardened to form non-overlapping, horny elytra which protect folded hindwings and abdomen. Many fly readily; others flightless. Metamorphosis complete. Larvae varied.

Green Tiger-beetle *Cicindela campestris* CICINDELIDAE BL 11–15 mm. Prominent eyes; large jaws overlap at rest. Preys on insects. Active in sunshine, spring; sandy heaths, moorlands. Larva with large, powerful jaws; lives in burrow 15–30 cm long, seizes insect prey as it passes. T, ex Ic. [1]

Wood Tiger-beetle *Cicindela sylvatica* CICINDELIDAE BL 15–19 mm. Preys on other insects. Active in summer; sandy heaths, moors, forest edges. Larva predatory like *C. campestris*. T, ex Ic. [2]

Violet Ground-beetle *Carabus violaceus* CARABIDAE BL 22–26 mm. Nocturnal, hunting on foot. Feeds on other insects, including heather leaf-beetles, also earthworms. Jun–Aug; widespread, heaths, moorlands. Larva elongate, with 2 cerci; also predatory. T, ex Ic. [3]

ground-beetle *Carabus glabratus* CARABIDAE BL 22–30 mm. Broad pronotum, smooth elytra often tinged steely blue. Runs freely, preys on insects. Summer; drier mountains. Larva also predatory. T, ex Ic. [4]

ground-beetle *Miscodera arctica* CARABIDAE BL 6–8 mm. Thorax wider than long, short in proportion to elytra. Preys on other insects. Active in summer; high moors, mountains. Larva in drier places, predatory. T, ex Ic. [5]

ground-beetle *Pterostichus adstrictus* CARABIDAE BL 9–11 mm. Stout, pronotum slightly narrower than parallel-sided elytra. Esp active in sunshine, summer; mountains, moorlands. Larva preys on other insects. T, ex De, ?Ne. [6]

rove-beetle *Stenus geniculatus*
STAPHYLINIDAE BL 4–5 mm. Eyes large,
protuberant; elytra parallel-sided, short,
exposing abdomen. Runs very fast.
Summer; widespread, including moorlands, but in dry places. Larva straight-
bodied, slender, cerci at tip of abdomen;
lives in moss. T, ex Ic. [7]

dung-beetle *Aphodius lapponum*
SCARABAEIDAE BL 5·5–7 mm. Elytra
parallel-sided. Scavenger. Mar–Jul;
moorlands, rough grassland. Larva in
sheep dung. nBr, Ic, CE, FS. [8]

Minotaur Beetle *Typhaeus typhoeus*
SCARABAEIDAE BL 11–20 mm. Elytra
grooved; thick, spiky legs; 2 horns (♂
long, ♀ much shorter). Summer; sandy
heaths, moorlands. Buries rolls of dung,
esp of rabbit or sheep, laying egg in each
roll. Larva in dung. sBr, Ir, Fr, Ge, rare
Sw. [♂ 9]

Bee Chafer *Trichius fasciatus*
SCARABAEIDAE BL 10–30 mm. Body
covered with yellow-brown hair. Aug–
Sep; moorlands, mountains, often on
flowers of thyme. Larva in rotting wood.
T, ex sBr, Ic, De, ?Ne. [10]

click-beetle *Ampedus balteatus* ELATERIDAE
BL 7–9 mm. Legs short, thin. If falls on
back, bends body backwards and springs
up with audible click. Summer; rotting
wood in conifers. Larva, or 'wireworm',
elongate, slender, orange-brown; feeds
on rotting wood and leaf litter. T, ex Ic.
[11]

Glow-worm *Lampyris noctiluca*
LAMPYRIDAE BL ♂ 10–13 mm, ♀ 10–18
mm. Front of thorax semicircular,
covering head, with transparent spot over
eyes; ♀ wingless, more pointed, woodlouse-
like, with 3 segments on underside
strongly luminous. ♀ glows to attract ♂
(egg, pupa and ♂ also all glow slightly).
Nocturnal, hiding by day, summer;
grassy areas, heaths. Adult and larva suck
liquid from paralysed slugs, snails. T, ex
Ic. [♂ 12] [♀ 13]

Oil-beetle *Meloe proscarabaeus* MELOIDAE
BL 10–32 mm, ♂ much smaller than ♀
swollen with eggs. Head sharply
constricted behind eyes; thorax sculptured
with coarse marks; elytra very short,
exposing abdomen; all bluish-black or
metallic purple; overlapping. Exudes evil
smelling fluid from joints. Summer;
widely distributed. ♀ lays thousands of
eggs in cracks in ground, often near bee
nest. On hatching, larva tries to catch
hold of bee; if carried into nest, it feeds
on eggs, larvae, honey. T, ex Ic, No.
[♂ 1]

Bluish Oil-beetle *Meloe violaceus*
MELOIDAE BL 14–36 mm, ♂ much smaller
than ♀ swollen with eggs. Similar to *M.
proscarabaeus*, but more violet-blue, with
finer marks on thorax. Summer;
widespread, including grassy banks with
heathers. Life history as *M. proscarabeaus.*
T, ex Ic. [♂ 2]

ladybird *Coccinella hieroglyphica*
COCCINELLIDAE BL 3–4·5 mm. Typical,
round, ladybird shape, head partly hidden.
Variable, yellow or reddish with black
markings; legs black. Summer; heaths,
moorlands, esp near conifers. Larva
elongate, active; preys on aphids, other
small insects. T, ex Ic. [3]

Pine Longhorn-beetle *Asemum striatum*
CERAMBYCIDAE BL 10–18 mm. Antennae
long, head narrower than thorax, elytra
each with 6 longitudinal ridges, dull black,
with downy covering. Summer; coniferous
woods at all altitudes. Larva fleshy,
elongate, with front of thorax broad;
protuberances over body help movement
in tunnels; bores in conifers. T, ex Ic.
[4]

leaf-beetle *Chrysolina cerealis*
CHRYSOMELIDAE BL 6–9 mm. Ovoid,
convex; body with metallic lustre,
longitudinal stripes of coppery-red and
green on elytra. Summer; moorlands,
mountains. Adult, larva feed on thyme.
T, ex Ic, Sw, No, but rare Br, De, Ge,
Fi. [5]

Heather Leaf-beetle *Lochmaea suturalis*
CHRYSOMELIDAE BL 6–7 mm. Dark brown
or black-brown, with yellowish elytra.
Jul–Aug; moorlands, heaths; feeds on
heathers, larva on young shoots; may kill
plants. T, ex Ic. [6]

reed-beetle *Plateumaris discolor*
CHRYSOMELIDAE BL 10 mm. Generally
black with coppery or metallic-green
elytra; red near tips of antennae. May–
Jun; wet moors, in *Sphagnum* moss.
Larva in root of cottongrass. T, ex Ic. [7]

Large Pine-weevil *Hylobius abietis*
CURCULIONIDAE BL 9–13 mm. Long
rostrum with elbowed antennae; dull
black, with patches of yellow or reddish
on elytra, reddish legs. May–Jun; conifer
woods, esp pines, eating bark on young
shoots and buds. Larva feeds in decaying,
fallen pines. T, ex Ic, De. [8]

weevil *Micrelus ericae* CURCULIONIDAE
BL 1–2·5 mm. Long, orange-brown
rostrum with elbowed antennae; body
greenish-black, white underside, orange-
brown legs. Aug–Sep; moorlands,
mountains. Adult and larva mine in
heather stems. T, ex Ic. [9]

weevil *Strophosomus sus* CURCULIONIDAE
BL 4·5–6 mm. Head square, elytra pitted;
shiny black. Apr–Sep; drier moorlands.
Adult and larva mine in heather stems.
T, ex Ic. [10]

weevil *Otiorhynchus arcticus* CURCULIONIDAE
BL 5–7 mm. Short rostrum, elbowed
antennae with 1st segment long; all black.
Mainly nocturnal, summer; mountains.
Larva lives in grasses, roots. Br, Ir, Ic,
Fi, Sw. [11]

Spruce Bark-beetle *Ips typographus*
SCOLYTIDAE BL 4–6 mm. Head not visible
from above; squat, parallel-sided;
posterior of elytra has scoop-like area
with 3 small teeth on either side; brown,
covered with yellowish down. Summer;
coniferous woods. ♀ burrows under bark
to lay eggs in central tunnel, larvae excavate
'fish skeleton' side-galleries. T. [12]

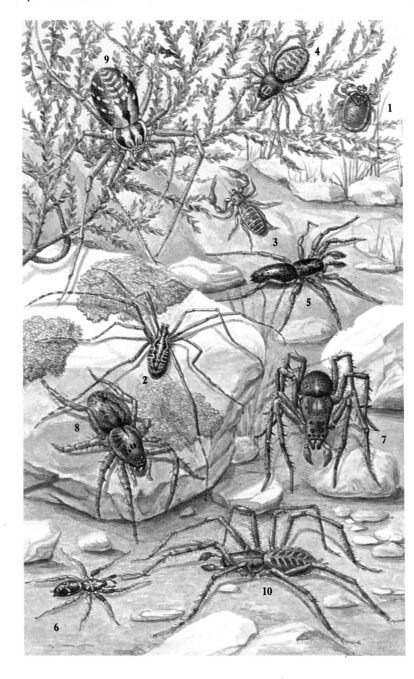

Castor Bean or **Sheep Tick** *Ixodes ricinus* IXODIDAE L ♂ 2 mm, unfed ♀ 3–4 mm, fully fed ♀ 11 mm. Dark red-brown, with tough, leathery skin. Important parasite of sheep, cattle, also other mammals, birds; transmits several diseases. Lays thousands of eggs. Each stage (6-legged larva, 8-legged nymph, adult) feeds on blood for few days, then rests to digest. T. [1]

harvestman *Mitopus morio* PHALANGIIDAE L 4–8 mm. ♂ blackish, with transverse rows of whitish abdominal tubercles; ♀ creamy-yellow, with dark brown or black, notched band on back. Aug–Oct; sea-level to mountains. Scavenger. Red mites *Leptus* sometimes attached to legs. T. [2]

false scorpion *Neobisium muscorum* NEOBISIIDAE L 3 mm. Small, reddish, with 4 eyes; pair large 'pinchers'. Open areas or woods, sea-level to mountains, in litter, moss, under stones. T, ex Ic. [3]

spider *Dictyna arundinacea* DICTYNIDAE L 3 mm. Carapace dark brown; abdomen yellowish-white, with deep brown or greyish markings at middle and sides. May–Jun; widespread, often abundant in gorse, heather. Builds meshed web around and enclosing tops of twigs, stems. Sexes often together. T, ex Ic. [4]

spider *Zelotes apricorum* GNAPHOSIDAE L 5–9 mm. Glossy black. Apr–Jun; widespread in open areas, including moors, mountains, in heather, grass, under stones. Moves quickly when disturbed. Builds no snare, but hunts insects on ground. T, ex Ic, Fi, Sw. [5] (Several similar spp.)

ant-mimic *Micaria pulicaria* GNAPHOSIDAE L 2–4 mm. Brownish-black spider, with red-green iridescent hairs, white abdominal markings. Active in sunshine, May–Aug; ubiquitous. Associates with ants; runs with 1st pair of legs like antennae. Builds no snare, but hunts insects on ground. T, ex Ic. [6]

wolf-spider *Pardosa trailli* LYCOSIDAE L 6–8 mm. Very dark brown; patterns obscure. On mountain screes. Moves quickly; hides under stones. Builds no snare, but hunts prey on ground in bright sunshine. ♀ carries cocoon held by spinnerets: habit characteristic of wolf-spiders. Br. [7]

wolf-spider *Trochosa terricola* LYCOSIDAE L 7–14 mm. More robust, with shorter legs, and less active than other Lycosidae; red-brown body fairly distinctive. All year; open, dry heaths, in mat-grass and limestone grassland, also coniferous woodland. Ground-living; prowls at night for insects. T, ex Ic. [8] (Several similar spp.)

crab-spider *Philodromus histrio* THOMISIDAE L 6–8 mm. Handsome dark red-brown with yellow-white markings, easily overlooked as coloration matches heather. Apr–Jun; heaths, dry moorland. Builds no web, but grabs prey within reach. Often on large cocoon, also effectively camouflaged in heather. T, ex Ir, Ic. [9]

labyrinth-spider *Agelena labyrinthica* AGELENIDAE L 8–12 mm. Carapace dark brown with darker markings; abdomen dark greyish, with pale band in middle, light angular stripes, long spinnerets. Jun–Aug; heaths, rough ground, in gorse, long grass. Spins large sheet-web with tubular retreat; egg sac enclosed in chamber full of passages (labyrinths), which house ♀ until she dies. T, ex Ic. [10]

spider *Textrix denticulata* AGELENIDAE
L 6–7 mm. Looks like a wolf-spider, but long spinnerets distinctive; carapace dark brown, with light band in middle; abdomen light yellow or red-brown, with notched band enclosing reddish stripe. Most of year; widespread, often abundant in lowlands, including heaths. Moves quickly when disturbed. Builds small sheet-web under loose stones, esp on stone walls. T, ex Ic, Fi. [1]

spider *Coelotes atropos* AGELENIDAE
L ♂ 7–9 mm, ♀ 9–12 mm. Carapace dark brown, blackish at front; abdomen brown, with blackish markings, including central black stripe and oblique bars. May–Jul; locally abundant, esp on mountains, under stones in damp situations. Builds rather matted web, with retreat hole and small sheet at lower edge. Young remain in nest until following spring. T, ex Ir, Ic, Fi, No. [2]

spider *Episinus truncatus* THERIDIIDAE
L 3–4 mm. Carapace yellowish, with dark brown markings; leaf-like abdominal pattern variable in colour. May–Aug; heaths, grassland, on low vegetation. Builds simple, H-shaped web of irregular threads. T, ex Ic. [3] (*E. angulatus* similar, but less distinctive pattern. T, ex Ic, Lu, Be, No.)

spider *Nesticus cellulanus* NESTICIDAE
L 3–6 mm. Pale, with long, slender legs. Most of year; only in damp, dark places, in drains, caves, esp under stones deep in rock screes. Builds web of criss-cross threads with sticky droplets that trap crawling insects. Egg sac large, spherical, held by spinnerets. T, ex Ic. [4]

spider *Meta merianae* TETRAGNATHIDAE
L 4–10 mm. Carapace light brown, with black margins and central band; abdomen rather variably black, dark brown and white with obscure, leaf-like

pattern; 2 yellow spots on underside distinctive. Most of year; usually in dark, damp places, esp culverts, sides of overhanging banks. Builds orb-web, but no retreat: signal thread leads from web to spider. [var *celata* 5]

spider *Araneus cornutus* ARANEIDAE
L 5–8 mm. Colour variable, esp ♂, but carapace light brown with indistinct markings; abdomen cream or pinkish with brown or sepia, leaf-like pattern. Probably all year; widespread in both uplands, lowlands. Builds orb-web on plants near water; lives in silken retreat connected to web by signal thread, ♂ sometimes with ♀. T. [6]

spider *Araneus quadratus* ARANEIDAE
L ♂ 6–8 mm, ♀ 9–15 mm. Carapace with broad central band; abdomen large, rounded, fairly distinctive; colour variable, but often rust-red with cream spots, brownish leaf-like pattern. Aug–Sep; heaths, rough grassland. Builds orb-web in heather, gorse. ♀ esp large when full of eggs. T, ex Ic. [7] (*A. diadematus* similar, in same habitats, but distinguished by more angular abdominal shoulders. T.)

money-spider *Drapetisca socialis*
LINYPHIIDAE L 3–4 mm. Mottled grey, very variable; melanic forms frequent near industrial areas. Jul–Nov; on tree trunks, branches, esp conifers, birches, beech. Builds network of very fine threads on bark, which traps crawling insects. T, ex Ic. [8]

money-spider *Walckenaera acuminata*
LINYPHIIDAE L 3 mm. One of many small, black spp, most of which can be identified only through microscope. ♂s sometimes have odd-shaped heads: *W. acuminata* is extreme example, with all 8 eyes on long, slender turret. All year; open areas, woodland, including heaths, conifers. T, ex Ic. [9]

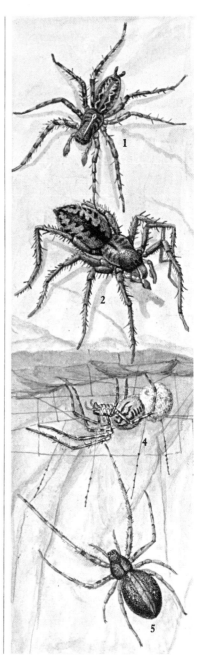

Midwife Toad *Alytes obstetricans*
DISCOGLOSSIDAE L <5·5 cm. Small, with
warty skin. Pupil of eye vertical slit. Loud,
monosyllabic, bell-like whistle, regularly
repeated. Damp places, <c2100 m.
Breeds Apr–Aug, esp May; mates on land,
after which ♂ looks after eggs wrapped
round hindlegs; tadpoles live in ponds.
Food worms, insect larvae. Fr, Lu, Be,
swGe, (rare sBr). [1]

Alpine Salamander *Salamandra atra*
SALAMANDRIDAE L 11·5 cm (av) <16·5 cm.
Slender body, flattened head, vertical
grooves on flanks. Active at night; damp,
cool places under rocks and in thick
vegetation, 580–1800 m. Breeds Jul–Aug;
young born alive on land. Food worms,
slugs, insects. seFr, sGe, Cz. [2]

Alpine Newt *Triturus alpestris*
SALAMANDRIDAE L ♂ 9 cm, ♀ 10 cm
<12 cm. ♂ has low, black and white
crest, more spots than ♀. In spring in
ponds, mostly in hilly country; rest of
year on land, hiding by day, wandering
by night. Enters water after spring thaw,
mates Mar–May. Food small crustaceans,
insects and larvae, worms, slugs. Exudes
distasteful secretion when handled. eFr,
Lu, Be, Ne, Ge, Cz, Po. [♂ 3]

Palmate Newt *Triturus helveticus*
SALAMANDRIDAE L 8 cm (av), ♀ <10 cm.
Olive-green or brown above; pale yellow
below, lightly spotted; ♂ has slight crest,
5 mm filament at tail-tip, webbed hind
feet. Ponds, edges of lakes, on acid soils.
Breeds Feb–May, depending on area;
courting ♂ vibrates tail rapidly; eggs
wrapped in leaves. Food invertebrates.
Br, Fr, Lu, Be, Ne, wGe. [4]

Sand Lizard *Lacerta agilis* LACERTIDAE
L <24 cm. Back pale brown or grey, with
3 rows of black spots, central row white-
bordered; underparts creamy-white;
flanks and underparts of breeding ♂
greenish. Dry open country, esp sandy
heathland, dunes. Hibernates autumn–
spring; often colonial. Mates May–Jun,
much aggression between ♂s; eggs laid
Jun–Jul. Food small invertebrates. T, ex
Ir, Ic, but rare Br. [non-breeding ♂ 5]

Viviparous or **Common Lizard** *Lacerta
vivipara* LACERTIDAE L 11 cm (av) <18
cm. Grey-brown above; ♂ reddish below,
♀ grey or creamy; usually central stripe
along back. Climbs and swims well.
Heaths, banks, woodlands, old walls.
Hibernates autumn–spring. Mates Apr–
May, much aggression among ♂s; young
born alive Jul–Aug. Food insects and
larvae, spiders, other invertebrates. T, ex
Ic, nFS. [♂ 6]

Slow-worm *Anguis fragilis* ANGUIDAE
L 40–52 cm. Shiny blue-grey to brown
with lateral dark lines; ♀ usually darker
below. Heaths, woods, hedgerows,
gardens, coastal districts; burrows in
ground, basks in sun. Hibernates
autumn–spring. Mates Apr–Jun, ♂s very
aggressive, ♂ and ♀ intertwine. Food
slugs, worms, spiders, insects and larvae.
Many vertebrate predators. T, ex Ir, Ic,
nFS. [7]

Smooth Snake *Coronella austriaca*
COLUBRIDAE L 50 cm (av) <74 cm. Back
brown, grey or reddish. Prefers light,
sandy soils with dense heather, in woodland
or open country, but mostly in hilly areas.
Hibernates Oct–Mar. Mates Mar–Apr;
young born Aug–Sep. Food lizards. T, ex
Ir, Ic, but rare Br, only in s. [8]

Adder, Viper *Vipera berus* VIPERIDAE
L ♂ 50 cm (av) <60 cm, ♀ 60 cm (av) <84
cm. Dense undergrowth on dry heaths,
moors, favouring sunny spots. Hibernates
autumn–spring. Mates Apr–May; ♂s
very aggressive, dance with head raised.
Food birds' eggs, nestlings, frogs, newts,
slugs, worms, insects. Venomous bite can
kill man. Eaten by some larger birds. T, ex
Ir, Ic, nFS. [♂ 9]

Asp Viper *Vipera aspis* VIPERIDAE L 46–
61 cm, ♂ <76 cm. Broad, almost
triangular head, thin neck, thick body;
colour variable, but grey, yellowish or
brown, pattern of dark cross bands along
flanks. Undergrowth on hills, mountains.
Hibernates Oct–Apr. Mates Apr–May.
Food mice, voles, nestlings, lizards.
Venomous bite rarely fatal to man. sFr,
sGe. [10]

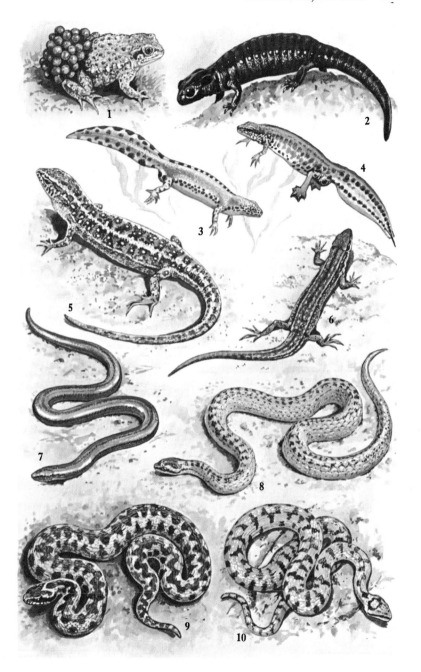

Red-throated Diver *Gavia stellata*
GAVIIDAE L 53–58 cm. Small head,
uptilted bill; stripes on hind neck, red
throat looks black at distance, plain back;
in winter, white face and underparts, grey
back speckled white. Wailing clamour
when nesting; guttural, quacking calls.
Moor/tundra lakes, pools, coastal lagoons;
winters mainly on sea. Nest scrape on
ground, or mound of rotting vegetation by
or in water, 2 eggs, May–Jul. Food fish,
molluscs, crustaceans, insect larvae.
Summer nBr, Ic, FS; winter T, ex Fi,
nSw. [summer **1**]

Black-throated Diver *Gavia arctica*
GAVIIDAE L 58–69 cm. Straight bill; grey
head and hind neck, black throat edged
with stripes, black-brown back with
squarish white spots in 2 patches; in
winter, greyish crown and hind neck with
blacker forehead, blackish back ('scaly' in
imm), white underparts. Wailing clamour
when nesting; barking calls. Moor/tundra
lakes, often with islands; winters mainly
on sea. Nest scrape variably lined with
rotting vegetation, 2 eggs, Apr–Jul. Food

fish, crustaceans, worms, molluscs.
Summer nBr, FS; winter T, ex Ir, Ic, Fi,
nSw. [summer **2**]

Great Northern Diver *Gavia immer*
GAVIIDAE L 68–81 cm. Large head, heavy
bill; green-black head and neck with 2
striped collars, black back chequered
white; in winter, blackish crown, white
cheeks and underparts, grey-brown back.
Wailing clamour when breeding; barking
calls. Mountain and forest lakes, often
with islands; winters mainly on sea. Nest
like black-throated, 2 eggs, May–Jul.
Food fish, crustaceans, worms, molluscs.
Summer Ic; winter Br, Ir, Ic, Fr, Be, Ne,
wGe, De, No. [summer **3**]

Slavonian Grebe *Podiceps auritus*
PODICIPEDIDAE L 31–35 cm. Largest of 3
smaller grebes, straight bill, longish neck;
glossy black head, broad golden stripes
extending into 'horns', chestnut neck and
flanks; in winter, dark above and white
below with flattened blackish crown to
eye-level. Rippling trill when nesting.
Northern ponds, lakes, quiet rivers;

winters mainly on sea. Nest of floating
vegetation, 4–5 eggs, May–Jul. Food insect
larvae, fish, crustaceans, molluscs.
Summer nBr, Ic, FS; winter Br, Ir, Fr,
Be, Ne, De, Ge, Po, sSC. [summer **4**]

Golden Eagle *Aquila chrysaetos*
ACCIPITRIDAE L 75–90 cm, ♂ smaller than
♀. In flight, projecting head, broad wings
with spread upcurved primaries, large
squarish tail; dark brown with yellowish
tinge on head; imm with white in wings,
white base to tail. Yelping, whistling,
barking notes near nest. Mountains, rocky
moors, forested plains. Bulky nest of
sticks, heather, bracken, on ledge or tree,
esp pine, 2 eggs, Mar–Jun. Food
mammals and birds, to size of deer and
herons, also carrion. nBr, ePo, nFS.
[adult **5**]

Gyrfalcon *Falco rusticolus* FALCONIDAE
L 50–56 cm, ♂ smaller than ♀. In flight,
broad wing-bases and blunt tips; 3 colour
forms: (1) dark grey with lighter blotches
and bars, whitish below with black streaks,
barred flanks; (2) paler with black-
streaked, whitish head; (3) white with
some black markings, dark primaries;
imm browner, more heavily marked.
Generally silent. Mountains, rocky moors,
edges of coniferous forests, coasts. Nest
scrape on rocky ledge or in old tree nest
of other large bird, 3–4 eggs, Apr–Jun.
Food birds; also lemmings, other
mammals. Ic, nFS, winter sFS. [dark
♂ **6**]

Peregrine *Falco peregrinus* FALCONIDAE
L 38–48 cm, ♂ much smaller than ♀.
Rather short and tapered tail, long pointed
wings, dashing flight with shallow beats,
long glides; black crown, sides of head
and moustache, slate-grey back, buff-
white underparts barred black, streaked
on upper breast; imm much browner,
streaked below. Chatters near nest.
Mountains, rocky moors, tundra, coastal
cliffs, coniferous forests. Nest scrape on
rocky ledge, in old cliff or tree nest of
other large bird, on ground on tundra
hummock, 3–4 eggs, Mar–Jul. Food birds;
also mammals, amphibians. T, ex Ic, Ne,
rare in south, only summer nFS. [♂ **7**]

Goshawk *Accipiter gentilis* ACCIPITRIDAE
L 48–61 cm, ♂ much smaller than ♀.
Like huge sparrowhawk, with rounded
wings, long tail; dark brown above, with
whitish line over eye, banded tail; whitish
below, closely barred dark brown, with
conspicuous white undertail-coverts; imm
redder-brown above, buff below with bold,
dark brown, drop-like streaks. Generally
silent, but buzzard-like cry and harsh,
chattering alarm when breeding. Conifer
forests, also broadleaved and mixed woods,
esp near open ground. Rather flat-topped
nest of sticks, lined with green leaves,
in tree, esp pine or beech, 2–3 eggs, Apr–
Jun. Food mainly mammals and birds to
size of hares, grouse, ducks, owls. T, ex Ir,
Ic, but rare Br. [♀ 1]

Sparrowhawk *Accipiter nisus*
ACCIPITRIDAE L 28–38 cm, ♂ smaller
than ♀. Short rounded wings, long tail,
flies with rapid beats interspersed with
glides; ♂ slate-grey above, with white
spot on nape, dark brown bands on tail,
whitish below finely barred with red-
orange, and pale rufous cheeks; ♀ dark
brown above, with whitish stripe over and
behind eye, whitish below closely barred
with warm brown; imm browner above,
whitish to buff below with bold, ragged
bars of brown and red-brown blotches,
more streaked on throat. Generally silent,
but many chattering, cackling and
whistling notes when breeding. Forest
edge or open country with scattered
woodland, chiefly coniferous or mixed.
Nest platform of twigs in tree, esp conifer,
oak, birch, 4–5 eggs, Apr–Jul. Food birds
to size of small ducks, partridges, woodpeckers; also small mammals, insects.
T, ex Ic, but only summer nFS. [♂ 2]

Hen Harrier *Circus cyaneus* ACCIPITRIDAE
L 43–51 cm, ♂ smaller than ♀. Slim, with
long, narrow, pointed wings, long tail; ♂
largely grey above with white rump,
white below with grey head, but wings

with black tips and blackish trailing edges;
♀ and imm dark brown, with owl-like
face, white rump, banded tail, blackish-
streaked underparts. Generally silent, but
chatters, squeals, when breeding. Moors,
heaths, marshes, crops. Ground nest of
heather, reeds, sedges, grasses, 4–6 eggs,
Apr–Jul. Food birds and mammals, esp
pipits, voles, to size of grouse, young
rabbits. nBr, Ir, Fr, Lu, Be, Ne, Ge, Cz,
Po, sSw, summer FS. [♂ 3] [♀ 4]

Montagu's Harrier *Circus pygargus*
ACCIPITRIDAE L 40–46 cm, ♂ smaller
than ♀. Even slimmer than hen harrier,
with narrower wings, more buoyant flight;
♂ largely grey above with grey rump,
white below with dark head and rusty
streaks on flanks, but wings with black
tips and black bar in middle; ♀ and imm
very similar to hen harrier, but less owl-
like face, dark crescent on cheeks, less
white on rump. Softer, higher-pitched
chattering notes near nest. Heaths, dry
moors, young conifer plantations, reed-
marshes, crops. Ground nest of grasses,
sedges, 4–5 eggs, May–Jul. Food
amphibians, reptiles, eggs, small birds,
mammals. Fr, Lu, Be, Ne, De, Ge, Cz,
Po, rare sBr, sSw. [♂ 5] [♀ 6]

Merlin *Falco columbarius* FALCONIDAE
L 26–33 cm, ♂ smaller than ♀. Small,
compact, with rather short, broad-based,
pointed wings, dashing flight; ♂ slate-
blue above with broad black tip to tail,
greyish-black wing-tips, reddish-buff nape
and underparts, latter streaked black; ♀
and imm dark brown above with barred
brown and creamy tail, whitish below with
red-brown streaks. Generally silent, but
chattering and other calls near nest.
Moors, hills, dunes. Nest scrape on
ground under heather, bracken or grass,
or in old crow nest in tree, 5–6 eggs,
May–Jul. Food mainly small birds, some
insects, small mammals. nwBr, Ir, Ic, FS;
winter T, ex Fi, nSw, No. [♂ 7] [♀ 8]

Red/Willow Grouse *Lagopus lagopus*
TETRAONIDAE L 36–41 cm, ♀ smaller than
♂. Red *L. l. scoticus*: ♂ red-brown, with
red eye-wattle, dark brown wings, black-
sided tail, becoming darker in winter; ♀
yellower-brown in summer, with broad
black barring. Willow *L. l. lagopus*:
summer ♂ red-brown above and on breast,
but with white wings and underparts;
summer ♀ yellow-brown barred with black,
less white below; in winter, both sexes all
white apart from black on tail (like ♀
ptarmigan). Crowing 'go-back, go-back';
flight call 'kowk-ok-ok-ok'. Tundra with
scrub, moors, peat-bogs. Nest scrape on
ground, sometimes lined grasses, heather,
6–11 eggs, Mar–Jul. Food shoots, buds,
flowers, berries, esp heathers, bilberries,
crowberry; also insects, earthworms, slugs.
nBr, Ir (red), FS (willow). [♂ red 1]
[♂ willow summer 2]

Ptarmigan *Lagopus mutus* TETRAONIDAE

L 33–36 cm. Summer ♂ mottled black-
brown above and on breast, with red eye-
wattle, black-sided tail, white wings and
underparts, the dark areas becoming grey
barred with black in autumn; summer ♀
tawny with less white below, browner in
autumn; in winter, both sexes all white
apart from black on tail and, ♂ only,
black from bill to eye. Clock-winding
sound when disturbed, also hoarse croak
and belching 'song'. Mountains, tundra.
Nest scrape on ground, scantily lined
grasses, 5–9 eggs, May–Aug. Food shoots,
leaves, berries, esp bilberries, crowberry,
heathers; also insects. nBr, Ic, nFS.
[♂ summer 3] [♀ summer 4] [♂ winter 5]

Hazel Grouse *Bonasa bonasia*
TETRAONIDAE L 34–37 cm. Slight crest,
longish tail; upperparts greyish in north,
red-brown farther south, barred and
spotted black and brown, with white lines
at sides of throat and across shoulders;

grey tail with black band at end; underparts whitish, marked with brown; ♂ also
white-bordered, black throat. High,
whistling calls. Coniferous or mixed
forests with shrub layer. Nest scrape on
ground, lined grasses, 6–10 eggs, May–Jul.
Food shoots, leaves, esp birches. eFr, Lu,
Be, Ge, Cz, Po, sFS. [♂ **6**] [♀ **7**]

Black Grouse *Tetrao tetrix* TETRAONIDAE
L ♂ 50–56 cm, ♀ 40–43 cm. ♂ blue-
black with red eye-wattle, lyre-shaped
tail, white wing-bar and undertail-
coverts; ♀ brown, barred black, with
white wing-bar and rather long, forked
tail. ♂ at lek (display ground) has
bubbling, dove-like song, other barking
and sneezing notes. Edges of moors,
forest clearings, heaths, rushy pastures,
usually with scattered trees. Nest almost
bare scrape on ground in thick vegetation,
6–10 eggs, May–Aug. Food shoots, buds,
leaves, berries, esp birches, larches, pines,
bilberries, heathers. T, ex sBr, Ir, Ic,
wFr. [♂ **8**] [♀ **9**]

Capercaillie *Tetrao urogallus*
TETRAONIDAE L ♂ 84–89 cm, ♀ 58–64 cm.
♂ huge, bearded, turkey-like, with long
tail fanned in display, mainly slate-grey
with whitish belly, red eye-wattle, brown
wings, white shoulder-patch, glossy green
breast; ♀ mottled and barred orange-buff,
black and whitish, with orange-chestnut
breast, long rounded tail. ♂ song
accelerates to climax like pulling of cork
and pouring of liquid; other calls include
retching sound and, of ♀, pheasant-like
'kok-kok'. Coniferous forests with good
undergrowth, esp on hills. Nest scrape
scantily lined plants, often between tree
roots, sometimes in heather, 5–8 eggs,
May–Jul. Staple food shoots and buds of
conifers; but other plants, some insects, in
summer. nBr, eFr, Ge, Cz, Po, FS.
[♂ **10**] [♀ **11**]

Crane *Grus grus* GRUIDAE L 110–115 cm.
Long neck extended in flight, long legs;
grey, but for black and white head (red
inconspicuous), with blackish flight-
feathers, drooping plumes over tail; juv
darker, with brown head and neck.
Trumpeting call. Bogs, wet moors,
marshes, often near forests. Nest heap of
vegetation, 2 eggs, Apr–Jun. Food seeds,
berries, insects, earthworms, frogs, young
birds, small mammals. Summer De, Ge,
Po, FS; passage Fr, Lu, Be, Ne, Cz. [1]

Dotterel *Eudromias morinellus*
CHARADRIIDAE L 20–22 cm, ♂ smaller,
duller than ♀. Often tame, colourful but
inconspicuous; blackish crown, white
superciliaries and throat, grey-brown back
and breast, separated from chestnut and
black underparts by white band; in winter,
and juv, mainly brown, with faint
superciliaries, breast-band. Twittering
whistle, other calls. Tundra, mountains,
moors; arable in Ne. Nest scrape bare or
lined lichens, moss, 2–3 eggs, May–Jul
(♂ incubates). Food insects, spiders.
Summer, nBr, Ne, Cz, nFS; passage sBr,
Fr, Be, Ge, Po, sFS. [summer ♀ 2]

Golden Plover *Pluvialis apricaria*
CHARADRIIDAE L 27–29 cm. Upperparts
spangled black and gold, divided from
black underparts by white band, much
less clear-cut in southern populations; in
winter, whitish below, mottled golden;
juv paler above, browner below. Clear,
liquid whistle; piping alarm, rippling
song. Tundra, moors, heaths; winters
farmland, estuaries. Nest scrape variably
lined heather, lichens, 3–4 eggs, Apr–Jul.
Food invertebrates, seeds, berries. Summer
nBr, nIr, Ic, De, Ge, FS; winter Br, Ir,
Fr, Be, Ne, De; passage T. [northern
summer ♂ 3] [southern summer ♀ 4]

Dunlin *Calidris alpina* SCOLOPACIDAE
L 17–19 cm. Small, hunched; slightly
downcurved bill; note chestnut back,
black belly-patch; in winter, brown-grey
above, white below with greyish breast.
Nasal 'tree'; when nesting, 'wirr-wirr-
wirr', 'quoi-quoi', purring trill. Tundra,
moors with peaty pools, lowland mosses,

saltmarshes; winters coasts, estuaries. Nest
cup in tussock, lined grass, 4 eggs, Apr–
Jul. Food insects, molluscs, crustaceans,
worms. Summer nBr, Ir, Ic, De, nGe,
nPo, FS; winter Br, Ir, Fr, Be, Ne, De,
Ge, swSC; passage T. [summer 5]

Broad-billed Sandpiper *Limicola
falcinellus* SCOLOPACIDAE L 16–17 cm.
Small, skulking; short legs, long bill with
kinked tip; creamy snipe-like streaks,
forked superciliary; in winter, like dunlin
but for shape, whiter throat and superciliary, black shoulder. Harsh, trilling calls.
Moorland bogs with cottongrass. Nest cup
in tussock, lined leaves, 4 eggs, Jun–Jul.
Food insects, molluscs. Summer nFS;
passage De, Ge, Cz, Po, sFS. [summer 6]

Greenshank *Tringa nebularia*
SCOLOPACIDAE L 30–32 cm. Slightly
upturned bill, long green legs; dark brown
and white streaked and spotted, with
white wedge up back; in winter, greyer
above, whiter below. Loud 'tew-tew-tew'.
Moors, open forest; passage marshes,
estuaries. Nest scrape lined leaves, debris,
4 eggs, May–Jun. Food invertebrates,
frogs, fish. Summer nBr, nFS; winter sBr,
Ir, wFr; passage T, ex Ic. [summer 7]

Curlew *Numenius arquata* SCOLOPACIDAE
L 53–59 cm. Large, with long, downcurved bill (♀ longer than ♂); streaked
brown with white rump. Ringing 'cour-
lee'; long bubbling trill. Moors, heaths,
rough grassland, open forest; winters on
estuaries. Nest hollow, lined-grass, 4 eggs,
Apr–Jul. Food invertebrates, fish, berries.
Summer T, ex Ic, Lu, nFS; winter T,
ex sGe, Cz, Po, Fi, Sw, nNo. [8]

Whimbrel *Numenius phaeopus*
SCOLOPACIDAE L 38–41 cm. Like small,
dark curlew, with shorter, kinked bill,
striped crown; juv darker still. Rapid,
whinnying titter; also bubbling trill,
mournful 'teeeeu'. Moors, tundra, open
forest or scrub; on passage, coasts and
adjacent fields. Nest hollow in open, lined
grass, heather, 4 eggs, May–Jul. Food as
curlew; many insects in summer. Summer
nBr, Ic, nFS; passage T, esp coastal. [9]

Spotted Redshank *Tringa erythropus*
SCOLOPACIDAE L 29–31 cm. Slender,
upright, with long bill, dark red legs;
black, spotted white above, white wedge
up back; in winter, grey above, spotted
white on wings, whitish below, orange legs.
Distinctive 'tchu-eet'. Open marshy forest,
tundra scrub; winters estuaries. Nest
scrape lined leaves, 4 eggs, May–Jul. Food
aquatic insects; also worms, molluscs, fish,
frogs. Summer nFS; winter sBr, sIr, wFr,
Ne; passage T, ex Ic. [summer 1]

Green Sandpiper *Tringa ochropus*
SCOLOPACIDAE L 22–24 cm. Stoutish,
with black underwings, bold white rump,
green legs; blackish above, speckled
whitish in summer. Distinctive 'weet,
weet-weet'; trilling song. Marshy woodlands; passage/winter by streams, ponds,
saltmarsh channels. Uses old tree nest of
other bird, 4 eggs, Apr–Jul. Food insects;
also other invertebrates, algae. Summer
Ge, Cz, Po, sFS; winter sBr, wFr;
passage T, ex Ic. [summer 2]

Wood Sandpiper *Tringa glareola*
SCOLOPACIDAE L 19–21 cm. Slender, with
pale underwings, whitish rump, yellow
legs; spotted white above in summer.
Diagnostic 'chiff-iff-iff'; trilling song in
flight. Tundra, boggy moors; passage on
marshes. Nest scrape lined grass, leaves,
rarely in old tree nest, 4 eggs, May–Jul.
Food worms, insects, spiders, molluscs.
Summer De, nGe, FS, rare nBr, ?Po;
passage T, ex wIr, Ic. [summer 3]

Common Sandpiper *Actitis hypoleucos*
SCOLOPACIDAE L 19–20 cm. Short legs,
constant bobbing, low flight with bowed
wings flicking; olive-brown above, white-
sided tail. Shrill 'twee-wee-wee'; song
'kitti-weewit' repeated. Rocky streams,
lake edges, open or wooded, mostly
upland; passage/winter by lowland rivers,
lakes, saltmarsh channels. Nest scrape
lined plants, debris, 4 eggs, Apr–Jul. Food
invertebrates, tadpoles. Summer T,
ex seBr, Ic, Lu, Ne, De; winter sBr,
eIr, wFr; passage T, ex Ic [summer 4]

Snipe *Gallinago gallinago* SCOLOPACIDAE
L 26–27 cm. Skulking; long bill held
down in zigzag flight; mottled black and
rufous, with buff stripes, some white at
sides of tail. Rasping 'scaap'; song 'chip-
per, chip-per'; bleating 'drumming' by
spread tail in display-flight. Wet moors,
marshes, from tundra to lowlands; also
saltmarshes in winter. Nest hollow lined
grass, 4 eggs, Apr–Aug. Food worms;
also insects, molluscs, crustaceans, seeds.
T, but only summer Cz, Po, FS. [5]

Great Snipe *Gallinago media*
SCOLOPACIDAE L 27–29 cm. Bulkier than
snipe, with broader wings, shorter bill
held up in straighter flight; mealy head,
heavily barred underparts, much white on
tail. Usually silent; bubbling chorus of
♂s on display ground. Swamps, tundra
scrub; passage on heaths, stubble, marshes.
Nest scrape lined grass, 4 eggs, May–Jul.
Food worms; also molluscs, insects.
Scarce summer nePo, sFi, nSw, No;
passage eFr, Ne, De, Ge, Cz, Po, sSw. [6]

Jack Snipe *Lymnocryptes minimus*
SCOLOPACIDAE L *c*19 cm. Small with short
bill; skulks, seldom flies far; dark central
crown-stripe, brighter stripes and purplish
gloss on back, no barring on flanks.
Usually silent, but summer song like
cantering horse in sky. Bogs, in tundra,
scrub, open forest; in winter, as snipe.
Nest scrape lined grass, 4 eggs, Jun–Aug.
Food worms, molluscs, insects, seeds.
Summer nFS; winter Br, Ir, Fr, Be, Ne;
passage T, ex Ic. [7]

Red-necked Phalarope *Phalaropus
lobatus* PHALAROPODIDAE L 16·5–18 cm,
♂ smaller, duller than ♀. Dainty, tame,
swims habitually; bill black, needle-like;
orange patch contrasts with white throat,
grey head; in autumn, streaky grey above,
white below, black eye-patch. Call 'whit'.
Marshes, lakes, in tundra or forest.
Nest in tussock, lined grass, 4 eggs, May–
Jul (♂ incubates). Food small invertebrates. Summer nBr, Ic, nFS; passage T,
ex Lu, Cz; only on coast, scarce. [♀ 8]

Arctic Skua *Stercorarius parasiticus*
STERCORARIIDAE L 43–47 cm. Hawk-like
seabird; adult with central tail-feathers
projecting 5–9 cm; very variable from
dark form all black-brown to light form
with blackish cap and dark brown upperparts, creamy cheeks and hind neck, white
underparts, often with dark breast-band;
imm dark or barred and mottled.
Miaowing, squealing, chattering when
breeding. Moors, tundra, shingle, mainly
near coast; otherwise at sea. Colonial;
nest scrape in heather or moss, 2 eggs,
May–Aug. Food small mammals, birds,
insects, spiders, berries, leaves, moss;
terns and gulls chased to disgorge fish.
Summer nBr, Ic, coastal FS; passage all
coasts. [dark 1] [light 2]

Long-tailed Skua *Stercorarius longicaudus*
STERCORARIIDAE L 51–56 cm. Like light
form of arctic skua, but smaller, slighter,
adult with thinner central tail-feathers
projecting 13–20 cm; also neater black

cap, yellower cheeks, whiter underparts
without breast-band. Shrill yelping when
breeding. High moors, tundra, stony fells,
bogs at forest edges; otherwise at sea.
Colonial; nest scrape like arctic skua,
2 eggs, Jun–Jul. Food small mammals, esp
lemmings; also small birds, eggs, small
fish, earthworms, berries, leaves. Summer
nFS; scarce passage all coasts. [3]

Black-headed Gull *Larus ridibundus*
LARIDAE L 35–38 cm. White leading edge
to pointed wings; white and grey, with
red bill and legs, chocolate hood in
summer, white head with blackish marks
round eye in winter; juv like winter adult,
but some brown on crown and back,
black-tipped tail, yellower bill and legs.
Strident 'kwarr', other harsh notes, mainly
when breeding. Many wet habitats from
moorland pools to lowland bogs, coastal
marshes; in winter, coasts or freshwater
and fields inland. Colonial; ground nest
shallow scrape to heap of vegetation, 2–3

eggs, Apr–Jul. Food includes fish, crustaceans, molluscs, worms, insects, seeds, bread, refuse. T, ex nFS, but only summer Fi, most SC. [summer **4**]

Common Gull *Larus canus* LARIDAE L 40–41 cm. White and grey, with white-spotted, black wing-tips, greenish-yellow bill and legs, head streaked grey in winter; juv browner with broadly black-tipped tail. Shrill whistling, squealing calls when breeding. Chiefly moorland bogs, islands in upland lakes; in winter, coasts or inland fields. Usually colonial; ground nest lined scrape to heap of vegetation, 2–3 eggs, Apr–Jul. Food as varied as black-headed gull. Summer nBr, nIr, wIc, Ne, De, Ge, nPo, FS, locally elsewhere; winter T, ex Fi, but only coastal SC. [summer **5**]

Snowy Owl *Nyctea scandiaca* STRIGIDAE L 53–66 cm, ♂ much smaller than ♀. Diurnal, large, round-headed; white variably flecked and barred with brown; ♂ sometimes nearly pure white. Generally silent, but shrieks and chatters when breeding. Arctic tundra, high fells, mountains; in winter, also moors, coastal marshes. Nest scrape on hummock, 4–10 eggs, Apr–Jun. Food mainly mammals, esp lemmings, hares; also birds to size of mallard, grouse. Ic, nFS, rare nBr. [♂ **6**] [♀ **7**]

Short-eared Owl *Asio flammeus* STRIGIDAE L 37–38 cm. Mainly diurnal, in open country; wings long and narrow with dark patch at 'elbow', ear-tufts barely visible; pale tawny above blotched with dark brown, buff below streaked on neck and breast; fierce, whitish face with dark areas round yellow eyes. Resonant song 'boo-boo-boo', barking notes, wing-clapping, only when breeding. Moors, upland bogs, heaths, marshes, dunes. Ground nest among tall vegetation, 4–8 eggs, Mar–Jul. Food small mammals, esp voles; also small birds, insects. Summer T, ex sBr, Ir, sFS; winter T, ex most FS. [**8**]

Eagle Owl *Bubo bubo* STRIGIDAE
L 64–71 cm, ♂ smaller than ♀. Partly diurnal; large, bulky, with prominent 'ears', orange eyes; tawny, boldly barred and streaked blackish. Song 'boo-hu' (2nd syllable lower) repeated at intervals, far-carrying. Open or wooded country, esp mountains, moorland crags, rocky coniferous forests. Nest scrape on ground or ledge, in hollow tree or old nest of other bird, 2–3 eggs, Mar–May. Food mammals, birds to size of roe deer, buzzard, capercaillie, other owls; also reptiles, frogs, fish, beetles. eFr, Ge, Cz, Po, FS. [1]

Long-eared Owl *Asio otus* STRIGIDAE
L 34–36 cm. Largely nocturnal; easily confused with short-eared owl when long 'ears' not visible, but face elongated, cat-like, with orange eyes; body slenderer, darker above, more extensively streaked below; in flight, more compact with less prominent 'elbow' patches. Song low, drawn-out, cooing moan 'oo-oo-oo'. Forests, copses, chiefly conifers, esp spruce, pine; also hunts over open country. Uses old nest of other bird or squirrel, 4–5 eggs, Feb–Jun. Food small mammals, birds, insects; common victim of goshawk, eagle owl. T, ex Ic, nFS, but only summer Fi, most SC. [2]

Tengmalm's Owl *Aegolius funereus* STRIGIDAE L 25–26 cm. Mainly nocturnal; rather small, with large, rounded head, pale face with blackish border, yellow eyes, white eyebrows; chocolate-brown above spotted with white, whitish below mottled with brown; juv chocolate with white eyebrows. Liquid, musical song 'pu-poo-pu-poo'. Mainly coniferous forests, often in mountains. Nests in tree hole, often old nest of black woodpecker, 3–6 eggs, Apr–Jun. Food small mammals, birds. eFr, Ge, Cz, Po, FS. [3]

Pygmy Owl *Glaucidium passerinum* STRIGIDAE L c16·5 cm. Partly diurnal; bold, aggressive, often jerks tail up; tiny (smaller than starling) with small, rounded head, whitish face, yellow eyes, white eyebrows; dark brown above spotted with buff, grey-white below streaked with

dark brown. Noisy, including whistling 'keeoo', bullfinch-like piping. Forests, chiefly coniferous, often in mountains. Nests in tree hole, often old nest of woodpecker, 4–6 eggs, Mar–May. Food mainly small birds; also small mammals, insects. eFr, sGe, Cz, Po, FS. [4]

Hawk Owl *Surnia ulula* STRIGIDAE
L 36–41 cm. Diurnal; perches conspicuously on tree or wire, less upright than other owls, often jerking tail; hawk-like in flight with short, pointed wings, long tail; face greyish, bordered with black; blackish-brown above spotted and barred with white, pale below barred blackish. Chattering, hawk-like cries near nest. Coniferous forests, birch scrub with isolated conifers. Nests in tree hole, esp hollow at end of broken bough or old nest of black woodpecker, also disused nest of other bird, 3–10 eggs, Apr–Jun. Food mainly small mammals; also birds, insects. nFS, wandering south in winter. [5]

Ural Owl *Strix uralensis* STRIGIDAE
L 59–63 cm. Often diurnal; like huge, long-tailed, greyish-white tawny owl *S. aluco*, boldly streaked dark brown; head large and rounded, face greyish, eyes black-brown. Calls include harsh 'kayvick', barking 'kow'. Forests, esp coniferous, in more open areas. Nests in hollow tree, old nest of other large bird, sometimes on ground between tree roots, 3–4 eggs, Mar–May. Food small mammals, esp voles, also birds to size of grouse, other owls; some insects. Mainly Fi, Sw, rare eGe, Cz, Po, No. [6]

Great Grey Owl *Strix nebulosa* STRIGIDAE L 67–71 cm. Often diurnal; shape like Ural owl, but larger still; grey, mottled darker and lighter above and streaked below; face heavily lined, with white brows between yellow eyes, blackish patch on chin. Shrill 'ke-wick' call and deep hooting recall tawny owl. Coniferous forests. Nests in old nest of hawk or crow, or where tree-trunk broken off, 3–5 eggs, Apr–May. Food small mammals, esp mice, voles, to size of squirrels; occasionally birds. nFS, rare nePo. [7]

Nightjar *Caprimulgus europaeus*
CAPRIMULGIDAE L 26–27 cm. Nocturnal,
with erratic, silent flight; tiny bill, huge
gape, broad head, long wings and tail;
mottled and barred grey, brown and buff,
camouflaged on ground; ♂ white spots on
tips of wings, outer tail. Churring song,
rising and falling for as long as 5 mins;
also 'coo-ik', 'quik-quik-quik'. Open
woods, esp coniferous, heaths, moors,
dunes. Nests on bare ground, 2 eggs,
May–Aug. Food moths, beetles, flies.
Summer T, ex nBr, Ic, nFS. [♂ 1]

Black Woodpecker *Dryocopus martius*
PICIDAE L 45–46 cm. Crow-sized,
angular shape; all black, but ♂ crimson
crown, ♀ crimson patch on nape; eyes
pale yellow, bill pale with darker tip.
Strident, ringing 'chok-chok-chok', other
whistling and yelping calls; drums loudly
on dead wood. Old forests, esp coniferous,
also beech. Nest large hole excavated in
tree (later used by owls, jackdaw,
goldeneye), 4–6 eggs, Apr–May. Food

mainly wood-boring insects, larvae. eFr,
Lu, Be, Ne, Ge, Cz, Po, FS. [♂ 2]

Three-toed Woodpecker *Picoides
tridactylus* PICIDAE L 22–23 cm. Black
and white head, with black on cheeks, ♂
yellow on crown; mainly black wings,
broad whitish stripe right down back,
white underparts barred black on flanks;
juv greyer, mottled black on back. Often
silent, but weak 'tchik', chattering 'kek-
ek-ek'; drums rather slowly. Coniferous
forests in mountains and arctic, also
willow/birch. Nest hole excavated in tree,
4–5 eggs, May–Jul. Food insects, larvae.
FS, rare eFr, sGe, Cz, sPo. [♂ 3] [♀ 4]

Horned Lark *Eremophila alpestris*
ALAUDIDAE L 16–17 cm. Yellow face
and throat, black breast-band and cheeks,
♂ also black 'horns', but pattern obscured
in winter; pinkish-brown above, whitish
below; juv duller, more spotted. Calls
pipit-like; song high-pitched warble, high
in air or on ground. Tundra, stony grassland above tree-line; winters on coast,

adjacent stubble. Cup nest of grass, plant down, by tussock or stone, 4 eggs, May–Jul. Food seeds, buds, insects, larvae; small molluscs, crustaceans, in winter. Summer nFS; winter eBr, Fr, Be, Ne, De, nGe, nPo, sSw, coastal. [summer ♂ **5**]

Meadow Pipit *Anthus pratensis*
MOTACILLIDAE L 14·5–15 cm. Olive-brown above, whitish below, heavily streaked; white-sided tail, pale brown legs. Calls 'tseep', 'tissip'; song gathers speed, ends in trill, during 'parachuting' descent. Moors, rough grassland; winters on marshes, farmland, coasts. Cup nest of dry grass, hair, in tussock, 3–5 eggs, Apr–Aug. Food insects, larvae, spiders, some seeds. Summer T; winter T, ex Cz, Po, FS. [**6**]

Red-throated Pipit *Anthus cervinus*
MOTACILLIDAE L 14·5–15 cm. Darker above than meadow pipit, with heavily streaked rump; in summer, reddish on throat, sometimes breast, sides of head. Calls 'chup', hoarse 'skeeez'; song higher-pitched than meadow pipit's. Swampy tundra, cultivation, birch/willow scrub; marshes on passage. Nest like meadow pipit's, 5–6 eggs, Jun–Aug. Food insects, larvae, small molluscs, some seeds. Summer nFS; passage mainly De, Ge, Cz, Po, FS. [summer **7**]

Water/Rock Pipit *Anthus spinoletta*
MOTACILLIDAE L 16–16·5 cm. Larger than meadow pipit, longer bill, dark legs. Song louder, with more pronounced trill. Cup nest of grasses, hair, under plant or in rocky crevice, 4–6 eggs, Apr–Jul. Food small invertebrates, some seeds. Water *A. s. spinoletta*: greyish above, with white superciliary, white-sided tail; whitish below, flushed pink in summer, streaked in winter. Mountain pastures; winters on lowland marshes. Summer eFr, sGe, Cz, sPo, winter west to sBr, Fr, Be, Ne. [summer **8**]. Rock *A. s. petrosus/littoralis*: darker, more olive and streaked (pinkish below in FS), with grey-sided tail. Rocky shores; adjacent moors, tundra. Br, Ir, Fr, nDe, summer FS.

Waxwing *Bombycilla garrulus*
BOMBYCILLIDAE L 17·5–18 cm. Mainly
pinkish-brown, with prominent crest,
black bib, grey rump and short, yellow-
tipped tail; undertail-coverts chestnut,
wings dark with white and yellow marks
(also small, red waxy blobs); starling-like
flight; juv duller, streaked below, with
smaller crest, no bib. Most characteristic
call is high, thin trill. Northern forests,
esp coniferous, birch: in winter, wherever
berry-bearing trees, shrubs (*eg* rowan,
cotoneaster), often in gardens. Cup nest
of conifer twigs, moss and grasses, in
tree, 4–6 eggs, May–Jul. Food in summer
also berries, esp bilberries, crowberry,
juniper, and insects. Summer nFS;
winter T, ex Ic, rare wBr, Ir, Fr, but
numbers variable. [1]

Dartford Warbler *Sylvia undata*
SYLVIIDAE L 12·5–13 cm. Small, dark,
skulking, with long, white-edged, blackish
tail, often cocked; ♂ has slate-grey head,
red eye-ring, dark brown upperparts,
dull purplish-brown underparts, with
white spots on throat in winter; ♀ and juv
paler, browner. Chattering song, often in
dancing flight, recalls whitethroat *Sylvia
communis*; various other churring, rattling,
ticking notes. Heaths, where rank heather,
gorse or bramble. Cup nest of grasses,
heather, moss, wool, thistledown, low in
shrub, 3–4 eggs, Apr–Jul. Food insects
and larvae, spiders. sBr, Fr. [♂ 2] [♀ 3]

Arctic Warbler *Phylloscopus borealis*
SYLVIIDAE L *c*12 cm. Distinguished from
other, often much commoner, green-
brown, yellow and whitish *Phylloscopus*
by combination of broad, yellow-white
superciliary extending almost to nape, dark
line through eye, whitish throat, one or
two whitish wingbars (sometimes lost
through wear), pale legs. Trilling song not
unlike cirl bunting *Emberiza cirlus* or

lesser whitethroat *Sylvia curruca*; calls
include hard 'zik', hoarse 'tseeip'. Wet
and dry arctic forests, esp coniferous,
birch, often near water. Domed nest with
side entrance, of grasses, moss, leaves,
usually on ground but sometimes low in
shrub, 5–6 eggs, Jun–Aug. Food insects
and larvae, esp mosquitoes. Summer
nFS [4]

Goldcrest *Regulus regulus* SYLVIIDAE
L *c*9 cm. Tiny, plump, with 'surprised'
expression and black-edged, orange (♂)
or yellow (♀) crown; greenish above, with
2 white bars and broader black band on
wings, dull whitish below; juv lacks head
markings. Call shrill, high 'zee-zee-zee';
song equally thin and high repetition of
double note with terminal flourish.
Coniferous and mixed woods, also parks
and gardens with isolated conifers; in
winter, sometimes broadleaved woods and
hedgerows. Thick cup nest of moss,
lichens, feathers, bound to supporting
twigs with spiders' webs, near end of
conifer branch or in ivy, 7–10 eggs, Apr–
Aug. Food spiders, insects, larvae and
eggs. T, ex Ic, nFS. [♂ 5] [♀ 6]

Firecrest *Regulus ignicapillus* SYLVIIDAE
L *c*9 cm. Greener above, whiter below
than goldcrest, with additional black stripe
through eye and bold white line above it,
more extensive bright orange-red (♂) or
orange-yellow (♀) crown; juv has
indication of head stripes on head but
lacks coloured crest. Call 'zit-zit-zit',
lower-pitched, stronger, less often repeated
than goldcrest's; song also stronger
repetition of one note without terminal
flourish. Coniferous or broadleaved woods,
but esp evergreens. Nest like goldcrest,
7–11 eggs, May–Aug. Food as goldcrest.
Resident sBr, Fr, Lu, Be, Ne; summer
De, Ge, Cz, Po. [♂ 7] [♀ 8]

Whinchat *Saxicola rubetra* TURDIDAE
L 12·5–13 cm. Short-tailed, upright,
perching prominently, distinguished from
stonechat by bold white superciliary, white
patches at base of tail; ♂ streaked brown
above, warm buff below, with additional
white down sides of throat and on wings;
♀ paler with buffish superciliary, smaller
wing-patch; juv has spotted breast, no
wing-patch. Scolding 'tic-tic' not as hard
as stonechat's; song brief warble. Upland
pastures, moors, hillsides, esp among
bracken, to heaths, meadows, marshes.
Cup nest of grass and moss, on ground in
rank vegetation, 5–7 eggs, May–Jul. Food
insects and larvae, spiders, earthworms.
Summer T, ex Ic. [♂ 1] [♀ 2]

Stonechat *Saxicola torquata* TURDIDAE
L 12·5–13 cm. Plumper, more upright
than whinchat; ♂ with black head and
throat, white half-collar, dark upperparts
with narrow white wing-stripe and whitish
rump, chestnut underparts; ♀ and juv
streaked brown above, with no white on
neck or rump, dull reddish below with
variable black markings on throat. Calls
'hweet, tsak-tsak', like 2 stones knocked
together; song musical warble. Moors,
rough hillsides, heaths, wasteland, dunes,
esp among gorse, brambles; in winter,
extends to farmland. Cup nest of grass,
moss, wool, feathers, on or near ground
in dense bush, 5–6 eggs, May–Jul. Food
insects and larvae, spiders and eggs,
worms, some seeds. Summer T, ex Ic,
nGe, nPo, FS, rare De; winter Br, Ir, Fr,
Lu, Be, Ne. [♂ 3] [♀ 4]

Wheatear *Oenanthe oenanthe* TURDIDAE
L 14·5–15 cm. Summer ♂ blue-grey
above, buff below, with broad black patch
through and behind eye, white line above
it, black wings, white rump extending to
sides of otherwise black tail; ♀ and
autumn ♂ browner, without contrasting
black on cheeks and wings, but same tail-
pattern; juv similar but more spotted.

Call 'weet-chack-chack', harder than
stonechat's; song short, rattling warble
of rich and harsh notes. Mountains, stony
hillsides, moors, upland pastures, downs,
cliffs, dunes. Cup nest of grasses, moss,
feathers, deep in rock hole or rodent
burrow, 5–6 eggs, Apr–Jul. Food insects
and larvae, spiders, centipedes, molluscs.
Summer T. [♂ 5] [♀ 6]

Bluethroat *Luscinia svecica* TURDIDAE
L c14 cm. Chestnut patches at base of
tail; summer ♂ with bright blue throat
separated from white underparts by black
and chestnut bands, spot in centre either
chestnut (Scandinavian race *L. s. svecica*)
or white (central European race *L. s.
cyanecula*); ♀ and autumn ♂ show traces
of blue and chestnut merging into
irregular dark breast-band; juv spotted.
Calls chat-like mixture of tacking and
plaintive notes; song rich, varied,
reminiscent of nightingale *L. megarhynchos*.
Tundra, bogs with birch/willow scrub,
damp heaths, reedy ditches. Cup nest of
grasses and moss, often on bank or under
bush, 5–7 eggs, May–Jul. Food insects,
molluscs, worms, some seeds and berries.
Summer Fr, Be, Ne, Ge, Cz, Po, nFS;
passage also eBr, Lu, De, sFS.
[♂ Scandinavian 7] [♀ 8]

Ring Ouzel *Turdus torquatus* TURDIDAE
L 24–24·5 cm. ♂ black, with white
gorget, light patch on closed wings; ♀
browner, with narrower, whitish crescent;
juv lacks gorget, spotted like young
blackbird *T. merula*, but greyer. Clear,
piping call, also blackbird-like tacking
and chatter; song repetition of single or
double piping note. Moors, mountains,
esp rocky slopes or outcrops. Cup nest of
grasses, moss and leaves, on ground or
ledge or under bush, occasionally in tree,
4–5 eggs, Apr–Jul. Food worms, insects,
molluscs, also berries and fruit in autumn.
Summer nwBr, Ir (local), eFr, sGe, Cz,
sPo, nFi, wSC; passage T, ex Ic, ePo,
eFi. [♂ 9] [♀ 10]

Siberian Tit *Parus cinctus* PARIDAE
L 13–13·5 cm. Looks scruffier than most
tits; dark brown crown and nape, paler
reddish-brown upperparts and flanks, off-
white cheeks and underparts with large,
sooty throat-patch merging into breast.
Call buzzing 'eeez-eeez-eeez'. Coniferous
forests, also birch. Nest of moss, hair, in
tree hole, often partly excavated, 6–10
eggs, May–Jul. Food insects, larvae,
spiders, seeds. nFS. [1]

Crested Tit *Parus cristatus* PARIDAE
L *c*11·5 cm. Pointed crest whitish
speckled with black; white cheeks with
curved black mark behind eye, bordered
by narrow line extending from neat
black throat-patch; back and wings brown,
underparts whitish with buff flanks.
Characteristic call low, purring trill; also
high 'zee-zee-zee' like other tits.
Coniferous or mixed woods, in lowlands
or mountains. Nest of moss, hair, in hole
partly excavated in rotten stump or dead
branch, 5–8 eggs, Apr–Jun. Food insects,
larvae, spiders, some conifer seeds,
juniper berries. T, ex Ir, Ic, nFS, but
only nBr. [2]

Coal Tit *Parus ater* PARIDAE L *c*11·5 cm.
Looks small, with short tail; large white
patch on back of black head, whitish
cheeks, black throat extending to upper
breast; otherwise olive-grey above with
2 white wing-bars, whitish below with
buff flanks; juv has yellowish nape-patch,
cheeks, underparts. Plaintive piping call
and other notes, some goldcrest-like; song
'teechu-teechu-teechu' faster, more piping
than great tit's *P. major*. Woods, parks,
gardens, esp among conifers. Nest of
moss, hair, in hole in tree stump, wall,
bank or ground, 7–11 eggs, Apr–Jun.
Food insects, larvae, spiders, some seeds;
also meat, scraps. T, ex Ic, nFS. [3]

Siskin *Carduelis spinus* FRINGILLIDAE
L *c*12 cm. Yellow patches at base of tail;

♂ streaky yellow-green, paler below, with black crown and chin, yellow wing-bar and rump; ♀ duller, greyer, more streaked, no black on head; juv browner, strongly streaked. Shrill, squeaky calls; song musical twitter ending in long creaky note. Coniferous or mixed woods, esp spruce; in winter, chiefly birches, alders, often by streams. Cup nest of twigs, grass, moss, wool, hair, feathers, often near end of high branch, 3–5 eggs, Apr–Jul. Food mainly tree seeds; also berries, some insects. Summer Br (mainly n), Ir, eFr, De, Ge, Cz, Po, FS (ex far north), irregular Be, Ne; winter T, ex Ic, nFS. [♂ 4] [♀ 5]

Redpoll *Carduelis flammea* FRINGILLIDAE L 12–13 cm. Streaky grey-brown, with red forehead, black chin, ♂ also pink flush on breast; rump brown or pink to whitish, wing-bars buff to white, flanks lightly to heavily streaked; juv indistinct chin-patch, no red. Flight calls high-pitched, metallic twittering 'chuch-uch-uch' and plaintive notes; song twittering interspersed with rolling 'errrr', ending in rippling trill. Birch/alder scrub, pine woods, heaths, tundra, sea-level to mountains. Untidy cup nest of twigs, grass, down, feathers, high in tree or near ground in bush, 4–6 eggs, May–Jul. Food seeds; also insects, larvae. Summer Br, Ir, Ic, nFS, rare Fr, Ne, Cz, Po; winter T, ex nFS. [♂ 6] [♀ 7]

Arctic Redpoll *Carduelis hornemanni* FRINGILLIDAE L 12·5–13 cm. Similar to redpoll, but looks frosted, esp on head; greyer back contrasts with clear white rump, wing-bars; whiter underparts less streaked, ♂ with only pale pink tinge on breast. Twittering slower, more deliberate. Birch/willow scrub, open tundra; trees in winter. Cup nest of twigs, grass, down, feathers, in low bush or on ground by rock, 4–6 eggs, Jun–Jul. Food seeds, insects. Summer nFS; winter sFS, De. [♂ 8]

Little Bunting *Emberiza pusilla*
EMBERIZIDAE L 13–13·5 cm. Compact,
short-tailed; in summer, red-brown crown
and cheeks outlined with black; otherwise
brown above with darker streaking,
whitish below with fine black streaks on
upper breast and flanks; ♀ duller, with
pale superciliary. Call repeated 'tik'; song
varied, musical, robin-like. Birch/willow
scrub on tundra, swamps and clearings in
forests. Cup nest of leaves, moss, grass,
hair, on ground in rank vegetation, 4–5
eggs, Jun–Aug. Food seeds; insects in
summer. Summer nFi, rare nSw; vagrant
elsewhere. [♂ 1] [♀ 2]

Rustic Bunting *Emberiza rustica*
EMBERIZIDAE L 14·5–15 cm. White
underparts with breast-band of bright
chestnut spots extending down flanks;
upperparts also chestnut, streaked black;
summer ♂ has black cap and cheeks, with
white stripe behind eye; ♀ duller,
browner-headed. Call sharp 'tsip, tsip';
song short, dunnock-like warble. Wet
moors and heaths with scattered trees,
thickets at edges of swampy forest, often
near streams. Cup nest of grass, moss,
horsetails, on or near ground in rank
grass or bush, 4–5 eggs, May–Jul. Food
seeds; insects in summer. Summer Fi,
nSw; vagrant elsewhere. [♂ 3] [♀ 4]

Lapland Bunting *Calcarius lapponicus*
EMBERIZIDAE L 15–15·5 cm. Summer ♂
black on head, throat, breast, flanks,
divided from chestnut nape by buff
zigzag widening into white; ♀ and winter
♂ much duller, streaked, with yellow bill,
pale crown-stripe, variable chestnut on
nape and wings. Piping 'teu', 'ticky-tik-
teu'; short, lark-like song in flight. Open
tundra, high moorland, with birch,
crowberry; winters on coastal stubble,
saltings. Cup nest of grass, moss, feathers,
in side of hummock, 4–6 eggs, May–Jul.
Food seeds, mainly insects in summer.
Summer nFS; winter eBr, Fr, Be, Ne,
De, nGe, nPo; passage nBr, Ir, sFS.
[summer ♂ 5] [♀ 6]

Snow Bunting *Plectrophenax nivalis*
EMBERIZIDAE L c16·5 cm. Summer ♂

white, with black back, wing-tips, central
tail, also black bill and legs; summer ♀
less white, with head and back grey-
brown flecked black; in winter, variably
reddish-sandy on head and breast, white
wing-patches, creamy underparts,
yellowish bill. Rippling twitter, piping
'teu'; song short, loud, musical, in flight
or perched. Rocky areas, screes, from sea-
level to mountain tops; winters on coasts.
Cup nest of grass, moss, hair, feathers,
deep in crevice, 4–6 eggs, May–Jul. Food
insects in summer, sandhoppers, grain,
other seeds. Summer nBr, Ic, nFS;
passage/winter T, coastal. [summer ♂ 7]
[summer ♀ 8]

Brambling *Fringilla montifringilla*
FRINGILLIDAE L 14·5–15 cm. Chaffinch-
like, but white rump, less white on wings
and tail; summer ♂ has black head and
back, orange breast and shoulders; ♀ and
winter ♂ mottled brown above, variably
chestnut-buff on breast and wings.
Characteristic spring call repeated,
greenfinch-like 'dzwee'. Birch and open
conifer forests, also tundra scrub; winters
in stubble, beechwoods. Chaffinch-like
cup nest of moss, grass, feathers, wool,
decorated with lichens, often in conifer,
5–7 eggs, May–Jul. Food insects, larvae
in summer; seeds, berries, beechmast
in winter. Summer FS, ex sFi, sSw,
rare De; winter T, ex Ic, Fi, nSC.
[summer ♂ 9] [♀ 10]

Twite *Carduelis flavirostris* FRINGILLIDAE
L 13–13·5 cm. Linnet-like, mainly buff
streaked with black-brown, but darker,
tawnier in summer; less white in wings
and tail, reddish-buff throat; ♂ rump
pink, brighter in summer; bill greyish,
but yellow in winter. Call nasal, twanging
'tsooeek', much twittering in flight; song
linnet-like jangle. Moors, upland pastures,
bracken slopes, barren coasts; winters on
salt-marshes, coastal stubble. Bulky cup
nest of grass, wool, feathers, on or near
ground in heather, gorse, rocks, 5–6 eggs,
Apr–Aug. Food mainly seeds; some insect
larvae in summer. Summer nBr, Ir, No;
winter T, ex Ic, Fi, nSC, mainly coastal.
[summer ♂ 11] [♀ 12]

Pine Grosbeak *Pinicola enucleator*
FRINGILLIDAE L 20–20·5 cm. Like large
crossbill with straight stout beak, flat
crown, 2 white wing-bars, long tail; ♂
pinkish-red, with grey back and belly,
dark brown wings and tail; ♀ greenish-
gold instead of red, more grey-brown on
back; juv yellowish-brown. Piping call
'tee-tee-teu'; song loud whistling notes,
interspersed with harsh twangs. Mainly
coniferous and mixed forests, also birch or
juniper scrub. Large bullfinch-like nest of
loose twigs with cup of roots, grass,
usually fairly low in conifer or birch, 3–4
eggs, May–Jul. Food berries, seeds, buds;
also insects in summer. Summer nFS,
winter sFS. [♂ 1] [♀ 2]

Crossbill *Loxia curvirostra* FRINGILLIDAE
L *c*16·5 cm. Crossed mandibles, heavy
head, short tail, parrot-like actions; ♂
brick-red (more orange when young),
brighter on rump, with dark-brown wings
and tail; ♀ yellow-green with yellower

rump, underparts; juv green-grey,
strongly streaked. Call loud, incisive 'chip-
chip-chip'; song of trilling, creaking,
chipping notes. Coniferous woods, esp
spruce, also pine, larch. Cup nest of
twigs, grass, moss, wool, hair, feathers,
often high in conifer, 3–4 eggs, Jan–Jul.
Food seeds of spruce, pine, larch; also
berries, other seeds, insects, caterpillars.
T, ex Ic, nFS, but only after periodic
invasions Ir, nFr, Lu, Be, Ne. [♂ 3]
[♀ 4]

Parrot Crossbill *Loxia pytyopsittacus*
FRINGILLIDAE L 16·5–17 cm. Slightly
larger than crossbill, with deep, arched
bill giving top-heavy look (but Scottish
crossbill intermediate); plumages similar.
Call deeper, stronger 'chup-chup-chup'.
Pine forests. Nest similar to crossbill's,
but more substantial, 3–4 eggs, mainly
Mar–May. Food seeds, esp pine, rarely
spruce, larch; also berries. sFS, rare Po;
in winter, south to Ge, Cz. [♂ 5]

Siberian Jay *Perisoreus infaustus*
CORVIDAE L 30–31 cm. Rusty-red wing-patch, rump, flanks, undertail-coverts and outer feathers of long, graduated tail, this colour conspicuous in flight; dull brown head; greyer back, wings, central tail, underparts. Coniferous forests, birch woods, village outskirts in winter. Cup nest of twigs, bark, grass, lichens, feathers, in conifer, often near trunk, 4 eggs, Apr–Jun. Food insects, slugs, small rodents; berries in autumn, scraps in winter. nFS. [6]

Nutcracker *Nucifraga caryocatactes*
CORVIDAE L 31–32·5 cm. Long pointed bill, shortish tail; jay-like, undulating flight on broad wings; all dark brown flecked with white, apart from blackish wings, white-tipped black tail, conspicuous white undertail-coverts. Harsh 'krar' and other notes; rather silent when nesting. Coniferous forests, or where conifers predominate, often perching on tree-tops; in winter, also in broadleaved woods, more open country. Cup nest of twigs, moss, grass, lichens, in conifer, usually near trunk, 3–4 eggs, Mar–May. Food mainly conifer seeds; also hazelnuts, berries, insects, young birds. eFr, sGe, Cz, Po, sFS; winter also De, nGe, sometimes farther west. [7]

Raven *Corvus corax* CORVIDAE
L 62–65 cm. All black, glossed green and purple; distinguished from other black crows by large size, much stouter bill, shaggy throat, wedge-shaped tail. Distinctive call 'pruk'. Mountains, moors, with or without trees; also sea-cliffs, more locally wooded lowlands. Large cup nest of sticks, moss, grass, leaves, wool, on rock ledge or tree fork, 4–6 eggs, Feb–May. Food mainly carrion; also small mammals, birds' eggs, frogs, molluscs, insects, some seeds. T, ex seBr, Lu, Be, Ne, local Fr, Ge. [8]

Pygmy Shrew *Sorex minutus* SORICIDAE
BL 45–60 mm, TL 32–45 mm, HF 9–12
mm. Shrews, located by high-pitched
squeaks, distinguished from mice and
voles by very small size and long, pointed
nose; ears almost hidden. Pygmy, mainly
grey-brown with greyish-white underside,
is smaller than equally widespread
common shrew *S. araneus* and water
shrew *Neomys fodiens* (HF >12 mm) and
bigger than rare least shrew *S. minutissimus*
of FS (HF <9 mm). Open country,
woodland among grass, heather, scree.
Diurnal and nocturnal; feeds on small
insects, esp larvae, and other invertebrates.
T, ex Ic. [1]

Northern Bat *Eptesicus nilssoni*
VESPERTILIONIDAE BL 48–52 mm, TL 38–47
mm, FA 38–46 mm. Brown with yellowish
sheen, yellower underneath; tragus (lobe
inside ear) short, blunt; tail-tip projecting
slightly beyond membrane. Mainly
woodlands, roosting in buildings, tree
holes. Sometimes flies by day; food flying
insects. FS, also recorded Ge, Cz, Po. [2]
(Whiskered bat *Myotis mystacinus*, smaller
and generally dark grey, also extends
beyond Arctic Circle in Sw.)

Norway Lemming *Lemmus lemmus*
CRICETIDAE BL 13–15 cm, TL 15–19 mm.
Mottled black and yellow pattern variable,
but distinctive. (Wood lemming *Myopus
schisticolor* smaller, dark grey, with rusty
streak on back.) Squeals. Open mountain
country, tundra, runways in grass
conspicuous after snow melts; extends
to lower ground and woodland in 'lemming
years', when enormously abundant, more
active by day and sometimes swims. Feeds
on grasses, sedges, dwarf shrubs. Preyed
on by raptors, owls, skuas, foxes. FS. [3]

Ruddy Vole *Clethrionomys rutilus*
CRICETIDAE BL 80–100 mm, TL 25–35 mm.
Distinguished from grey-sided vole
C. rufocanus by lighter red-brown above,
extending to flanks; from similar, more
southern bank vole *C. glareolus* by shorter,
hairier tail. (Young of all *Clethrionomys*
greyer than adults, more difficult to
identify except by teeth.) Tundra, open
woodland, esp birch, also pine. Moderately

active by day and night, but tends to hide among vegetation; climbs; feeds on berries, buds, seeds, leaves. nFS. [4]

Grey-sided Vole *Clethrionomys rufocanus* CRICETIDAE BL 100–120 mm, TL 30–40 mm. Larger than other *Clethrionomys*, with grey flanks and red-brown confined to narrow zone on back; tail longer, less hairy than ruddy vole *C. rutilus*. Mountains, tundra, open woodland from pine to birch and willow, among dwarf shrubs, scree. Moderately active by day, with runways in grass; climbs; feeds on varied vegetation, esp shoots of dwarf shrubs. FS. [5]

Field Vole *Microtus agrestis* CRICETIDAE BL 90–130 mm, TL 30–45 mm. Grey-brown with soft, shaggy fur; ears and tail shorter, eyes smaller, than *Clethrionomys*; similar root vole *M. oeconomus* (FS, s coast of Baltic) has longer tail; common vole *M. arvalis* (s of Baltic, Orkney) difficult to distinguish, but less shaggy, with tail less clearly 2-coloured. Wherever dense grass, sedges or rushes provide cover and food. Preyed on by many birds, foxes, stoats. T, ex Ir, Ic. [6]

Red Squirrel *Sciurus vulgaris* SCIURIDAE BL 19–24 cm, TL 15–20 cm. Only squirrel except where American grey squirrel *S. carolinensis* (Br, Ir) or smaller, grey, nocturnal flying squirrel *Pteromys volans* (Fi). Red-brown, dark brown, black or grey, prominent ear tufts in winter. Chatters, scolds, whistles. In coniferous forest, also beech. Diurnal; travels fast through trees. Feeds on conifer seeds, also buds, fungi, nuts, beechmast. T, ex Ic. [7]

Mountain Hare *Lepus timidus* LEPORIDAE BL 45–60 cm, TL 5–8 cm, EL 6–9 cm. Greyer in summer than brown hare *L. capensis*, with shorter ears, no black on tail; white in winter (ex Ir, Faeroe); black on ear tips distinguishes from rabbit *Oryctolagus cuniculus*. Mountains, moorland, among grass, dwarf shrubs; also open woodland, farmland, in absence of brown hare (*eg* Ir, most of FS). Feeds on most ground vegetation, in winter also on bark. nBr, Ir, FS, (wBr, Ic). [8]

Wolf *Canis lupus* CANIDAE BL 100–130 cm, TL 30–40 cm, SH 70–80 cm. Confusable only with Alsatian dog: note erect ears, drooping tail; colour variable, usually grey-brown, but may be almost white in far north. Howls, esp in winter; also growls, yelps, but hunts silently; tundra, mountains, open woodland. Hunts in small packs by day when undisturbed, more solitary and nocturnal when persecuted; feeds mainly on deer, also domestic stock, small mammals, birds. Few survive west of Russia. Cz, Po, Fi. [1]

Arctic Fox *Alopex lagopus* CANIDAE BL 50–65 cm, TL 28–33 cm, SH 30 cm. Slightly smaller than red fox *Vulpes vulpes* (throughout FS, but not Ic); ears short, blunt; fur shades of grey or brown in summer, usually white in winter, never reddish, never with black markings. Barks, yelps. Tundra, in winter esp near coasts. More sociable than red fox and more often seen by day; feeds on small mammals, birds, molluscs, carrion. Ic, nFS. [2]

Brown Bear *Ursus arctos* URSIDAE BL 150–250 cm, TL 6–14 cm, SH 90–110 cm, WT 105–265 kg. Only bear in Europe except wholly white polar bear *Thalarctos maritimus* (Spitsbergen, only rarely on n coasts of SC, Ic). Colour varies from light to very dark brown. Big footprints and scratched trees reveal presence; covers large distances with ambling run or trot. Usually silent except for low grunts. Mainly forests, but wanders extensively in open mountain country and tundra; hibernates in den among rocks or fallen trees. Solitary, nocturnal, but hunts by day where undisturbed; bathes, swims, but rarely climbs; omnivorous, feeding on carrion, rodents, birds, eggs, fish, grubs, roots, bulbs, fruit, nuts. Cz, Po, FS. [3]

Pine Marten *Martes martes* MUSTELIDAE BL 40–55 cm, TL 22–27 cm, SH 15 cm. Body long and slender, ears small but pointed and erect; prominent pale yellowish throat. Only marten in Br, Ir, FS; south of Baltic, very similar beech marten *M. foina* has pure white throat. Mainly coniferous forest, spending much time in trees but also hunting on ground; den among rocks or in hollow tree. Mainly nocturnal; feeds on rodents, including squirrels, and birds. T, ex Ic. [4]

Wolverine, Glutton *Gulo gulo* MUSTELIDAE BL 70–80 cm, TL 12–15 cm, SH 40–45 cm. Like large badger *Meles meles*, but fur brown, and pale forehead and flanks characteristic; much larger and heavier than pine marten. Forest, tundra, mountains, mostly on ground but occasionally climbing trees; den in thick bushes or among rocks. Usually nocturnal, but active by day in winter; feeds mainly on carrion, also small mammals, birds, berries. FS. [5]

Stoat *Mustela erminea* MUSTELIDAE BL 20–30 cm, TL 8–12 cm, ♀ much smaller than ♂. Very long and slender, legs short, tail prominent, always with black tip; brown above, yellowish below, demarcated by straight line; in N and E Europe turns pure white in winter, except tail-tip (ermine), but in S and W whitening only partial or sporadic. Chatters; shrill alarm. All forest and open habitats with ground cover (grass, heather, scree, walls); nests in holes. Often hunts in groups, mainly at night, but also by day; climbs well; feeds chiefly on rodents, esp voles. Occasionally taken by large birds of prey. T, ex Ic. [6]

Weasel *Mustela nivalis* MUSTELIDAE BL 13–23 cm, TL 4–7 cm, ♀ much smaller than ♂. Smallest carnivore, much more elongate than any rodent or shrew; as stoat, but generally smaller with shorter tail, no black tip, demarcation between upperside and underside often (not always) wavy; turns white in winter only in far north. All habitats from mountains to lowlands, needing little cover; nests in holes, among tree roots, in heaps of stones. Mainly solitary, active day and night; climbs trees; feeds on rodents in their runways. Sometimes taken by predatory birds. T, ex Ir, Ic. [7]

Wild Cat *Felis silvestris* FELIDAE BL 50–80 cm, TL 25–35 cm, SH 35–40 cm. Like large tabby cat, but pattern always striped, never blotched; tail thicker, blunt and more distinctly ringed; feet usually pale. Purrs, mews, growls. Forests; den among rocks or in hollow tree. Nocturnal; hunts mainly on ground, though climbs and leaps skilfully in trees. Feeds on rodents, birds, frogs. nBr, Fr, Lu, Ge, Cz, Po. [1]

Lynx *Felis lynx* FELIDAE BL 80–130 cm, TL 11–25 cm, SH 60–75 cm. Larger than wild cat, with relatively longer legs, much shorter tail lacking clear rings; tufted ears and cheeks; spotting variable, least in north, most in Carpathians. Footprints distinctive, similar to those of domestic cat (no claw marks) but twice the size. ♂ in spring utters high-pitched howl ending in moan. Coniferous forests, esp in mountains; den in cave or hollow tree. Nocturnal; mainly on ground, where creeps rather than runs, but often climbs on low branches. Feeds on hares, rodents, birds, young deer. Cz, Po, FS. [2]

Roe Deer *Capreolus capreolus* CERVIDAE BL 100–120 cm, TL 2–3 cm, SH 65–75 cm. Smaller than other native deer; pale rump conspicuous, esp in winter, tail invisible; coat red-brown in summer, grey-brown in winter; fawns spotted at first. Only ♂ has antlers, rarely more than 3 points on each, shed in early winter, regrown by spring. Sharp bark most frequent sound. Lowland, mountain forests with good undergrowth, often emerges at night to feed on open ground. Solitary or in small groups. Feeds mainly by browsing on deciduous trees and shrubs; also eats grass, nuts, fruits. T, ex Ir, Ic. [3]

Elk *Alces alces* CERVIDAE BL 200–280 cm, TL 4–5 cm, SH 150–210 cm, ♀ smaller than ♂. Largest deer, with high shoulders, very long legs, large drooping muzzle; grey-brown to near black, legs usually paler than body; no pale patch around tail; calves unspotted. Only ♂ has antlers, flattened, shed in winter, regrown by late summer. ♂ utters trumpeting roar in autumn. Coniferous forests with deciduous undergrowth, esp in summer on banks of lakes, rivers. Mainly solitary, but herds in winter. Active by day and night; often in water, even dives. Feeds on variety of vegetation in summer, on conifers in winter. eGe, Cz, Po, FS. [4]

Reindeer *Rangifer tarandus* CERVIDAE BL 190–210 cm, TL 15 cm, SH 105–120 cm. Grey-brown in summer, paler grey or almost white in winter, but very variable (domesticated stock in Lapland smaller and still more variable). Both sexes have antlers, shed by ♂ in early winter, retained by ♀ until early summer; secondary branching of lowest forward branch characteristic. ♂ roars during autumn rut. Tundra, mountains, open woodland, migrating south in autumn. Gregarious, esp in winter; walks, trots, gallops. Feeds on ground vegetation, esp lichens in winter. Ic, FS. [5]

Feral Goat *Capra* (domestic) BOVIDAE BL 100–120 cm. Very variable, but mostly derived from primitive domestic breeds: small, long-haired, often piebald. Both sexes have horns usually twisted outwards. Open mountains, moorland, sea-cliffs, often on ledges inaccessible to domestic sheep. Sociable, but adult ♂s solitary for much of year. Feeds by grazing and browsing. Br, Ir. [6]. Only other goat-like mammal of region, chamois *Rupicapra rupicapra*, has slender horns curving at ends; contrasted head-markings; body brownish-yellow in summer, blacker in winter; limited to mountain woods and open, rocky slopes in Cz, Po, (eFr, swGe)

FURTHER READING

The following are among the publications consulted in preparing this book. Unavoidably the list is selective. In seeking additional information on particular aspects of any system it is helpful first to take the appropriate article in a general encyclopaedia, *eg* the *Macropaedia* volumes of the *Encyclopaedia Britannica* and go to the references listed at the end of the article. The following list gives at least one book per topic in the order of the ecological essay and the field guide.

The Living World of Animals (Reader's Digest, 1970, London)

Our Magnificent Wildlife (Reader's Digest, 1975, London). Prepared in conjunction with the World Wildlife Fund

Warne's Natural History Atlas of Great Britain, A. Darlington (Frederick Warne, 1969, London)

Britain's Structure and Scenery, L. Dudley Stamp (Collins, 1946, London)

A Beast Book for the Pocket, E. Sandars (Oxford University Press, 1944, London)

Woodland Ecology, E. G. Neal (Heinemann Educational Books, 1953, London)

Blandford Colour Series: *eg Woodland Life*, G. Mandahl-Barth, A. Darlington (ed.) (Blandford Press, 1972, London)

Dune and Moorland Life, L. Lyneborg, A. Darlington (ed.) (Blandford Press, 1973, London)

Heathland Ecology, C. P. Friedlander (Heinemann Educational Books, 1960, London)

The Highlands and Islands, F. Fraser Darling and J. Morton Boyd (Collins, 1964, London)

Ice Ages, Recent and Ancient, A. P. Coleman (Macmillan, 1926, London)

Productivity and Conservation in North Circumpolar Lands, A. W. Fuller and P. G. Kevan (eds.) (International Union for Conservation of Nature and Natural Resources: new series no. 16.) Papers on the production and conservation of arctic plants and animals and the role of human resources.

Arctic and Alpine Environments, W. H. Osburn and H. E. Wright (jt. eds.) (Indiana University Press, 1968). Papers on the climatology, geology and ecology of tundras

The ecology of arctic and alpine plants. Billings, W. D. and Mooney, H. A. *Biol. Rev.* **43**: 481–529 (1968). A review of the physiological ecology of tundra flowering plants

Flora Europaea, 4 vols, T. G. Tutin (ed.) (Cambridge University Press, 1964–72, Cambridge)

The Wild Flowers of Britain and Northern Europe, R. Fitter, A. Fitter and M. Blamey (Collins, 1974, London)

The Concise British Flora, W. Keble Martin (Ebury Press and Michael Joseph, 1969, London)

A Field Guide to the Trees of Britain and Northern Europe, A. Mitchell (Collins, 1974, London)

Trees and Bushes of Europe, O. Polunin and B. Everard (Oxford University Press, 1976, London)

Flowers of Europe, O. Polunin (Oxford University Press, 1969, London)

Grasses, C. E. Hubbard (Penguin, 1968, London)

The Oxford Book of Invertebrates, D. Nichols, J. Cooke and D. Whiteley (Oxford University Press, 1976, London)

The Young Specialist looks at Molluscs, H. James (Burke, 1965, London)

A Field Guide to the Insects of Britain and Northern Europe, M. Chinery (Collins, 1973, London)

Grasshoppers, Crickets and Cockroaches of the British Isles, D. R. Ragge (Warne, 1965, London)

A Field Guide to the Butterflies of Britain and Europe, L. G. Higgins and N. Riley (Collins, 1970, London)

The Moths of the British Isles, Two volumes, R. South (Warne, 1961, London)

Flies of the British Isles, C. W. Colyer and C. O. Hammond (Warne, 1968, London)

Ray Society publications: *eg British Spiders*, G. H. Locket and A. F. Millidge (Ray Society, British Museum, 1951-53, London)

Bees, Wasps, Ants and Allied Orders of the British Isles, E. Step (Frederick Warne, 1932, London)

Beetles of the British Isles, E. F. Linssen (Frederick Warne, 1959, London)

The British Amphibians and Reptiles, M. Smith (Collins, 1954, London)

A Field Guide to the Birds of Britain and Europe, R. Peterson, G. Mountfort and P. A. D. Hollom (Collins, 1954, London)

Man and Birds, R. K. Murton (Collins, 1971, London)

A Field Guide to the Mammals of Britain and Europe, F. H. van den Brink (Collins, 1967, London)

The Handbook of British Mammals, G. B. Corbet and H. N. Southern (eds.) (Blackwell, 1977, Oxford)

ACKNOWLEDGEMENTS

page

6 A. D. Schilling/NHPA
11 Bruce Coleman/Ulrike Schneiders
11 Heather Angel
19 Bruce Coleman/Hans Reinhard
23 Jacana/Jean-Philippe Varin
26 Brian Hawkes/NHPA
26 Heather Angel
30 Heather Angel
34 Heather Angel
39 Stephen Dalton/NHPA
41 Heather Angel
43 Walter Murray/NHPA

43 Heather Angel
50 Brian Hawkes/NHPA
51 R. Everts/Zefa
52 Arnold Darlington
59 Brian Hawkes/NHPA
65 Brian Hawkes/NHPA
65 Walter Murray/NHPA
67 Bruce Coleman/Douglas Botting
69 M. Savonius/NHPA
75 Werner Mohn/Zefa
77 Bruce Coleman/Sven Gillaster

INDEX

Page references in **bold**
refer to illustrations.

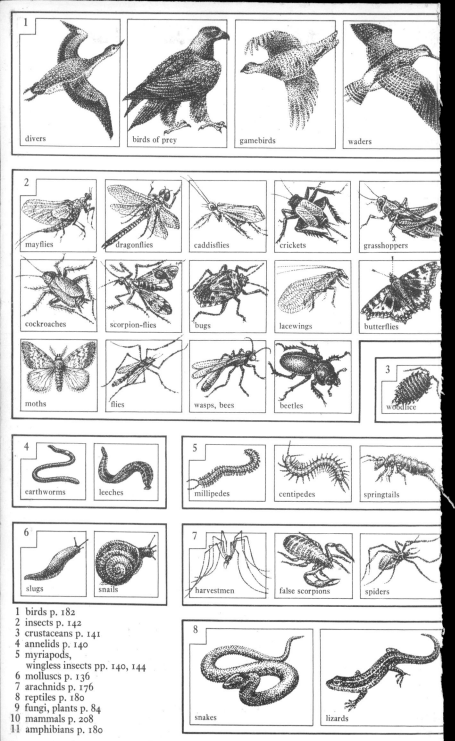

1
divers | birds of prey | gamebirds | waders

2
mayflies | dragonflies | caddisflies | crickets | grasshoppers
cockroaches | scorpion-flies | bugs | lacewings | butterflies
moths | flies | wasps, bees | beetles

3
woodlice

4
earthworms | leeches

5
millipedes | centipedes | springtails

6
slugs | snails

7
harvestmen | false scorpions | spiders

8
snakes | lizards

1 birds p. 182
2 insects p. 142
3 crustaceans p. 141
4 annelids p. 140
5 myriapods,
   wingless insects pp. 140, 144
6 molluscs p. 136
7 arachnids p. 176
8 reptiles p. 180
9 fungi, plants p. 84
10 mammals p. 208
11 amphibians p. 180